SOCRATES

a life worth living

PHILOSOPHY FOR
YOUNG PEOPLE

SOCRATES

a life worth living

DEVRA LEHMANN

PHILOSOPHY FOR YOUNG PEOPLE

SEVEN STORIES PRESS

New York • Oakland • London

A TRIANGLE SQUARE BOOK FOR YOUNG READERS
PUBLISHED BY SEVEN STORIES PRESS

Maps on pages xii and 16 are based on Adobe Stock images.

Hackett Publishing Company takes no responsibility for the
modifications to the map on page 32.

Endsheets: Théodore Caruelle d'Aligny. *The Acropolis, Athens: The Pnyx,
Areopagus, Acropolis and Mount Hymmettos,* 1845. The Art Institute of Chicago.

SEVEN STORIES PRESS
140 Watts Street
New York, NY 10013
www.sevenstories.com

Library of Congress Cataloging-in-Publication Data
NAMES: Lehmann, Devra, author.
TITLE: Socrates : a life worth living / Devra Lehmann.
DESCRIPTION: New York : Seven Stories Press, [2022].
Includes bibliographical references.
Audience: Grades: 10-12.
IDENTIFIERS: LCCN 2021061962
ISBN 9781644211366 (hardcover)
ISBN 9781644212615 (paperback)
ISBN 9781644211373 (ebook).
SUBJECTS: LCSH: Socrates—Juvenile literature.
Philosophers—Greece—Biography—Juvenile literature.
Philosophy, Ancient—Juvenile literature.
CLASSIFICATION: LCC B316 .L44 2022
DDC 183/.2—dc23/eng/20220302.
LC record available at https://lccn.loc.gov/2021061962

Teachers may order free
examination copies of Seven Stories Press titles.
Visit https://www.sevenstories.com/pg/resources-academics
or email academics@sevenstories.com.

Book design by Stewart Cauley and Beth Kessler

Printed in the USA

9 8 7 6 5 4 3 2 1

Contents

PART THREE
The Last Days

MAPS

Acknowledgments

I AM GRATEFUL TO THE MANY SOCRATIC MIDWIVES to this book. First are my students, who have shown me again and again their passion for meaningful discussions about big ideas—as well as their need for books to help them navigate our rich intellectual heritage. Next are the many people who have been my own guides. Tirosh Feldman kept me challenged and helped me identify what I was trying to say. Karen Klockner responded to my disastrous first drafts with her magnificent blend of compassion and honesty. Debra Nails graced me with her breathtaking erudition and exactitude, providing me with a wealth of source material, answering my endless questions, and setting me right where I went wrong. Geoff Bakewell, Mark Anderson, and Yona Gonopolsky contributed articles, advice, expertise, and encouragement, and Sylvie Dumont patiently explained the ins and outs of using images from the generous collection of the American School of Classical Studies at Athens.

Andy Ross, my agent, was energetic in finding my work a home at Seven Stories, where Dan Simon, Ruth Weiner, and Lauren Hooker greeted it warmly. Lauren is the superb reader that every writer wants in an editor. She asked just the right questions, ferreted out the inconsistencies, and polished out the roughness. Conor O'Brien copyedited with an acuity that saved me from many an excess, ambiguity, and stupid mistake; Beth Kessler and Stewart Cauley gave the finished work a beautiful, bold design; and Tal Mancini proofread with patience and care.

Friends and family have contributed in more subtle but no less important ways. I treasure long walks and good talks over knitting and coffee with many wonderful companions. Your friendship has provided sustenance and sanity, especially as the certainties of youth have receded. Hindy, you have also contributed your photographic skills, and I thank you once again for your help. Danny, Roni, Ariella, Matanel, J.J., Naama, and Noam, you warm me with your love and keep me on my toes with the ping-pong of your discussions and the zaniness of your humor. Omer, Eyal, Nehara, and Aluma, I hope that you will always see the world through your bright, curious eyes. Maybe one day you'll read Bubby's books. Mom, I hope that you enjoy this fruit of your many sacrifices, and Gil, thanks for your priceless attempts at rap and your pride in your little sister. Ron, it all begins and ends with you.

In e. e. cummings's beautiful words, my father, Asher Sorrel Wolfe, was a man who "lived his soul." He died just as I began writing my first draft, and I felt his presence at every stage of the work. He is the person to whom I am most indebted for my love of reading, writing, and thinking, and I have dedicated this book to his memory.

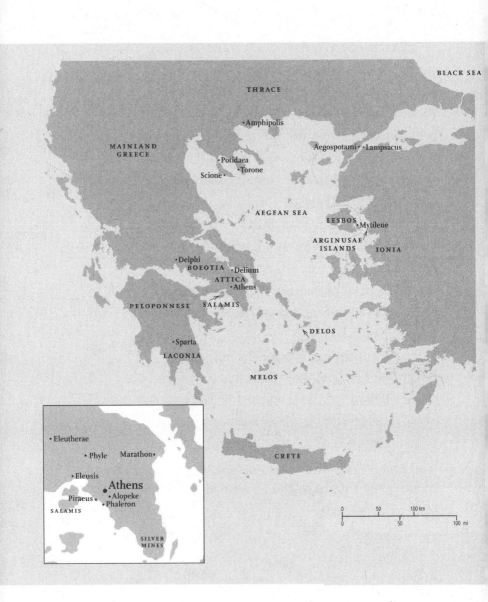

Mainland Greece
and the Aegean,
with inset of Attica

Prologue

EVEN NOW, IN HIS FINAL HOURS IN A GRIM prison cell, Socrates kept asking his questions. About fifteen men had occupied the room since the early morning, their dread steadily mounting as the sun made its course across the sky. But Socrates had engaged his visitors in such animated conversation, and his manner had been so probing, so lively, so full of good cheer— in short, so much the way it always was—that he had turned the day into a curious sort of celebration. His friends had almost forgotten where they were and what was about to occur.

For years these men had followed Socrates around Athens. He had drawn them into spirited discussions in the marketplace and craftsmen's workshops, the athletic facilities and judicial precincts, the homes of wealthy men and the shady banks of a river. Most of these friends were locals, but others had come from far away to seek him out. And they were not the only ones who had flocked to his side. Socrates engaged trendsetters and intellectuals, aristocrats and slaves, shoemakers, ne'er-do-wells, artists, politicians, writers, and even occasionally a woman, unusual at a time when public life was almost exclusively male. These individuals had not come to him for answers, for he had surprisingly few of those to give. Instead, he offered questions and the opportunity to think. What is virtue? What is friendship? What is beauty?

All of that was coming to an end. The visitors had nurtured their hopes for several weeks, but the last rays of light were fading in the west, and now the outcome was inevitable. Socrates, their dear friend, was about to die. They could already hear the prison official making his way down the passage that ran between the rows of cells. The man's steps were slow and deliberate, but soon enough he appeared in the doorway, careful not to spill the liquid in the clay cup he was holding. The visitors closest to him instinctively drew away. The cup was small, but the poison it contained would kill even the strongest man within minutes. Only the prisoner, sitting on his bed, maintained his composure. "Well, my good man," Socrates said, "you are an expert in this; what must one do?"

So began the final moments of the philosopher's life. Ever since it was first set into words by Socrates's most famous follower, Plato, the scene has inspired countless writers and artists; even people who know virtually nothing else about Socrates have heard of his fatal ingestion of hemlock in a prison cell in Athens. Perhaps they know, too, of the legal proceedings that led to that final scene: the accusation that Socrates had spurned the gods and corrupted the youth of Athens, the fervent speech that Socrates delivered before a packed and unruly courtroom, the majority vote of the jury to declare him guilty, and the jury's subsequent decision, with an even larger majority, to impose the death penalty.

Courtroom drama is riveting, and willing martyrdom is poignant. But it would be a disservice both to Socrates and ourselves to focus only on the end of his story. Socrates lived during one of the most glorious periods in history, the lightning flash of a few decades when Athens blazed onto the scene as a democracy, an international power, and a center of art and thought. He was a vital part of that spectacular setting, which shaped him and which he shaped in return. And although he didn't quite invent philosophy, he set Western thought on a radically new course, which it has followed ever since.

These are the usual reasons for learning about bygone men and women: they lived in important times, thought important thoughts, performed important deeds. If we care about how the past influences who we are today, these matters are well worth our attention. But what makes Socrates especially compelling is the way he leaps out of the past. His questions and his search for answers are as vital today as they ever were.

They are vital because they all lead to what, for Socrates, was the ultimate question, one too precious for any of us to leave to chance: How can we construct lives of meaning? Socrates believed that to live meaningfully, we must pursue what is good and true. Obviously, if we are to engage in that pursuit, we must first be able to identify which things are good and true and which things are not. Our starting point, in other words, must be careful thinking. Only

reason yields the knowledge that we need to
make moral decisions, and only moral decisions,
in their totality, create a life of meaning.

Socrates exhibited a breathtaking integrity as he
pursued his own life of meaning, even as the world
he knew began to crumble around him. Almost
two and a half thousand years later, his personal
example has lost none of its power or relevance.

HEAD OF SOCRATES.
Roman copy after a
Greek original ca. 320
BCE by Lysippos. State
Collection of Antiquities
and Glyptothek Munich.
Photograph by Renate
Kühling.

PART ONE

The Path to the Questions

CHAPTER I

THE CITY OF GODS
AND HUMANS

SEVENTY YEARS BEFORE THAT SCENE IN the Athenian state prison, a man named Sophroniscus and a woman named Phaenarete festooned the doorway of their home with an olive wreath. The year was approximately 469 BCE, and the place was the *deme*, or district, of Alopeke, part of the *polis*, or city-state, of Athens. The polis occupied the eastern Greek peninsula known as Attica, and its nucleus, the large city that was also called Athens, was a mere mile or so to the northwest of the couple's home.

The decoration on the couple's door was an announcement: Phaenarete had given birth to a boy. The baby received his name when he was ten days old, once he had proven strong enough to survive the perils of newborn life.

(Facing page) Detail from the *Lansdowne Bust of Athena of Velletri*, second-century CE Roman copy after a Greek original ca. 430–420 BCE by Kresilas. Los Angeles County Museum of Art. *See page 8.*

Sophroniscus and Phaenarete chose "Socrates," which combined the notion of wholeness (*sos*) and power (*kratos*). The gods must have been favorably disposed. As he grew, the boy showed every sign of strength and intelligence—although with his thick lips, flat nose, broad nostrils, and wide-set, bulging eyes, he would never be handsome.

Sophroniscus, as far as we know, was a stonecutter. Like other workmen, he probably maintained his workshop in a front room of the house, but if he followed the usual pattern, he had little to do with the early rearing of his son. For most Athenian men, home was a place for eating, sleeping, and recovering from illness; the real business of life, beyond the need to make a living, consisted of gathering in the public spaces of the city for conversation, political activity, and athletic pursuits. Phaenarete's life was completely different. Like other women, she mostly stayed at home, where she engaged in the endless tasks of maintaining the household. As she spun, wove, and sewed to produce the family's clothing, Socrates played at her feet.

The little boy's everyday life was constricted and dark. The mud-brick house contained only the barest essentials, and the unglazed windows were usually shuttered to keep out the sun and rain. But Socrates soon understood that he was part of a much bigger, more wondrous world. He learned that his family descended from Daedalus, the greatest human craftsman who had ever lived—the same Daedalus who had cleverly fashioned two sets of wings so that he and his son, Icarus, could escape the evil king Minos on the island of Crete. The story ended sadly, with the tragic death of Icarus, but Daedalus was a brilliant inventor, certainly a worthy man to have as an ancestor. And since Daedalus was the descendant of another craftsman, the metal-working god Hephaestus, and Hephaestus was the son of Zeus, Socrates could trace his ancestry all the way back to the most powerful god of all.

There were a great many gods, and they were everywhere. Socrates's home, like every other one in Athens, featured an altar to Hestia, the goddess of the hearth, and temples and shrines to one deity or another dotted the city and countryside. Even the naked landscape spoke of the gods' presence. The cone-shaped Mount Lycabettus to the northeast of Socrates's home was more than just a stony protrusion on the Athenian plain; it was really a rock that

Athena, the goddess of wisdom, had accidentally dropped when she heard some bad news. The Areopagus, an outcropping to the northwest, was where Ares, the god of war, had been tried and acquitted by his fellow gods for the murder of Poseidon's son.

But the best story of all concerned the Acropolis, the plateau that rose in the middle of the city. Athens was beautiful even in its earliest days, and the gods Athena and Poseidon each laid claim to the place as a personal possession. Since the city could not belong to both gods at once, they challenged one another to a contest: each god would present the residents with a gift, and the one who presented the better gift would win. Escorted by a procession of locals, the two gods climbed the Acropolis, and the contest began. Poseidon, the god of the sea, went first. He struck the side of the cliff with his trident, and out gushed a bountiful stream of water. The spectators were awed—not surprisingly, since no city can survive without water. But the awe turned to dismay when the people discovered that the water was as salty as the sea. Poseidon's gift was useless. Next came Athena, who caused an olive tree to sprout from the unpromising soil. This time the people's awe was justified, since the olive tree provided food, oil, and wood. Athena won the contest. The city was hers, and she graced it with her name.

That special connection explained why Athena was the focus of the polis's most thrilling holiday. Socrates enjoyed frequent breaks in his quiet routines at home, since each of the gods demanded at least one festival of his or her own. But nothing came even close to the festival for Athena, the Great Panathenaea, an event so grand that it came only once every four years. The holiday's high point was a joyous procession along a wide avenue that led to the Acropolis, and just about everyone in Athens participated, even women, visitors, slaves, and foreign-born residents, none of whom were entitled to citizenship. Socrates rode high on his father's shoulders, above the garlanded baskets that bobbed on the heads of distinguished young women, where he could spot a genuine ship gliding through the city streets. Attached to the mast was a special gift for the goddess, an ornate *peplos*, a body-length robe that a select group of maidens had painstakingly woven and embroidered over the previous months. That peplos would adorn the city's most sacred object, an ancient wooden statue of Athena that was carefully tended atop the Acropolis,

ATHENA: Because
Athena was the
protectress of their
city, Athenians liked
to emphasize her
military character. On
this statue, the helmet
draws attention to her
identity as goddess
of war, and the small
breastplate recalls her
role in defeating the
Gorgon Medusa.

*The Lansdowne Bust
of Athena of Velletri,*
second-century CE
Roman copy after a
Greek original ca. 430–
420 BCE by Kresilas.
Los Angeles County
Museum of Art.

where Athena's olive tree still stood next to Poseidon's saltwater spring. As everyone knew, that hallowed statue had fallen, fully fashioned, directly from the heavens.

The gods gave Socrates a sense of identity and shaped his experience of space and time. But the wondrous world beyond Socrates's mud-brick home was inhabited by regular people too—regular people who had achieved extraordinary things. His own parents could tell him about the spine-tingling events that had taken place only about ten years before he was born, when Persia, the most formidable empire the world had ever known, was attempting to conquer Greece. The Persians had failed at their first attempt in 490 BCE, and this time, in 480, they were making sure to do a thorough job. They had returned with a crushing force on both land and sea, and the chances for Greece looked slim. As the enemy moved southward through the mainland, one polis after another fell to its knees, and soon nothing would stand between Persia and Athens.

The terrified Athenians sent messengers to Delphi, about seventy-five miles to the northwest, to seek guidance from the oracle of Apollo. Oracles were priests or priestesses regarded as mouthpieces for the gods, but they were not known for straightforward communication. In this case, the oracle's response was especially cryptic: "Safe shall the wooden wall continue for thee and thy children." After a few days of heated debate, the Athenians concluded that the "wooden wall" referred to the wooden vessels of their navy, and the people resolved to construct two hundred new ships. The expense would have been prohibitive had it not been for a happy coincidence: silver had just been discovered in the southeastern corner of Attica. The original plan had been to distribute the unexpected bounty among all the people, but they voted to build the new ships instead. It was a wise decision.

As the invaders approached, the Athenians who were not actively fighting in the army or navy fled to the island of Salamis, just across the water to the south. The abandoned city lay defenseless, and from the hills of Salamis, the horror-struck refugees watched their homes, shops, civic buildings, and temples rise in flames. The situation at sea looked somewhat better. Although the Athenian navy was relatively inexperienced, its leaders quickly understood that Persia's large fleet and imposing maneuvers, so devastating in open waters, would become handicaps in a constricted space. The straits between Salamis and the mainland were perfect, and into those waters Athens lured its heedless enemy. Seizing their advantage, the scrappy Athenians mercilessly rammed the Persian ships. In the chaos of swirling waves, sinking vessels, and drowning soldiers, the Greek victory was unmistakable.

The Persians renewed their attack the following year, and once again the Athenians fled to Salamis and watched their city burn. But that summer, with the help of its allies, Athens achieved another major victory. Although smaller confrontations with Persia continued for many years, the existential threat was over, and all of Greece felt the relief. The Athenians were jubilant. Yes, their once stately city had been left in ruins, and yes, they had suffered many casualties. But they had triumphed in several decisive battles, even without significant support from their fellow Greeks. Athens had saved not only itself but the entire Greek world.

The euphoria was still strong when Socrates was born, and part of what kept it alive was a conviction that the victory was not just a piece of miraculous luck. Athens was unique, and the victory had resulted from that uniqueness. And here was another tale of human triumph that

Socrates heard from his elders—a subtler story than the dramatic defeat of Persia, but more momentous in the long term. That story began in the seventh century BCE, when the establishment of overseas trade routes widened the gap between rich and poor. Commerce enriched the large landowners who produced crops for export, but peasant farmers, who could not compete, fell into debt and lost their land. The peasants had no way to improve their situation. All political power rested in a governing council that met on the Areopagus. The men who convened there were aristocrats, and their decisions invariably reflected their own interests. Another assembly, the Ekklesia, drew on a broader swath of the population, but it had no real power, because its agenda and proceedings were controlled by the council on the Areopagus.

By the beginning of the sixth century BCE, the situation had become so explosive that even many aristocrats recognized the need for change. Reforms took hold over a long and difficult period, and by the end of the century, the central government had undergone a radical transformation. The Ekklesia opened to more of the population than it had before and operated along a new set of rules. Now all citizens had the right to attend a meeting, address the crowd, and vote on an issue under consideration, and each citizen, no matter how rich or poor, had just one vote. Just as importantly, the council on the Areopagus no longer controlled the Ekklesia's proceedings; executive control over the assembly shifted to committees that represented the entire body of citizens. Even so, these new committees never eclipsed the Ekklesia itself; the citizens in their entirety held direct, supreme power over the polis's decisions. The people's power was enhanced by many other reforms as well. Most political positions were filled by lottery, so all citizens had a chance of holding public office at some point in their lives, and the judicial system gave all citizens the right to air their grievances before a jury of their fellows.

The new system fell grievously short of today's standards. A citizen had to be a freeborn male over seventeen years of age with two Athenian parents, and that requirement excluded whole categories of adults—women, obviously, but also slaves and foreign-born residents. Slaves alone composed fully half the total population; in ancient warfare, winners took possession of losers, and captives became slaves when they did not have the good fortune to be ransomed. Of the 300,000 to 400,000 people who lived in the polis when Socrates was about fifty or sixty years

**THE BOULE
AND PRYTANY:**
The Ekklesia had two
executive committees.
The five-hundred-
member Boule was
responsible for setting
the Ekklesia's agenda,
and the fifty-member
prytany chaired the
Ekklesia's sessions and
executed its decisions.
Modern calculations
suggest that more than
half of all citizens served
on those committees
at some point in their
lives (JACT, p. 212).
The picture below
shows a model of the
Old Bouleuterion, the
building where the
Boule met for much of
Socrates's life.

*Model of the Old
Bouleuterion*, ca. 500
BCE. Petros Demetriades
and Kostas Papoulias.
American School
of Classical Studies
at Athens: Agora
Excavations.

old, only about 30,000 qualified for citizenship.
Nonetheless, at a time when most people lived
under the arbitrary authority of kings and other
rulers, the Athenians had achieved something
phenomenal. All Athenian citizens, regardless of
their economic background or social status, held
the potential to shape their political reality. The
Athenians did not yet call their creation by the
name we would give it; their term was *isonomia*,
or equality under the law. But in response to
the grievous rifts within their society, they had
created the world's first democracy.

To the Athenians, it was obvious that their
two stories of achievement, the establishment
of democracy and the victory against Persia,
were related. The historian Herodotus, a
contemporary of Socrates, later described the
prevailing view:

*[F]reedom is an excellent thing; since
even the Athenians, who, while they
continued under the rule of tyrants, were
not a whit more valiant than any of their
neighbours, no sooner shook off the yoke
than they became decidedly the first of all.
These things show that, while undergoing
oppression, they let themselves be beaten,
since then they worked for a master; but so
soon as they got their freedom, each man
was eager to do the best he could for himself.*

Democracy had given the Athenians something worth defending, and their victory against Persia proved that nothing would stand in their way.

How lucky Socrates was to have been born in the polis of Athens! Formidable gods had vied to possess it, and heroic humans had defended it, confronted its failings, and shaped it to reflect their values. There could be no doubt that Athens had been singled out for a special destiny. Soon enough, the polis was to experience one of those rare golden ages in history, an intense period of almost unbelievable political, military, economic, intellectual, and artistic achievement. It was a heady time and place for a child to begin his life.

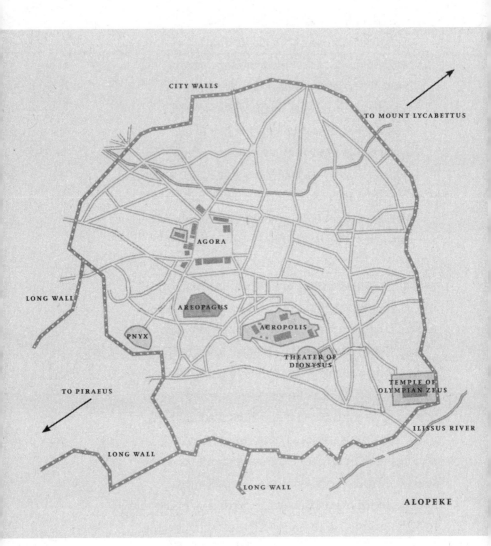

The city of Athens

CHAPTER 2

THE WAY TO CITIZENSHIP

ATHENS DID NOT MAINTAIN A comprehensive school system, but virtually all boys from citizen families received at least some formal education. When Socrates was six or seven years old, Sophroniscus made arrangements with the private instructor of his choice, and the little boy dutifully set off for his lessons each day. Socrates was finally emerging from his mother's close supervision, but he was never alone. Schoolboys were escorted by a *paidagogos*, a slave or hired man who ensured their physical safety and handled any disciplinary problems. Families that could not afford a slave or hired man, and Socrates's family was probably one of these, assigned the job to a responsible male relative.

The curriculum for all boys consisted of the three major subjects that were deemed essential to the life of a citizen. The first subject, literacy, enabled citizens to maintain public records, understand public notices, and cast written ballots. To master the basic skills, Socrates balanced a wax-covered tablet on his knees and used a stylus to carve letters in the soft surface. Bright students like him caught on quickly, and the repetitive exercises probably tried his patience. If he displayed the same exuberant wit as a schoolboy that he possessed as an adult, he would have paid the price. Vase paintings of the period depict teachers holding sandals in their hands, poised to strike naughty pupils into submission.

A more interesting part of the literacy curriculum was the memorization of highly regarded poetry. Memorization has fallen out of fashion in today's schools, but its benefits were patently clear to Athenian teachers. A student who had committed great texts to memory could draw almost effortlessly upon an enormous repertoire of elegant vocabulary and phrasing to enhance his own speaking and writing. Besides, great works of literature offered the uplifting role models of distinguished heroes. As astounding as it seems to us today, some boys learned the entire *Iliad* or

Odyssey by heart, and Socrates may well have been one of them. As an adult, he frequently drew upon his fluent knowledge of Homer and other poets.

Socrates had more difficulty with music, the second component of the curriculum. Like other boys, he learned to sing and play an instrument, probably the lyre or a kind of flute, but the activity did not become a major part of his life. Only in his sixties did he resume his music lessons—and then described himself as having "disgraced" his teacher, "who is still trying to teach me to play." Nonetheless, Socrates shared his culture's high regard for the discipline. Music was a highlight of many public festivals and an integral part of the *symposium*, a formal men's-only dinner held in wealthy homes, and Greek poetry, including the *Iliad* and *Odyssey*, was generally sung to instrumental accompaniment. And music, like literacy, was thought to build character. Music cultivated a sensitivity to proportion, grace, and order that resulted in appropriate attitudes and behavior. A generation after Socrates, Plato warned that an unorthodox mixing of musical styles—"breaking the laws of music," as he put it—led inevitably to a "general disregard for the law." We might doubt that cause-and-effect relationship, but to Athenians it made perfect sense.

With his physical strength, Socrates was a natural at athletics, the third component of his schooling. He and his classmates practiced boxing and wrestling in their local *palaestra*, a colonnaded courtyard used for athletic training. For sports that required more space, such as running, long jumping, and discus- or javelin-throwing, they moved to one of the larger state-funded gymnasia that were located on the outskirts of town. Physical training helped to ensure the polis's military readiness, and just as importantly, it fostered the athletes who would bring honor to Athens. The Olympics, which took place every four years in the northwestern Peloponnese, Greece's large southern peninsula, were the oldest and most prestigious of the Greek sports competitions, but Athens hosted an important competition of its own during the Great Panathenaea. Sports events included boxing, wrestling, foot races, and— most exciting of all—chariot races, and the best athletes from all over Greece participated. Like other Greeks, the Athenians took these contests seriously. We have only to look at the word "athlete" to see the connection that Greeks drew between sports and competition. The word comes from

the Greek *athlon*, meaning "prize" or "reward";
the Greek word *athletes* meant literally "one who
competes for a prize."

Athletics were important for other reasons
too. Greeks prized the beauty of the male
body and the grace of its movements, and as
a result sportsmen competed in the nude.
Here, too, an English word captures the spirit:
"gymnasium" derives from the Greek *gymnos*,
meaning "naked." Greeks especially prized the
long jump for the fluidity of the athlete's flight,
which he executed to the accompaniment of
flute music. Athletics were also linked to the
life of the mind. The Great Panathenaea, the
Olympics, and other sports events included
artistic contests, recitations of literary works,
and spontaneous presentations by poets,
and the palaestrae and gymnasia served as
natural venues for scholarly debate. As an
adult, Socrates spent a great deal of time in
those facilities, where he drew passersby into
discussions that we might consider more suited
to a university seminar room than to the local
fitness center. An ancient Greek would have
been mystified by our culture's widespread
assumption that brain and brawn are
mutually exclusive.

ATHLETICS: Young men practice the long jump and discus-throwing on the outside of this two-handled cup, which was used for drinking wine at a symposium. At the center, a pair of javelins stands ready for use. One of the clothed figures is a flute player, and the other is a slave who is cleaning an athlete's skin.

Attic Red-Figure Kylix, ca. 510–500 BCE. Attributed to the Carpenter Painter, Greek, Attic. J. Paul Getty Museum. Image courtesy of the Getty's Open Content Program.

Socrates was expected to understand the interrelatedness of everything he studied. He was not just acquiring a set of discrete skills or chunks of isolated knowledge; instead, he was developing the means to live a full, well-rounded life. That ultimate goal, as the Greeks termed it, was a life of *arete*. "Virtue," the standard English translation of this word, nicely evokes the goodness of character that "arete" was meant to embrace. But "virtue" fails to capture the expansiveness of the original. "Arete" meant excellence in all aspects of life. To achieve arete was to distinguish oneself in body, mind, and soul.

It was a tall order. Did Socrates the schoolboy stand out in the challenge? The Greek historian Plutarch, who lived in the first century CE, maintains that the child was so impressive that he required no schooling at all. According to Plutarch, an oracle told Sophroniscus to let his son do whatever he wanted. Since Socrates already "had a better guide of life in himself than a thousand teachers and attendants," all Sophroniscus needed to do was to pray to the gods on the boy's behalf. The story, of course, is unlikely. The childhoods of illustrious figures have always provided fertile ground for fanciful tales, and when it comes to lively anecdotes, Plutarch is notoriously indiscriminate.

And yet Plutarch grounded his story in something that we do know about Socrates. From his earliest years, Socrates heard a sort of internal voice that warned him against taking specific actions. It might instruct him, for instance, not to associate with particular individuals or not to walk out of a room he was planning to leave; apparently, the warning was always about something he should *not* do. He heard this voice his entire life, and though other people sometimes mocked or mistrusted him because of his claim to possess it, he always obeyed its commands. He believed that the gods were behind it, and he referred to it as his *daimonion*, literally a "divine something."

Today it is hard to know what to make of Socrates's daimonion, and not just because of our modern tendency to doubt the existence of supernatural phenomena. Even within Socrates's thought, the daimonion seems out of place. Socrates's philosophical trademark is his emphasis on logical reasoning as the foundation of an ethical system, and obedience to a mysterious voice hardly counts as logical behavior. It is tempting to resolve the inconsistency by interpreting the daimonion's directives as the natural intuitions or hunches that we all experience from time to time. But no matter what we think, Socrates's own view was that the voice he heard somehow issued from the gods.

Socrates remained in school until the year he turned seventeen, when his father formally presented him before officials of the deme of Alopeke. After verifying that Sophroniscus was a citizen and Phaenarete the daughter of a citizen, the officials entered the young man's name on a formal list, and Socrates became a newly minted citizen of the proud polis of Athens. Although certain functions, such as serving on juries, would wait until he turned thirty, he was now subject to the many lotteries that determined the tasks of citizens, and he could now vote in the Ekklesia and hold most forms of public office in his deme and polis.

One of Socrates's first obligations as a citizen was to undergo military training. A century after his time, new recruits enrolled in a formal multiyear program. They spent the first year mastering the use of weapons and the second and third years patrolling the polis and its borders; at the end of the program, the young men qualified for full duty at home or abroad. The system was less organized in Socrates's day, but he certainly experienced some form of preparation. War, not peace, was the natural state of affairs in the Greek world, and the Athenian army was a people's militia, not a professional, full-time force. All citizens had to be available to serve until the age of sixty.

After finishing his military training, Socrates probably began working with his father. If Sophroniscus was indeed the stonecutter that tradition tells us he was, the young man may have spent his time crafting statues, chiseling letters, or even laying bricks; the Greek word for "stonecutting" included a full range of activities, some highly creative and others entirely prosaic. But no matter where Socrates found himself on this spectrum, the profession does not seem to have captured his heart or mind. We have no record of his having ever mentioned this work in his many discussions with his fellow Athenians.

The curious young man must have welcomed every opportunity to escape to the city, and when he did make it there, he would have often headed straight for the Agora. Literally the "place of assembly," the Agora was a government district, religious zone, marketplace, and social center rolled into one. The area had sustained heavy damage during the Persian assaults, but repairs and new construction had begun before Socrates's birth and continued throughout his life. As a minor, Socrates had needed an adult chaperone to enter the precinct, but now the border markers, which quaintly announced, "I am the boundary of the Agora," no longer stood in his way.

The Agora included the busy headquarters of the Ekklesia's administrative committees and the enormous law courts that handled, according to one fifth-century observer, "more public and private lawsuits and judicial investigations than the whole of the rest of mankind." Constantly changing notice boards kept citizens abreast of the latest news. Some of these notices were rapidly painted on wooden boards, but others were more laboriously engraved in stone—some, perhaps, by Socrates himself. The most welcoming places in the Agora were the *stoas*, the roofed and colonnaded porticos that were protected from the elements but open to fresh breezes. At the one that was later called the Stoa Poikile, the Painted Stoa, citizens wrangled over politics, rumor-mongers peddled the latest scandals, performers staged feats of juggling and fire-eating, and merchants hawked wares. Even serious intellectuals found the space hospitable. In the third century BCE, one of Socrates's intellectual heirs, Zeno of Citium, spent so much of his time in the Stoa Poikile that he and his followers became known as Stoics and their school of thought as Stoicism.

The Agora was so popular that citizens lingered there even when civic duty called them to the Ekklesia, which met on a nearby hilltop called the Pnyx. By the end of the fifth century, the city developed an ingenious solution. Just before the Ekklesia was scheduled to convene, a police force staffed by slaves fanned through the

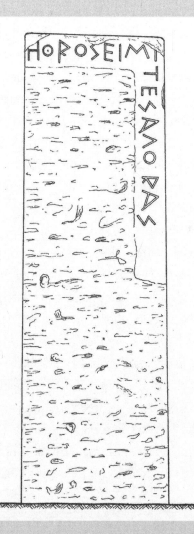

AGORA BOUNDARY MARKER: This sketch depicts one of two markers that archeologists found still standing in place. The inscription "I am the boundary of the Agora" runs along the top and right side of the stone.

Agora boundary stone found east of the Tholos, ca. 500 BCE. American School of Classical Studies at Athens: Agora Excavations.

Agora, brandishing a long rope dipped in red dye. Laggards scampered off to the Pnyx before the rope could touch them, since any citizen who bore the telltale red mark incurred a fine.

Unfortunately, just as Socrates was embarking on this intoxicating new life, tragedy struck. Sophroniscus died, leaving his son responsible for maintaining the family. Although Socrates was still quite young, he became his mother's legal guardian. Eventually he gave her in marriage to a second husband, Chaeredemus, with whom she had a son named Patrocles. Socrates may have had other siblings, but we know only about this half brother.

Good friends must have helped Socrates during this difficult time. He was especially close with a young man named Crito. The two were the same age and came from the same deme, and they had known each other for as long as either of them could remember. Their paths were diverging now. While Socrates neither possessed nor desired more than the barest essentials, Crito was immersing himself in agriculture and already amassing an enormous fortune. But this difference between the two men never destroyed their relationship. Until the very last day of Socrates's life, Crito remained his most intimate friend. Another young man from Socrates's childhood was Chaerephon, whose corpse-like appearance—tall, thin, and pallid—made him the frequent butt of jokes. His personality was unusual too; Socrates referred to Chaerephon as a "wild man" and described him as "impulsive in any course of action." Nonetheless, Chaerephon cared deeply about Socrates and was a steadfast, lifelong companion.

But the greatest source of comfort was the polis's culture of conversation. The Athenians were a famously opinionated lot, and anywhere they gathered, they delighted in staking out their positions. Socrates had already developed a keen intellect and a sharp tongue, and he could not have found a more congenial environment.

THE STOA POIKILE: The drawing below shows the stoa as it would have looked toward the end of Socrates's life. The structure received its name in the middle of the fifth century BCE, when the back wall was adorned with paintings that commemorated Athens's military triumphs.

Perspective drawing of the Stoa Poikile. W.B. Dinsmoor, Jr. American School of Classical Studies at Athens: Agora Excavations.

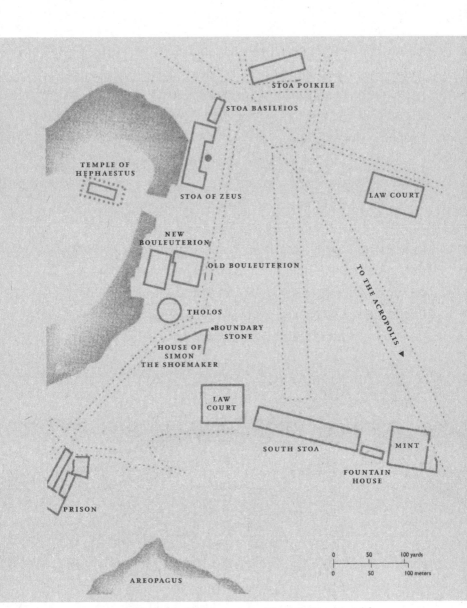

Highlights of the Agora toward the end of Socrates's life

This map is a modified version of the following source: Nails, Debra.
The People of Plato: A Prosopography of Plato and Other Socratics.
Hackett, 2002: p. 267. Original map used with the permission of
Hackett Publishing Company, Inc. All rights reserved.

CHAPTER 3

THE YOUNG INTELLECTUAL

ALTHOUGH SOME OF ATHENS'S MOST STIMULATING conversations arose spontaneously, in places like the Agora and gymnasia, other discussions were planned more deliberately. Wealthy citizens often hosted open houses to introduce prominent thinkers from abroad to Athenian audiences. Socrates eagerly attended those gatherings.

In a work titled *Parmenides*, Plato depicts Socrates as a very young man at a social event that has formed around the illustrious scholar Parmenides and his well-known student Zeno. The visitors have come from southern Italy to Athens in order to attend the Great Panathenaea, and they are staying at the home of a prosperous citizen. Zeno has authored a book, which he has brought to Athens for the first time, and a great number of locals have assembled in the hope that he will read it aloud to them. Zeno obliges, and an intense discussion, consisting mostly of exchanges between Socrates and Parmenides, follows on the heels of the reading.

It is far from certain that the specific gathering that Plato describes actually took place. Most of Plato's writings, including the *Parmenides*, belong to the genre of *dialogue*, a type of prose literature that he helped to popularize at the beginning of the fourth century BCE. Dialogues present lengthy philosophical conversations between two or more people, a group that in Plato's case almost always includes Socrates. Although the dialogues abound in historical information and present historically plausible situations, they are not historical records. Plato was present on only one of the occasions he depicts—Socrates's trial—and for a significant number of dialogues, his ability to bear witness was entirely out of the question: he was born about forty-three years after Socrates and did not get to know him until the last decade or so of Socrates's life. Plato was not yet alive when the discussion in the *Parmenides* purports to take place.

Of course, Plato's presence or absence does not necessarily determine the historical accuracy of his dialogues: most historians are not eyewitnesses to the events that they record. But Plato never set himself up as a historian in the first place. He wrote instead as a philosopher and literary artist, and when it served his purpose, he did not hesitate to devise fictitious conversations among real-life individuals. He seems to have used this device in the case of Socrates and Parmenides, who probably never met. The journey from southern Italy to Athens would have been quite arduous for a man as old as Parmenides would have been at the time.

Nonetheless, Plato evokes a reality that was thoroughly familiar to Socrates. Athens was no longer the sleepy backwater it had been before the victory against Persia. From all over the Greek world and even beyond it, individuals of all sorts poured into the city: politicians, merchants, artisans, athletes, writers, travelers, scoundrels, and—most riveting for Socrates— the thinkers we now call philosophers. Word of mouth spread quickly, and distinguished visitors found themselves thronged by locals eager for the latest news and ideas from far-flung places. The public reading of an unfamiliar book generated particular excitement, since ancient Greek books were handwritten scrolls and the reach of any single work was limited. In the *Parmenides*, Zeno has already achieved fame as a philosopher, and his book, which he wrote as a young man, is at least ten or fifteen years old. Even so, the book is making its appearance in Athens for the first time.

The *Parmenides* also offers a glimpse of Socrates as he made his transition to adulthood. Most striking is Socrates's phenomenal self-confidence. Parmenides is advanced in years, "already quite venerable, very gray but of distinguished appearance, about sixty-five years old"; Zeno is "close to forty, a tall, handsome man." Although Socrates has had at least one previous encounter with Parmenides—they met a day or two before, presumably at a similar gathering—Socrates does not know the visitors very well, and he is little more than a teenager. Nonetheless, as soon as Zeno finishes reading his book to the assembled crowd, Socrates is the first to jump in with a reaction. After confirming that he has indeed understood Zeno's argument, Socrates addresses his comments to Parmenides:

> *I understand that Zeno wants to be on intimate terms with you not only in friendship but also in his book. He has, in*

a way, written the same thing as you, but
by changing it round he tries to fool us into
thinking he is saying something different.
You say in your poem that the all is one,
and you give splendid and excellent proofs
for that; he, for his part, says that it is not
many and gives a vast array of very grand
proofs of his own.

Socrates is launching a grave charge. By rewording
Parmenides's ideas—by changing "one" into
"not many"—Zeno has intentionally deceived his
audience into believing his ideas original, and
Parmenides is complicit in this act of bad faith.
To this accusation, Socrates adds the barbs of his
provocative manner and speech. He does not
address Zeno directly, and he describes the visitors'
arguments in such grandiloquent language—
"splendid and excellent" and "very grand"—that he
appears to be laughing in their faces.

Zeno, it turns out, has a perfectly sound
explanation for his rewording of Parmenides.
He explains, good-naturedly enough, that he
wrote his book many years earlier to defend his
teacher against detractors. As a result, the book
naturally adheres to Parmenides's philosophy;
Zeno was neither stealing his teacher's ideas

nor attempting to present those ideas as his own. Furthermore, Zeno had not necessarily planned for the book to reach the general public. Someone else had taken that decision out of his hands by making an unauthorized copy.

Zeno does not take offense at Socrates's attack, but he might easily have done so. The young man disregards the civilities that the setting might suggest—politeness as a guest at a social gathering; deference to age, experience, and reputation; diffidence in the face of distinguished strangers. Certainly Pythodorus, the host of the gathering, is worried. As Plato describes him, Pythodorus "kept from moment to moment expecting Parmenides and Zeno to get annoyed." But the host's anxiety turns out to be unwarranted. Despite Socrates's manner, the two visitors listen thoughtfully to his comments and even show signs of appreciation; they "often glanced at each other and smiled, as though they admired him." Soon Parmenides makes his pleasure clear to Socrates himself. "[Y]ou are much to be admired for your keenness for argument!" Parmenides declares.

It is no surprise that Parmenides and Zeno perceive Socrates's intelligence; the young man is destined to become one of history's most important thinkers. Less predictable is the visitors' willingness to look beyond Socrates's swagger to discover a genuine inquisitiveness and even a seemly humility. When Parmenides challenges Socrates's ideas in the ensuing discussion, the young man readily acknowledges his confusion. Socrates worries that one of his theories, taken to its logical extreme, results in conclusions that seem trivial. "[W]hen I get bogged down in that," he confesses, "I hurry away, afraid that I may fall into some pit of nonsense and come to harm." Parmenides replies with a kindness born of his more advanced years. "That's because you are still young, Socrates . . . and philosophy has not yet gripped you, as, in my opinion, it will in the future, once you begin to consider none of the cases beneath your notice. Now, though, you still care about what people think, because of your youth." Later, when Socrates finds himself at another impasse, Parmenides offers more of his fatherly comfort and then demonstrates a method that will help the young man reach his desired goal.

The *Parmenides* may well be a product of Plato's imagination, but its depiction of Socrates passed muster with Plato's earliest readers, many of whom had known Socrates himself. The young man was cocky and provocative, but he earnestly sought the truth and harbored no illusions about finding it by himself. Fortunately, many people were able to discover Socrates's more endearing qualities beneath his abrasive exterior. The process, however, took patience, generosity, and insight, and not everyone who was to cross paths with Socrates possessed those qualities.

CHAPTER 4

THE NATURE
OF REALITY

GATHERINGS LIKE THE ONE IN PYTHODORUS'S
house introduced Socrates to the most pressing
intellectual concerns of his time. Foremost
among them was the question that Zeno and
Parmenides address in the *Parmenides*: What is
the true nature of reality?

The question may seem unnecessary. Isn't
reality simply the floor we stand on, the birds
we hear, the tomatoes we eat—the sum total
of what we apprehend through our senses?
But if we try to imagine reality as the ancient
Greeks experienced it, the question begins to
make more sense. Ancient Greeks were more
intimately acquainted than most of us today
with the constant flux in the physical stuff of
life. They saw how a seed planted in the fertile
ground sprouts into a stalk, how the grains at

the end of that stalk are harvested and ground into flour, and how that flour is mixed with other ingredients to make bread. They observed how fleece is sheared from the bodies of sheep and how the fibers are spun into yarn, woven into cloth, and sewn into a garment. They saw how living creatures that are nourished by crops eventually die and decay, nourishing new crops that feed new generations of life. Amid all this incessant transformation, the basic matter never changes and the cycles never vary. What, the ancient Greeks wondered, is the relationship between the changeability of nature and the permanence at its core?

Parmenides approached the question by dismissing all change as illusion. Reality consists of only one thing—the "one" that Socrates accused Zeno of rephrasing as "not many"—and that one thing is eternally unchanging, unmoving, and indivisible. In the *Parmenides*, Zeno presents his reason for supporting this notion. If reality were many rather than one, its parts—individual things—would be internally inconsistent. As part of a single entity, individual things would have to be "like" (similar to one another), but as differentiated parts of that single entity, they would have to be "unlike" (dissimilar to one another). Since it is impossible for a thing to be both like and unlike at the same time, reality must be one, not many.

Socrates expresses the same surprise that we might ourselves feel at this argument. He points out that his body has a right side and a left side, a front part and a back part, an upper half and a lower half. In this way he is many, not one. At the same time, he is a single member of a group that has gathered to speak together. In this way he is one, not many. Zeno is wrong to say that the one and the many cannot coexist.

But Socrates promptly qualifies his point. Zeno is mistaken only in regard to things we perceive through our senses; those things can and do embody opposites. When it comes to things we perceive solely through our minds, Zeno is absolutely right. Although the physical Socrates can be both one and many, the abstract concept of oneness does not admit multiplicity, and the abstract concept of multiplicity does not admit oneness. For that matter, all abstract concepts preclude their opposites. In our everyday sensory world, the fairest law always entails a measure of injustice, the most beautiful rose always exhibits a degree of imperfection, and the roundest hoop always contains flaws in its circularity. By contrast, justice, beauty, and circularity *themselves* are forever perfect and absolute.

Exactly how Socrates understood qualities like oneness and justice has been a subject of disagreement since ancient times. Plato is thought to have believed that those abstractions—usually called "Forms" in translations of his writings—have a reality of their own, clearer and more precise than the reality of our everyday experience, and in his dialogues, he often depicts Socrates expressing the same view. But Aristotle, Plato's student, denies that Socrates attributed any sort of independent existence to abstract qualities: "It was the others who made them separate, and called these separate entities the Forms of everything that exists."

It might be tempting to brush aside the entire issue. No matter who first articulated the idea of the Forms, isn't it just magical thinking to attribute any sort of independent existence to abstractions? And what would it mean, anyway, to say that beauty or redness or multiplicity exists apart from the things that we know through our senses—that those ideas exist like spirits in some dreamy, heavenly realm where everything is perfect? But Forms are not quite as outlandish as they may initially seem. We believe in absolute parallelism or perpendicularity even if the physical world never offers us perfect examples of either. We grasp the existence of an exact ratio between a circle's circumference and its diameter even if we can express only an approximation of pi. And we recognize, even as toddlers, that numbers have a life of their own. We count three marbles or three sticks, but we know that the idea of three is greater than any of those specific examples, greater than all the threesomes we can ever expect to encounter in our lives. If mathematical abstractions have this sort of independent reality, perhaps abstractions such as justice or beauty or redness do as well. After all, justice and beauty and redness might involve their own sets of exact measurements and proportions, and we do seem to sense those sorts of standards. Our day-to-day experience never brings us flawless examples of any of those qualities, and yet somehow we grasp those qualities well enough to recognize when a specific example falls short.

Thinkers like Parmenides and Zeno exposed Socrates to the notion that reality may be quite different from the sum of our sensory experience. But on his visits to Athens, Socrates also encountered an altogether different way to think about the nature of reality, one that gave much more weight to the material world. This other approach was cosmology, the study of the physical universe and its origins. The discipline arose during the sixth century BCE in Ionia, a Greek region along the western coast of Asia Minor, where several prominent thinkers attempted to identify the primal material out of which everything is made. In the history of philosophy, this material has become known as "substance," a word based on the Latin *substantia*, meaning "something that stands beneath." The term and its philosophical context may be unfamiliar, but the endeavor itself is not. We use the word "matter" instead of "substance," and we talk about quarks or stardust instead of the elements that the ancients identified, but we are still investigating the fundamental stuff of which the universe is composed.

The ancient cosmologists proposed many different theories about the nature of substance. Thales, who is widely considered the first philosopher of the Western tradition, believed that substance was water. Others disagreed. Some

THE FOUR ELEMENTS: One of the most famous of the cosmologists was Empedocles, who believed that different combinations of earth, air, fire, and water are responsible for everything we observe in the world. The idea influenced science and medicine for the better part of a thousand years. This image, with fire and air at the top and water and earth on the bottom, comes from the French edition of a thirteenth-century encyclopedic work in Latin, *De proprietatibus rerum* (*The Properties of Things*).

Bartholomaeus, Anglicus, active thirteenth century, et al. *Le propriétaire en francoys.* [Imprime au dit lieu de Lyon: Par honnorable homme maistre Mathieu Husz . . . , le xv. iour de mars, l'an 1491] Pdf. Retrieved from the Library of Congress, www.loc.gov/item/00522095/.

thought that substance was air, others thought that it was fire, and still others thought that it was a combination of earth, air, fire, and water. The parade of assertions may seem random, but the cosmologists based their ideas on careful observation. Thales, for instance, saw that people and animals survive by drinking freshwater and eating the crops that are nourished by rain. He noted that ice and steam revert to water through melting and condensation. And he knew that life begins in semen and amniotic fluid and ends in the oozing of a decaying corpse.

Some of the cosmologists' achievements were quite impressive. Thales predicted a solar eclipse, developed a basic understanding of electricity, and knew enough about triangles to estimate the height of a pyramid from the length of its shadow and the distance of a ship at sea from two sightings on land. Anaximander, who was deeply influenced by Thales, developed a theory of evolution that identified fish as the ancestors of human beings—a crude precursor of modern evolutionary theories, which also locate the earliest forms of animal life in water. Other cosmologists theorized that the world is composed of indivisible particles that move around in empty space. These particles, which they called atoms, come in many different shapes and clump together in various arrangements and densities to form everything that the universe contains.

But the cosmologists' most important achievement lay not in any specific theory or discovery but in the way they set the foundations for modern science. First, they rejected mythological explanations of nature. Instead of invoking the gods and their activities, the cosmologists accounted for natural phenomena *naturalistically*—in terms of nature itself without any appeal to outside intervention. Second, the cosmologists demonstrated the value of inference. To find the underlying causes of the phenomena they observed, they built up from what they already knew to arrive at what they did not yet know. And third, the cosmologists demanded rigorous proofs in the study of nature—proofs with the same sort of logical precision that people already expected in arithmetic and geometry. "Natural philosophy" is the name we now give to this early scientific approach to the universe.

Natural philosophy arrived in Athens by the time that Socrates celebrated his ninth birthday. The bearer was Anaxagoras, an Ionian whose insatiable curiosity led him to study many different natural phenomena, including thunder and lightning, sense perception, embryology, the saltiness of the sea, and the source of the Nile. Anaxagoras also developed his own theory of substance. In his view, substance was a composite of many different elements that swirl around in a kind of cosmic blender to produce all the individual things of our world. What first set the cosmic blender into motion and continues to regulate its operations was a force that Anaxagoras called Mind—*Nous* in the original Greek. Anaxagoras described Mind as a conscious agent:

> Nous *has control over all things that have soul, both the larger and the smaller. And* Nous *controlled the whole revolution, so that it started to revolve in the beginning. . . . And* Nous *knew . . . them all: the things that are being mixed together, the things that are being separated off, and the things that are being dissociated. And whatever sorts of things were going to be, and whatever sorts were and now are not, and as many as are now and whatever sorts will be, all these* Nous *set in order.*

These words might make Mind sound like
the all-present, all-knowing, and all-powerful
god that later came to dominate the Western
tradition, but Anaxagoras was not thinking in
religious terms. He granted Mind consciousness
but made no effort to personalize its power.
He never indicated that Mind experiences
emotions like compassion or anger or claimed
that it interacts in any way with people. Most
significantly, he never suggested that Mind
demands devotion or worship.

Anaxagoras spent twenty years in Athens.
We have no evidence that Socrates met him in
person, but we do know that as a young man,
Socrates delved into natural philosophy. In
Plato's *Phaedo*, which depicts Socrates's final
hours in prison, Socrates recalls that early
interest: "When I was a young man, I was
wonderfully keen on that wisdom which they
call natural science, for I thought it splendid to
know the causes of everything, why it comes to
be, why it perishes and why it exists." But this
pleasant memory gives way to a recollection of
profound disappointment. Socrates discovered
that his studies were bringing him only
superficial knowledge, not deep understanding.
He knew, for instance, that two is formed

when a single object is combined with another object, and he also knew that two is formed when a single object is split in half. How is it possible, he wondered, that contradictory processes—combining and splitting—lead to the same result? What is twoness, really? Natural philosophy described only the outer surfaces of things, not their essence.

As Socrates continues to recollect, however, he was not yet ready to abandon natural philosophy. His hopes surged when he heard someone reading about Mind from one of Anaxagoras's books. If Mind directs and causes everything, as Anaxagoras claimed, then the path to genuine knowledge was straightforward. Since Mind would always organize everything in the best possible way, the key to understanding the universe was to identify the best possible way for every single thing to be. "I was glad to think," Socrates remembers, "that I had found in Anaxagoras a teacher about the cause of things after my own heart, and that he would tell me, first, whether the earth is flat or round, and then would explain why it is so of necessity, saying which is better, and that it was better to be so. If he said it was in the middle of the universe, he would go on to show that it was better for it to be in the middle." In his enthusiasm, Socrates tracked down every one of Anaxagoras's books that was available in Athens. "I would not have exchanged my hopes for a fortune."

But Anaxagoras disappointed Socrates too. Anaxagoras never really invoked Mind to explain specific phenomena; instead of thinking about the best way for things to be, he focused on "air and ether and water and many other strange things." Socrates describes his frustration:

> *That seemed to me much like saying that Socrates' actions are all due to his mind, and then in trying to tell the causes of everything I do, to say that the reason I am sitting here is because my body consists of bones and sinews, because the bones are hard and are separated by joints, that the sinews are such as to contract and relax, that they surround the bones along with flesh and skin which hold them together, then as the bones are hanging in their sockets, the relaxation and contraction of the sinews enable me to bend my limbs, and that is the cause of my sitting here with my limbs bent.*

Anaxagoras's causes did not seem to be causes at all. Bones and sinews enable movement, but the reason movement happens in the first place is that a mind has decided on the best possible course. Socrates wanted to know *why*, not *how*.

After his hopes in Anaxagoras were dashed, Socrates stopped looking for answers in natural philosophy. Many years later, in his speech to the jury that condemned him to death, he disclaimed all interest in "things in the sky and below the earth." He added, "I do not speak in contempt of such knowledge, if someone is wise in these things . . . but, gentlemen, I have no part in it." Socrates was developing entirely new questions, ones that the thinkers he had encountered had not even begun to consider.

CHAPTER 5

QUESTIONS FOR AN AGE OF HUMANISM

SOCRATES'S QUESTIONS WERE DISTINCTLY Athenian. They arose from the same foundation that underlay the rise of democracy, the victory against Persia, the education for arete, and the gatherings at homes like Pythodorus's.

That foundation was a broad cultural temperament, and to understand it, we can look to Athenian architecture, always one of the best measures of the Athenian spirit. The most imposing building that Socrates knew from his earliest years was not the well-known Parthenon, the stately colonnaded temple whose majestic ruins still grace the Acropolis. Construction on the Parthenon did not begin until Socrates was about twenty-two years old, and the structure was completed only when he was in his early thirties. So although that temple has become the most famous symbol of ancient Athens, a different structure captured the polis's spirit when Socrates was beginning to formulate his essential questions.

This structure was the Temple of Olympian Zeus, the project of Hippias, a sixth-century tyrant who had dreamed of building the largest temple in the world. Almost half a century before Socrates was born, builders had laid a gargantuan foundation and begun working on columns that promised to soar into the sky. But the work had proceeded no further. In 510 BCE, Hippias was deposed and the project abandoned. Socrates could see the unfinished temple every time he walked from Alopeke to the center of Athens.

The site remained untouched even during the ambitious building spree that produced the Parthenon and transformed the city in the second half of the fifth century. The scope of that construction program suggests that neither money nor manpower was lacking; the Athenians just chose to devote their efforts elsewhere. And where they devoted their efforts is significant. The Parthenon and the other temples of the Acropolis are the most familiar products of the city's makeover, but many of the new buildings, located in the Agora, served the various needs of government and civic life: a new council chamber for one of the executive committees of the Ekklesia, a monument that served as a notice board, a prison, a mint, and several stoas, among other structures. All of these took precedence over Hippias's project. And yet Hippias's project was not just any building. It was meant to be a temple to a god, and not just to any god but to Zeus, the most powerful member of the pantheon. The Athenians were building shrines to their human institutions at the same time that they were neglecting the shrine to their mightiest god.

Aristotle sheds light on this neglect. The Temple to Olympian Zeus, he says, is a prime example of how a tyrant contrives to keep himself in power. By forcing people into the hard labor of a massive construction project, the tyrant destroys their ability to conspire against him; exhausted individuals lack the time and energy to organize a revolt against their oppressor. The Temple of Olympian Zeus, in other words, represented the presumptuous overreach of a ruler and the disempowerment of the people—the very antithesis of what the Athenians were trying to achieve through their democracy. By allowing the building to stand unfinished, the people were expressing their robust confidence in themselves.

The derelict temple bore witness to the Athenians' *humanism*—their profound faith in human potential. Athens devoted a lot of time, energy, and money to its temples, rituals, and festivals, but religion never dislodged the people's vigorous sense of themselves. Humanism led to the victory against Persia, which the people achieved through their strategic decisions and self-sacrifice; humanism gave rise to the social and political reforms of the sixth century, which the people instituted to address their society's terrible inequities; and humanism shaped the democracy, which affirmed that citizens have the ability and responsibility to govern themselves. Humanism animated Athenian education, which summoned young people to excellence in mind, body, and soul; and humanism explained the polis's meteoric rise as an economic, military, cultural, and political power. If Athens was a success story, it was the Athenians themselves who were its authors.

Ironically, Greek religion helped to nurture some of this vibrant humanism. Worship consisted mainly of following the intricate rules for sacrifices: pouring wine, milk, or olive oil upon the ground; placing fruits or cakes of grain upon the altar; or slaughtering an animal and burning specific parts of its body. These sacrifices acknowledged the gods' power, but not at the cost of diminishing the people's sense of themselves. An offering was a sort of business transaction, and worshipers felt an energetic faith in their own bargaining power. "Haven't I given you the tastiest bits of meat and the first portion of the wine?" they might have asked the gods. "Now you *owe* me what I'm requesting!"

Furthermore, as anyone familiar with Greek mythology knows, the gods were temperamental and self-centered. Worship was an ongoing

OFFERINGS TO THE GODS: On this jar, which was used for mixing wine with water, young men and a boy bring various offerings to an altar where a small fire burns. A flutist provides musical accompaniment.

Bell krater with scene of sacrifice, ca. 420 BCE. Pothos Painter, Greek, Attic. Yale University Art Gallery.

attempt to avert disaster; to offend the gods was to risk not only one's own welfare but the welfare of the entire community. This fearsome unpredictability might have crushed the people's confidence, but instead it gave them the latitude to make meaning for themselves. Worshipers had no expectation of forming a personal relationship with a just and loving deity. The gods offered no guidance about how to lead one's life or set up society, did little to help worshipers feel valued in an uncertain world, and extended no guarantee that human effort meant anything at all. The Athenians had no choice but to take charge of their own lives.

But humanism is a heavy responsibility. Without authoritative edicts from on high, people must themselves find answers to life's fundamental questions. What is the best way to achieve happiness? What differentiates justice from injustice, and what is the appropriate response to injustice? What are the limits of friendship? What differentiates courage from foolhardiness? To whom should one entrust positions of authority? How should one educate one's children? When all is said and done, what defines a good life?

These were the questions that intrigued Socrates. He had thoroughly imbibed the humanist spirit of his polis, and despite his tender years, he already understood that the human realm demands just as systematic an inquiry as the physical world of the natural philosophers or the rarified truths of a Parmenides or Zeno. The young man from Alopeke was about to forge a path through untrodden territory. In the first century BCE, Cicero, the great Roman statesman and philosopher, gave a memorable assessment of the new direction. Socrates, said Cicero, "was the first to call philosophy down from the heavens and set her in the cities of men and bring her also into their homes and compel her to ask questions about life and morality and things good and evil."

Socrates's new focus could not have better suited his time and place. The proud citizens of fifth-century Athens had grown accustomed to an extraordinary expectation, the idea that their lives were theirs to shape as they saw fit. The ultimate question for Socrates was how to shape a life worth living.

PART TWO

Asking the Questions

CHAPTER 6

THE GROWTH
OF A FOLLOWING

SOCRATES PURSUED HIS NEW PHILOSOPHICAL path with an intensity that affected all aspects of his behavior. He ate sparingly, went around barefoot, spent little time on grooming, and wore the same shabby peplos both day and night. In the winter, his *himation*, the heavy cloak that he donned over his peplos, did double duty as his bedtime blanket. As he strolled past market stalls heaped with trinkets and curiosities from near and far, he proudly declared, "How many things are there which I do not want." He was happy as long as he could devote himself to the questions he had begun to ask.

Since a meaningful life should be everyone's concern, Socrates did not want to pursue his quest alone. To reach as many people as possible, he abandoned the usual practices of other thinkers. He did not establish a formal school, develop

(Facing page)
Attic Red-Figure Column Krater, ca. 470–460 BCE. Agrigento Painter, Greek, Attic. J. Paul Getty Museum. Digital image courtesy of the Getty's Open Content Program.

an exclusive coterie, or limit his discussions to fashionable gatherings in wealthy homes. He engaged passersby on the street, in the Agora, at the palaestrae and gymnasia—wherever he could meet regular people going about their regular business. And he was quick to find wisdom where his contemporaries might not have expected it. He demonstrated that a slave who had never studied math could solve a problem in geometry, and he acknowledged his intellectual debt to two women, one who taught him about the art of love and the other who instructed him in the skill of persuasive speaking.

He came across ignorance and indifference as well. Most of his fellow Athenians never bothered to think about *how* they were living. Instead, they spent all their time pursuing careers, spending money, and trying to win the admiration of others. Awakening the public to its misdirected priorities became Socrates's personal mission. "Good Sir," he said to anyone who stayed long enough to listen, "you are an Athenian, a citizen of the greatest city with the greatest reputation for both wisdom and power; are you not ashamed of your eagerness to possess as much wealth, reputation and honors as possible, while you do not care for nor give thought to wisdom or truth, or the best possible state of your soul?"

Socrates was earnest, and his goals were honorable. But the passing years did little to soften the cocky, combative spirit that Plato depicts in Socrates's encounter with Zeno and Parmenides. Socrates often humiliated the individuals he challenged, and few of them forgot the affront—especially because it often took place in front of an audience. A crowd of spectators had begun to follow Socrates around Athens, and their numbers were growing.

The motivations of those spectators varied. Some people thrilled to Socrates's message. They agreed with his criticism of their culture and heeded his summons to worthier pursuits. Others enjoyed the logical combat. Socrates was a sharp thinker and debater, and it was an intellectual treat to watch him pick apart other people's arguments. A third group did not especially care about either the moral or cerebral side of Socrates's activity. This group simply liked to see Socrates take other people down a notch or two—and the older and more highly esteemed Socrates's targets, the greater the fun.

Teenagers especially enjoyed the spectacle of Socrates's encounters. Since these admirers were still too young to enter the Agora on their own, Socrates began to station himself just outside its perimeter. A favorite haunt was right next to one of the Agora's border stones, where a shoemaker named Simon kept a workshop. Intrigued by Socrates and the attendant crowd, Simon welcomed them into his premises and listened attentively to the proceedings. The shoemaker also took careful notes, which he eventually transformed into dialogues that focused on some of the subjects that Socrates discussed, including law, love, knowledge, poetry, beauty, and courage.

Most of Socrates's admirers were quite a bit wealthier than Simon, and this made perfect sense: the well-to-do had the greatest amount of leisure to follow Socrates about town. Eventually a teenager named Alcibiades, born into spectacular prosperity and privilege, became one of the philosopher's most ardent followers. This young man belonged to one of the polis's most prominent families, and his advantages continued even after his father died in battle. Alcibiades, then only six years old, became the ward of his mother's cousin, and this cousin was Pericles, the greatest statesman of the period. Alcibiades possessed such immense wealth that he eventually acquired several teams of horses that competed in chariot races, ancient Greece's most crowd-pleasing sport—and an undertaking so expensive that only the fabulously rich could enter even a single team. Exceptionally good looks topped off the young man's advantages. In a dialogue sometimes attributed to Plato, Socrates tells Alcibiades, "You fancy yourself the tallest and best-looking man around—and it's quite plain to see you're not wrong about that."

The attachment between Socrates and Alcibiades was well known, and it seemed to fit a familiar pattern known as *pederasty*. Ancient Athenians assumed that adult men felt physically attracted to adolescent boys. Men unabashedly frequented the palaestrae and gymnasia to watch boys practicing sports in the nude, and both the adults and the adolescents expected sexual relationships to develop. Today such a relationship would outrage most people. We worry about a dangerous imbalance of power, and we expect our society to protect young people from the physical advances of their elders. But where we perceive coercion by sexual predators, the Athenians saw something quite different. In their ideal notion of pederasty, the attachment was an essential part of a boy's education. The older man was meant to guide his beloved into the responsibilities of adulthood and citizenship.

As an adolescent, Socrates may never have been part of a pederastic pair. The Greeks prized physical beauty, and this was definitely not one of Socrates's strong points; besides, Plato shows him attributing his education in the art of love to a woman, not to a man. But when Socrates was in his early to mid-thirties, Alcibiades, about twenty years his junior, tried to involve him as the older man in a pederastic relationship. In a dialogue called the *Symposium*, Plato depicts Alcibiades, by then an adult, recalling those youthful hopes: "What I thought at the time was that what he really wanted was *me*, and that seemed to me the luckiest coincidence: all I had to do was to let him have his way with me, and he would teach me everything he knew—believe me, I had a lot of confidence in my looks." At the time, Alcibiades was still young enough to have an attendant to protect him from the advances of older men, but the boy was determined. He sent his attendant away and waited for Socrates to tell him "whatever it is that lovers say when they find themselves alone." Alcibiades did not get what he wanted. After engaging Alcibiades for some

PEDERASTY: A seated youth and his older male lover reach for a kiss on the interior of this drinking cup. When a guest received this vessel at a symposium, the image was covered in wine and would have been revealed as a pleasant surprise once the liquid was consumed. Since this is the same cup as the one with athletic scenes on pages 22 and 23, the message is clear: activities in the gymnasium naturally give way to pederastic relationships.

Attic Red-Figure Kylix, ca. 510–500 BCE. Attributed to the Carpenter Painter, Greek, Attic. J. Paul Getty Museum. Image courtesy of the Getty's Open Content Program.

time in a philosophical discussion, Socrates took his leave.

Etiquette demanded that Alcibiades, as the adolescent in the pair, remain passive, so he could do no more than offer strong hints and good opportunities. Soon he came up with the perfect plan. He would invite Socrates to a joint session at the gymnasium, where the two of them would be in physical contact while they were naked. Socrates accepted Alcibiades's invitation, and the pair engaged in an energetic wrestling match. To Alcibiades's delight, they found themselves alone. The circumstances were as favorable as they could be, but once again Socrates failed to respond as Alcibiades had hoped.

At this point, Alcibiades abandoned any pretense of passivity. He invited Socrates to dinner—"as if I were his lover and he my young prey!" he recalls, with surprise at his own audacity. It took some work, but at last he convinced Socrates to spend the night. With the lights out and the slaves dismissed, Alcibiades declared his love: "'I think,' I said, 'you're the only worthy lover I have ever had—and yet, look how shy you are with me! Well, here's how I look at it. It would be really stupid not to give you anything you want: you can have me, my

belongings, anything my friends might have.'"
But Socrates dodged this direct appeal, along
with the other attempts that followed, and gave
only the vaguest of answers: "In the future let's
consider things together. We'll always do what
seems the best to the two of us."

To desperate Alcibiades, that response was
invitation enough:

> His words made me think that my own had
> finally hit their mark, that he was smitten
> by my arrows. I didn't give him a chance to
> say another word. I stood up immediately
> and placed my mantle over the light cloak
> which, though it was the middle of winter,
> was his only clothing. I slipped underneath
> the cloak and put my arms around this
> man—this utterly unnatural, this truly
> extraordinary man—and spent the whole
> night next to him. . . . But in spite of all
> my efforts, this hopelessly arrogant, this
> unbelievably insolent man—he turned me
> down! He spurned my beauty, of which I
> was so proud. . . . I swear to you by all the
> gods and goddesses together, my night with
> Socrates went no further than if I had spent
> it with my father or older brother!

Alcibiades was humiliated, but his admiration for Socrates was stronger than ever. "Here was a man whose strength and wisdom went beyond my wildest dreams! How could I bring myself to hate him? I couldn't bear to lose his friendship."

On the surface, Socrates does not seem to have been Alcibiades's type at all. Socrates was not from a distinguished family, and he had little money; he obeyed a bizarre daimonion and paid little attention to his hygiene or appearance. Aside from wearing the same clothes all the time, he rarely bathed or combed his long, unkempt hair, and his ugliness was a poor match for Alcibiades's gorgeous looks. Socrates once teased Critobulus, the son of his good friend Crito, for his vanity, and Critobulus's retort said it all:

> *"What's this?" said Socrates. "You're bragging as if you were more beautiful than I am."*

> *"Of course," said Critobulus, "otherwise I should be uglier than any Silenus in the satyr-plays."*

Socrates fared badly even when he was stacked against the grotesque sileni and satyrs of Greek mythology, who were often portrayed onstage;

these were wild, animalistic men with a horse's tail and ears. What did Alcibiades find so irresistible?

Alcibiades himself provides the answer in the *Symposium*. During one of his attempts at seduction, he declared to Socrates, "Nothing is more important to me than becoming the best man I can be, and no one can help me more than you to reach that aim." Socrates's ugliness was immaterial, as were his relative poverty, unremarkable pedigree, and personal habits. The philosopher possessed the only thing that really mattered—a commitment to living a meaningful, ethical life. Alcibiades later earned notoriety as an opportunist and traitor, but as a young man he briefly caught sight, through Socrates, of what goodness might be.

The allure was powerful, and Alcibiades was not alone in feeling it. Even twenty-five or thirty years after Alcibiades's infatuation, idealistic young men continued to flock around Socrates. Critos's son was one of them. As a teenager, Critobulus attached himself to the philosopher, and even after joining his father in the supervision of the family's farms, he remained an avid disciple. Apollodorus, a marvelously successful businessman, withdrew from his

SATYRS: A satyr holds a wineskin in this painting from a drinking cup. Satyrs were eager followers of Dionysus, the god of wine, and often cavorted with Dionysus's female followers, the maenads. The satyr's animal side is reflected in his pointy ears as well as his long tail, which is only faintly visible in this image. Satyrs were usually depicted in an obvious state of sexual arousal, but here the wineskin blocks the view.

Attic Red-Figure Cup, ca. 520–510 BCE. Oltos, Greek, Attic. J. Paul Getty Museum. Image courtesy of the Getty's Open Content Program.

worldly affairs to become Socrates's constant companion. Antisthenes, who lived in the Piraeus, a port city about five miles away, walked to and from Athens each day so that he could benefit from Socrates's presence. Aristippus, who hailed from northern Africa, traveled to Greece to attend the Olympic Games, but there he heard such a glowing description of Socrates that he made his way to Athens to check out the reality himself—and then remained until almost the end of the philosopher's life. Phaedo's background was more troubled. As a prisoner of war, he had been forced into sexual slavery in Athens, where Socrates recognized his intellectual promise and may have persuaded Crito to pay for his release. After studying with Socrates for a number of years, Phaedo returned to Elis, his hometown in the northwestern Peloponnese, where he founded his own school of philosophy.

Today we are especially fortunate that two of Socrates's followers left substantial accounts of him. One of these followers was Xenophon, who lived in the countryside about nine and a half miles from Athens and in the early fourth century BCE led a distinguished career as a commander of Greek mercenary forces in Persia. Xenophon wrote extensively about many topics, including history, government, and horsemanship, and among his works are several dialogues that feature Socrates. Diogenes Laertius, who wrote early biographies of the philosophers, probably in the third century CE, records a lovely tradition about how Xenophon fell under Socrates's spell:

> They say that Socrates met him in a narrow lane, and put his stick across it, and prevented him from passing by, asking him where all kinds of necessary things were sold. And when he had answered him, he asked him again where men were made good and virtuous. And as he did not know, he said, "Follow me, then, and learn." And from this time forth, Xenophon became a follower of Socrates.

Although Xenophon's dialogues lack the nimble wit of Plato's work, they are an important source for our understanding of the philosopher's life and thought.

Plato, of course, is the second follower who left us an invaluable record of Socrates, and once again, Diogenes Laertius provides a description of a fateful first encounter. Although Plato was only twenty years old, he had already written a tragedy, and he was on his way to the great theater of Athens, the Theater of Dionysus, to enter his work in the dramatic competition that the polis held each year. Socrates happened to be standing in front of the theater that day, and Plato stopped to listen to what he was saying. The transformation was immediate. The young man consigned his manuscript to the flames, attached himself to Socrates as a disciple, and committed the rest of his life to philosophy.

The reality may not be quite what Diogenes Laertius reports. For Plato, at least, a less dramatic account appears in a letter that many scholars believe he wrote himself. Plato explains that as a young man he had planned to become a politician, but the machinations of Athenian politics—and especially the state's decision to execute Socrates—made him cast those plans aside: "At last I came to the conclusion that all existing states are badly governed and the condition of their laws practically incurable, without some miraculous remedy and the assistance of fortune; and I was forced to say, in praise of true philosophy, that from her height alone was it possible to discern what the nature of justice is, either in the state or in the individual." Plato's love of justice prompted him to abandon politics and follow the path that Socrates had forged.

In terms of Socrates's impact, it makes little difference whether Plato originally aspired to be a dramatist or a politician. Both stories touch on the same theme, the one that arises in the stories of all Socrates's followers. Socrates shook people to the core. They had never met anyone like him before, and they grasped, often instantly, that he could help them become better people. These young men yearned for lives of meaning, and through their attachment to Socrates, with his commitment to wisdom, truth, and the best possible state of the soul, they anticipated meaning in abundance.

CHAPTER 7

THE SOPHISTS

DESPITE THE MANY YOUNG MEN WHO aspired to learn from him, Socrates never thought of himself as a teacher. He was a man with a calling, not a merchant offering goods for sale, and he charged no fees for his services. At his trial many years later, he described the personal costs of his approach—and conveyed, all the while, a characteristically hearty sense of his own importance: "That I am the kind of person to be a gift of the god to the city you might realize from the fact that it does not seem like human nature for me to have neglected all my own affairs and to have tolerated this neglect now for so many years while I was always concerned with you, approaching each one of you like a father or an elder brother to persuade you to care for virtue." Years of this selfless behavior had left their mark: "I . . . have a convincing witness that I speak the truth, my poverty."

Socrates's manner and mission, however, often fell flat with the parents of his young followers. Who was that strange, ungroomed man who had entranced their sons, distracting them from what really mattered? Ambitious, well-heeled parents wanted to promote their families' interests, and they counted on their sons to garner as much political influence as possible. Those parents were much more impressed by a new group of thinkers who had begun to arrive in Athens toward the middle of the fifth century. The newcomers were itinerant teachers who went by the name of sophists, a word based on the Greek root *sophia*, or "wisdom," which also appears in the word "philosopher."

Unlike Socrates, the sophists did not hesitate to call themselves teachers or to charge for their services. They claimed that they could teach arete to anyone who paid their fees; Plato shows one of them even offering a money-back guarantee: "[A] student pays the full price only if he wishes to; otherwise, he goes into a temple, states under oath how much he thinks my lessons are worth, and pays that amount." For the sophists, wisdom was a commodity, like pottery or olive oil, acquired simply by laying out the cash. Socrates disdainfully defined the sophist as "a kind of merchant who peddles provisions upon which the soul is nourished."

Even worse, by "arete" the sophists meant something quite different from the all-around excellence that had been a traditional part of Greek culture. They were canny businessmen who understood the political aspirations of well-to-do Athenians and offered a concrete, no-nonsense way to make those aspirations come true. They knew that in the noisy, competitive democracy, the ability to promote one's own interests was almost synonymous with the ability to speak well. In the Ekklesia, citizens ascended the *bema*, the speaker's stand at the front of the Pnyx, and argued in favor of or against specific policies. In the courts, defendants and prosecutors stood before the jury and explained why justice was on their side. Anyone who hoped to stand out had to speak forcefully and convincingly. When the sophists promised to teach arete, what they really had in mind was *rhetoric*, the art of persuasive speaking. Prosperous parents snatched them up to teach their sons.

Now, mastering the art of rhetoric is not a bad thing in itself. The members of any group of people must communicate effectively in order to solve problems and share productive lives. But when a public speaker disregards truth and cares only about impressing an audience, rhetorical skills become dangerous weapons, tools of crass manipulation. Many of the sophists promoted that more sinister form of rhetoric. They knew that slick argumentation can disguise deficiencies in knowledge, reasoning, and integrity.

The sophists made light of everything that Socrates valued most. The modern English word "sophistry" captures Socrates's aversion: "sophistry" is the intentionally deceptive use of arguments that seem true but are actually false. In Plato's dialogue *Euthydemus*, Socrates is prevented by his daimonion from leaving the gymnasium one day, and as a result he unexpectedly meets two young sophists from abroad. After familiarizing himself with their style of argumentation, he playfully declares that he plans to hand himself over to them so that he can benefit from their instruction. He wryly sings their praises: "Not a single man can stand up to them, they have become so skilled in fighting arguments and in refuting whatever may be said no matter whether it is true or false." Later in the dialogue, one of the sophists,

Dionysodorus, provides an especially ludicrous example of his skill. He begins with a question to Ctesippus, a youth of Socrates's circle:

Tell me, have you got a dog?

Yes, and a brute of a one too, said Ctesippus.

And has he got puppies?

Yes indeed, and they are just like him.

And so the dog is their father?

Yes, I saw him mounting the bitch myself, he said.

Well then: isn't the dog yours?

Certainly, he said.

Then since he is a father and is yours, the dog turns out to be your father, and you are the brother of puppies, aren't you?

For unscrupulous sophists like Dionysodorus, arete had become a game of words in which truth played no part at all. The only goal was to win.

Many sophists were actually thoughtful philosophers, much more serious than the example of Dionysodorus suggests. Even so, Socrates found them offensive, and the problem was not just their insistence on fees or their focus on rhetoric. Socrates objected to the sophists' fundamental understanding of morality.

Most of us would reflexively agree with the statement "Murder is wrong." But *why* is murder wrong? One answer is that abstract values like good and evil are true in much the same way that abstract mathematical concepts are true. Just as assuredly as we know that one plus one equals two, we know that helping the poor is good and committing murder is evil. Another common answer is that we receive this knowledge from a good and all-powerful god. That god has forbidden murder, and we therefore know that murder is wrong. Both of these answers assume the existence of an *absolute* moral truth. This truth stands valid for all people in all times and places, regardless of what specific individuals might actually think or do. We can argue about the exact definition of murder—whether, for instance, it includes cases of self-defense or insanity—but the principle that murder is wrong remains forever unchanged. Because people are necessarily limited by time and place, they cannot create or modify this sort of principle. Absolute morality must somehow originate in a realm beyond our own.

The problem is that we cannot be sure that any such realm actually exists. Ultimately, belief in a transcendent realm is just that—a belief, and one that cannot be supported by provable facts. Many people in fifth-century Greece were becoming aware of this issue. Their gods had never been convincing moral authorities, and for well over a century, natural philosophers had been eroding traditional beliefs by explaining the cosmos without recourse to myth. At the same time, belief in an absolute morality independent of the gods—the idea that good and bad have the same sort of reality as mathematical concepts—grew increasingly unsustainable. With the Persian invasions and the development of trade routes across the Mediterranean, fifth-century Greeks had gained exposure to the sheer diversity of human culture. What passes for right and wrong in one society, they were learning, may look radically different in another society.

Socrates's contemporary, the historian Herodotus, avidly documented this cultural diversity. "Everyone believes his own customs to be by far and away the best," Herodotus remarks, and to demonstrate the point, he offers a fascinating example. Darius, the Persian king who organized the first invasion of Greece, met with two different groups, one composed of Greeks and the other of Callatians, a tribe from the Indian subcontinent. The king promised the Greeks any amount of money they named if they would agree to eat the dead bodies of their fathers. Thoroughly scandalized, the Greeks protested that no sum of money would tempt them to do anything so abhorrent. Darius next called in the Callatians and promised them any sum of money to burn the bodies of their fathers. The Callatians were just as horrified by this offer as the Greeks had been by theirs. As it turned out, it was a Greek custom to cremate the dead and a Callatian custom to eat the dead. Each group was just as certain of its own morality as it was of the other group's immorality.

Sophists were especially familiar with these challenges to absolute morality. As members of the intellectual elite, they knew the latest developments in natural philosophy, and as nomads in search of employment, they experienced firsthand the tendency of each society to assume that it held the monopoly on truth. Many sophists came to reject the notion of a universal moral system that people receive from on high. They saw instead a wide variety of local truths that human beings construct, whether consciously or unconsciously, from the ground up—the kind of truth we call *relative* because it exists only *in relation to* a specific cultural framework.

Protagoras, whom Plato identifies as the first professional sophist, exemplified his profession's belief in relative truth. First, Protagoras expressed his doubts about the traditional Greek divinities. "Concerning the gods," he said, "I am unable to know either that they are or that they are not or what their appearance is like. For many are the things that hinder knowledge: the obscurity of the matter and the shortness of human life." Second, in what has become his most famous statement, Protagoras expressed the idea that human beings situated in the real world—not abstract, universal forces— determine what is right and what is wrong:

"A person is the measure of all things—of things that are, that they are, and of things that are not, that they are not."

For a relativist like Protagoras, murder is wrong because we have *decided* that it is wrong and set up our society accordingly. We may have excellent reasons for this decision. We might argue, for instance, that no society can survive a murderous free-for-all; that if we kill others, we are likely to find the tables turned on us one day; that individuals cannot flourish when they are traumatized by random violence. But for a relativist, the best reasons in the world cannot change the basic fact that the wrongness of murder is a human invention.

Relativists are not by definition evil. Claiming that people construct morality themselves is not the same as claiming that morality is meaningless. Many relativists argue just the opposite: since the determination of right and wrong is entirely in our hands, we have the duty to set boundaries and revisit those boundaries as our circumstances change, and acting on that duty arguably shows a much greater respect for morality than the absolutist position allows. When people passively accept what they believe a higher authority has decreed, they are mindless automatons, not free agents who invest thought and effort into crafting moral lives. Although this argument has its appeal, it is undeniable that relativism opens the playing field to unprincipled people. If morality is just a human invention, then why not shape the rules to achieve whatever goals we have in mind, no matter how exploitative or cruel?

The gap between Socrates and this unscrupulous type of relativism takes dramatic form in the *Republic*, one of Plato's longest and most celebrated works. At the beginning of the *Republic*, Socrates asks his companions to define justice. Two of the definitions they propose are "speaking the truth and paying whatever debts one has incurred" and "to give to each what is owed to him," but neither definition withstands Socrates's examination. One of the flaws that Socrates exposes concerns the case of a borrowed sword. According to both definitions, returning that sword to its owner would constitute an act of justice. But would returning the sword still be just if the sword's owner has become insane? Surely in that case it would be a greater expression of justice for the borrower to keep the sword.

A third definition, "to treat friends well and enemies badly," also turns out to be flawed. Socrates points out that a horse is a good horse and a dog is a good dog when they live up to the excellence that is proper to their species. If either animal suffers mistreatment, it will be unable to live up to that standard. The same is true of human beings. People are good to the extent that they live up to human excellence, but they lose their ability to meet that standard when they suffer mistreatment. Now, since part of what constitutes human excellence is justice—in other words, the ability to think and act justly— the third definition collapses into absurdity. Claiming that justice means to treat one's enemy badly would be the same as claiming that a just person, through an act of justice, renders another person unjust. It is sometimes easy to get lost in Socrates's arguments, but a real-world example will clarify his point. A judge may decide to imprison a wrongdoer—or, in the language of the third definition, "to treat an enemy badly." The judge is acting in the name of justice, but the harshness of prison life may well turn the wrongdoer into a significantly more hardened criminal upon his or her release. If a punishment imposed in the name of justice impairs rather than corrects an offender's sense of right and wrong, it is fair to ask whether justice has in fact been served. Treating enemies badly, Socrates concludes, cannot be part of the definition of justice.

At this point, a sophist who has been listening to the discussion can no longer bottle his anger. Socrates later recalls how the hot-tempered Thrasymachus—whose name, fittingly, means "bold in battle"—bursts onto the scene: "He coiled himself up like a wild beast about to spring and he hurled himself at us as if to tear us to pieces." Thrasymachus is determined to set the record straight: everything he has heard so far has been total nonsense. Socrates and his companions are wrong to characterize justice as a lofty ideal. Instead, Thrasymachus asserts, "Justice is nothing other than the advantage of the stronger." In any society, he explains, powerful people establish the law to benefit only themselves. They convince the weaker members of society that obedience to the law serves the exalted purpose of justice, but in reality, this obedience brings everything to the strong and nothing to the weak. People who act justly are so wholly at the mercy of people who act unjustly that justice is really "very high-minded simplicity" and injustice is really "good judgment."

Socrates counters Thrasymachus's position with three different arguments. First Socrates attacks the claim that injustice is beneficial. Pursuing personal advantage at all costs would involve competing against anyone who stands in one's way. But truly knowledgeable people do not compete against one another; instead, they strive to emulate one another's words and deeds. Doctors aspire to act like the best doctors, and captains of ships aspire to act like the best captains of ships; by emulating their most skilled colleagues and engaging in professional collaboration, practitioners advance their craft or branch of knowledge. Because Thrasymachus advocates competition that benefits no one, neither the weak nor the strong, his version of justice exemplifies ignorance, not wisdom.

Socrates's second argument is that to achieve its ends, even injustice requires some degree of justice. A band of thieves plotting an ambush or a polis intent on conquest needs to act as a unit, and if people are to act as a unit, they must enjoy the harmony of friendship, trust, and a common purpose—in a word, justice. Evildoers who act unjustly among themselves provoke tensions that prevent their group from reaching its goal. The same argument applies even in the case of a solitary evildoer. A person whose thoughts, emotions, and desires are at war with one another—in other words, a person whose soul lacks internal justice—will be unable to achieve anything significant.

In his final argument, Socrates contends that a life without justice cannot be happy. He explains that things have both functions and virtues. A function is what a thing is meant to do and does better than anything else; the function of eyes, for example, is sight, and the function of a pruning knife is pruning. A virtue is the quality that enables a thing to perform its function well; the virtue of an eye is whatever leads to sight and not blindness, and the virtue of a pruning knife is whatever facilitates the cutting of a vine. The soul, too, has both a function and a virtue. The soul's function is ruling and deliberating in the management of one's life, and the soul's virtue is whatever corrals thought, emotion, and desire to achieve a shared goal—the same harmony, or internal justice, that Socrates has already identified in his second argument. Without this internal justice, the soul is unable to fulfill its managerial function, and a mismanaged life cannot bring happiness.

Socrates has now reached the bedrock of his thinking, an idea akin to a mathematical axiom in that it cannot be broken down any further and is taken as self-evidently true. This, for Socrates, is the premise that we all naturally desire happiness. In other dialogues, Plato shows him addressing some of the questions that hover around this premise. For example, what is the nature of this universally desired happiness? Why do some people consciously make decisions that bring them unhappiness? Those are important concerns, but here, in his rebuttal of Thrasymachus, Socrates simply builds upon the bedrock. "It profits no one to be wretched but to be happy," he points out, and with that he paves the way to his conclusion. "And so, Thrasymachus, injustice is never more profitable than justice."

Socrates, who is narrating the events a day after they occurred, vividly describes the impact of his arguments on his rival. After the first argument, Socrates observes, "Thrasymachus agreed to all this, not easily as I'm telling it, but reluctantly, with toil, trouble, and—since it was summer—a quantity of sweat that was a wonder to behold. And then I saw something I'd never seen before—Thrasymachus blushing." Socrates does not interpret this blush, but it would seem that Thrasymachus is beginning to waver in his position. Then, after concluding all three of his arguments, Socrates notices a radical change. "[Y]ou became gentle and ceased to give me rough treatment," the philosopher cheerfully reminds the sophist later in the dialogue. We never find out whether Thrasymachus actually switches over to Socrates's way of thinking, but it is impressive to see that two people with intensely antagonistic views have engaged in a serious discussion and will part as friends.

For his own part, Socrates remains steadfast in his understanding of morality. He still lacks the perfect definition of justice that he has been seeking, but he remains certain that one can be found. To his way of thinking, moral truths exist, even if we have not yet grasped them, and those truths are noble and universal. His certainty on this issue, along with his indifference to payment and his disgust at slippery rhetoric, set him apart from the sophists.

But these differences were apparent only to people who actually took the time to think about what Socrates was saying. On a superficial level, it was all too easy to confuse him with the sophists he deplored. For one thing, both he and the sophists employed the same method of argumentation, a rapid-fire series of questions that pushed discussion partners into unwanted positions. In the following sample, which comes from the *Republic*, Socrates is investigating an interlocutor's claim that a just person is especially talented at keeping money safe:

> *Isn't the person most able to land a blow, whether in boxing or any other kind of fight, also most able to guard against it?*

> *Certainly.*

> *And the one who is most able to guard against disease is also most able to produce it unnoticed?*

> *So it seems to me, anyway.*

> *And the one who is the best guardian of an army is the very one who can steal the enemy's plans and dispositions?*

> *Certainly.*

Whenever someone is a clever guardian,
then, he is also a clever thief.

Probably so.

If a just person is clever at guarding money,
therefore, he must also be clever at stealing it.

According to our argument, at any rate.

A just person has turned out then, it seems,
to be a kind of thief.

Through his questions, Socrates pushes his
interlocutor into a position that is patently
ridiculous. The philosopher's aim is legitimate:
he wants to expose the limits of the idea under
consideration so that a better idea can be
proposed in its place. Nonetheless, the shape
and tenor of the exchange recall Dionysodorus's
facetious argument that a dog was the father of
Ctesippus. By the end of Socrates's arguments,
many of his discussion partners felt, with
some justification, that they had been unfairly
manipulated—a feeling that was reinforced by
Socrates's brash and mocking tone. Like the
most shameless of sophists, he often gave the

impression that his real goal was to make fools of the people he engaged in conversation.

Another reason for confusing Socrates with the sophists was that they all attracted the same audience—mainly young, impressionable men who were eager to question the tried-and-true values of their elders. Although Socrates opposed the relativistic morality of the sophists, he did encourage a critical assessment of his polis's culture, and he made little room for the gods in his philosophy. All in all, then, it is no surprise that Socrates's vocal criticism of the sophists left almost no impression on his fellow citizens. For many, if not most, Athenians, that irksome, ugly man on the street, that poorly dressed, unwashed know-it-all, was just another scoundrel who duped the public with his slick tongue and corrupted his admirers with dangerous, newfangled notions.

CHAPTER 8

KNOWLEDGE
AND MORALITY

THE DISCUSSION IN THE *REPUBLIC* ILLUSTRATES
the way that Socrates went about his philosophical
work. He almost always began by asking the
people around him to define a specific quality,
and then he carefully examined each definition
to identify its strengths and weaknesses. In the
Republic he examines justice, but in different
dialogues he takes up other qualities. In *Greater
Hippias*, for example, a dialogue sometimes
attributed to Plato, Socrates engages a sophist
named Hippias in an effort to define the Greek
concept of *kalon*—a word for something highly
valued, usually translated as "the beautiful" or "the
fine." Over the course of the discussion, Hippias
proposes three different definitions. The first is a
beautiful girl, the second is gold, and the third is a

combination of wealth, health, and honor. Socrates exposes the weakness of each definition. The main problem is that Hippias fails to distinguish between a specific *example* of fineness—or as Socrates would say, "a fine thing"—and the abstract *notion* of fineness—"the fine itself." A beautiful girl may indeed be fine, but it is absurd to define fineness as a beautiful girl.

After Hippias's third attempt, Socrates expresses his exasperation—along with the kind of tongue lashing that humiliated his interlocutors and delighted his audiences. "Aren't you capable of remembering that I asked for the fine itself? For what when added to anything— whether to a stone or a plank or a man or a god or any action or any lesson—*anything* gets to be fine? I'm asking you to tell me what fineness is itself, my man, and I am no more able to make you hear me than if you were sitting here in stone—and a millstone at that, with no ears and no brain!" Only a definition with universal and eternal applicability, above and beyond the particulars of experience, will suffice.

Such a definition almost always proves elusive. Even when Socrates examines better proposals than Hippias's, they usually fail the test of logic, and the discussion ends in *aporia*—the term, originally from Greek, for a philosophical impasse. These endings can be frustrating. After following Socrates on the laborious ins and outs of his various arguments, readers may feel that it is only fair for him to provide some answers. But the lack of neat resolutions is one of the most forceful indications of Socrates's priorities. He did not view knowledge as the sophists did, as an object that can be readily transferred from a seller to a buyer or from a teacher to a student, and he was trying to get at the truth, not to win a verbal competition at any cost. As a result, he plunged into topics even when they promised no easy way out, and when he met with failure, he openly acknowledged it. The problem, he always insisted, was ignorance—not just the ignorance of his discussion partners but also his own. At the end of *Greater Hippias*, when he is no closer to a definition of kalon than he was at the beginning of the dialogue, he gives himself a typical scolding: "How will you know whose speech—or any other action—is finely presented or not, when you are ignorant of the fine? And when you're in a state like that, do you think it's any better for you to live than die?"

This self-reproach might seem excessive and the entire endeavor a bit silly. Often Socrates's insistence on the perfect definition, one that can withstand every single logical test he can conjure up, feels like useless quibbling about matters of no consequence—and an unfortunate confirmation, for many people, that philosophy is a pointless discipline. Socrates would have found this reaction preposterous. He was convinced that clear and accurate knowledge, the kind of knowledge that a definition represents, is the only path to goodness.

It is important to linger over this idea, because it is not at all self-evident. Many people draw a distinction between moral and intellectual qualities—or, in the anatomical terms we often use today, between the heart and the mind. In this popular view, goodness originates in the warm feelings of the heart; the colder, dispassionate mind operates independently of those feelings and sometimes at cross purposes to them. Religion and folklore often encourage this idea by portraying the simplest, most unschooled individuals as paragons of virtue. Too much education, we are led to believe, undermines our basic morality.

Socrates would have found this attitude absurd, and he offered a compelling argument for his position. Qualities of the soul, he observed, are neither beneficial nor harmful in themselves. Courage, for instance, saves lives, contributes to victory, and brings honor—but only when it is applied intelligently, in the right time and place. In the wrong circumstances, courage is really just a harmful recklessness. The same is true of moderation, generosity, mental quickness, and other attributes of the soul: they are good when they are applied appropriately and bad when they are applied inappropriately. Since knowledge enables us to differentiate between appropriate and inappropriate circumstances, knowledge is the decisive factor in a person's goodness.

But Socrates did not stop there. Knowledge, he argued, is not just essential to morality; knowledge actually *guarantees* morality. "[I]f someone were to know what is good and bad," he asserted, "then he would not be forced by anything to act otherwise than knowledge dictates." No one, according to Socrates, ever commits a wrong intentionally.

The claim seems improbable. We are all aware of times when we know we should not be doing something but proceed to do it anyway. We snack on a batch of freshly baked cookies despite a doctor's warnings. We copy answers from another student's test because we have failed to study sufficiently. We craft a careful lie after carelessly breaking an item that belongs to someone else. And grimmer examples abound. Hackers steal identities, politicians pocket bribes, terrorists destroy lives—and they all act with full knowledge and intent. How could Socrates maintain that all wrongdoing, without exception, amounts to an unintentional mistake?

Here, too, Socrates had a compelling argument. He began with a background question: How do we actually know whether a thing is good or bad? Standing firmly on his philosophical bedrock, his premise that we all naturally desire happiness, Socrates had a ready answer: the determining factor is pleasure or pain. A thing that brings pleasure is by definition good, and a thing that brings pain is by definition bad. This idea may be disturbing. We all know of pleasures that involve distasteful or dangerous self-indulgence—for example, enjoying too many drinks at a party from which one has to drive home. Did Socrates really mean to say that goodness amounts to sensual gratification? In the dialogue that bears his name, the sophist Protagoras voices this exact concern. When he hears Socrates define the good as the pleasurable, Protagoras adds a qualification: a person who has spent all his energy pursuing pleasure has lived a good life only "so long as he lived having taken pleasure in honorable things."

Socrates is baffled by this qualification: "Surely you don't, like most people, call some pleasant things bad and some painful things good?" he asks Protagoras. "I mean, isn't a pleasant thing good just insofar as it is pleasant, that is, if it results in nothing other than pleasure; and, on the other hand, aren't painful things bad in the same way, just insofar as they are painful?" What Socrates means is that his understanding of pleasure has already taken into account Protagoras's concern for honorability. If drinking at a party entails reckless driving afterward, then enjoying those drinks is by definition a degraded pleasure, one that is already alloyed by the pain it involves. Irresponsible excess is definitely not what Socrates means by the pleasure that he equates with goodness.

Now Socrates's idea that no one commits an intentional wrong begins to make sense. Since everybody naturally desires happiness, nobody knowingly pursues pain for its own sake. We always seek the things that we deem pleasurable, and we always choose what we consider to be a greater pleasure over a lesser one. As we determine our course of action, then, the real conflict is not between the pleasure we seek and the knowledge that we should avoid that pleasure ("I want a second cup of coffee" versus "I know that more caffeine will make me sleep poorly") but between one kind of pleasure and another kind of pleasure ("I want a second cup of coffee" versus "I want to have a healthy night's sleep"). The other choices that we make are similar. Do we want the comfort of avoiding surgery or the comfort of correcting a medical problem? Do we want the good grades we get by cheating or the genuine knowledge we gain by studying? Do we want the relief of lashing out at someone who has angered us or the possibility of reconciliation through more restrained behavior? Whenever we decide how to behave, we choose the pleasure we think is better.

At least in theory, the decision-making is simple. "Weighing is a good analogy," says Socrates. "[Y]ou put the pleasures together and the pains together, both the near and the remote, on the balance scale, and then say which of the two is more." Which pleasure is greater—indulging my desire for coffee or sleeping well tonight? Which pain is greater—disappointing my coffee craving or feeling jittery when I get into bed? But this is where our problems begin. Our balance scale is sometimes faulty, especially

A BALANCE SCALE: On this storage jug from the sixth century BCE, a man brings two containers on a scale into balance. He is aided by boys who tend to the ropes and pans on either side. Above the image, just below the decorative band on top, an inscription gives the name of the potter, Taleides, along with the words *Klitarchos kalos* ("Klitarchos is handsome"). Such *kalos* inscriptions, which usually name a boy old enough for a pederastic relationship, frequently appear on Greek pottery.

Terracotta amphora (jar), ca. 540–530 BCE. Taleides as potter, attributed to the Taleides Painter, Greek, Attic. The Metropolitan Museum of Art, New York.

when we weigh distant pleasures against more immediate ones. Just as nearby objects look larger than faraway objects, present pleasures seem greater than future ones. Since that coffee is available right now but my bedtime is still four hours away, I may mistakenly consider the coffee the greater of the two pleasures.

Now all the pieces are in place for Socrates's conclusion. Since pleasure defines what is good and pain defines what is bad, a mismeasurement of pleasure and pain is the same as a mismeasurement of good and bad. People do bad things because they have inaccurately assessed the choices they face. Wrongdoers are not departing from the best course of action but choosing to follow it; the problem is that they are mistaken about what constitutes the best course of action. After all, if a person truly knows which option is better, why would he or she ever fail to choose it? Socrates's claim, then, is not as absurd as it might initially seem. Accurate knowledge necessarily leads to good behavior. Socrates considered that link so tight that he sometimes dropped the language of cause and effect. Virtue does not just *result from* knowledge; virtue actually *is* knowledge.

CHAPTER 9

THE DEMOCRACY AND THE SPARTAN ALTERNATIVE

SOCRATES'S PROFOUND RESPECT FOR KNOWLEDGE led him in a direction that may seem quite troubling today: he became an outspoken critic of democracy. Our own standpoint in history gives us good reason to support democracy over other forms of government, but for many of us, democracy has become such an unquestioned orthodoxy that we have forgotten its flaws. To Socrates in the fifth century BCE, those flaws loomed large.

The essential problem, for Socrates, was the general public's ignorance. On his rounds about town, he had seen far too much faulty thinking, misinformation, and blithe indifference to matters of importance. "Are *they* the ones who know the truth—ordinary people?" he asks Hippias in *Greater Hippias*. Socrates's disdain is palpable.

Ordinary people—those who have not taken the trouble to know—have no grasp of the truth.

This ignorance made a mockery of majority rule. The procedure varied with the context—a raising of hands in the Ekklesia, a casting of ballots in the courts—but public decisions in Athens always rested on the largest number of votes. The Athenians liked majority rule for the same reasons we continue to favor it. The results are clear-cut, nobody's vote counts for more than anybody else's, and even though the outcome does not reflect everyone's wishes, more people support it than not, and disgruntled voters can hope to carry the day on another occasion. But as Socrates saw the situation, most people babble on about issues they have not studied and express opinions for which they possess no evidence. How, then, can they be trusted to vote intelligently, and why should their numbers, no matter how large, carry any weight? When ignorant individuals join to form a majority, the majority they form is ignorant too.

Social pressure made the problem worse. In the Ekklesia, the show of hands revealed each man's vote to his peers, and it was easier to support the views of one's group than to stake out a position that threatened friendships and other affiliations. But even when the ballot was secret, as in the courts, individuals often succumbed to a collective mentality. The force of the crowd was overwhelming. "[T]he very rocks and surroundings echo the din of their praise or blame and double it," Socrates remarked, and he wondered whether anyone could withstand the pressure. "What private training can hold out and not be swept away by that kind of praise or blame and be carried by the flood wherever it goes, so that he'll say that the same things are beautiful or ugly as the crowd does, follow the same pursuits as they do, and be the same sort of person as they are?"

Socrates also worried about the way that Athens selected its leaders. To the extent that leaders were elected, he objected to their selection on the same grounds that he objected to majority rule: How could an ignorant majority be trusted to choose the best candidates? But elections played only a tiny role in ancient Athens. The only elected officials were the military generals, or *strategoi*, as well as certain financial officers—the handful of public jobs that were considered to require special expertise. All other officials were appointed by means of an ingenious lottery machine called a *kleroterion*. To

Socrates, this way of selecting leaders was just as absurd as relying on the public's votes.

The kleroterion consisted of a large rectangular stone slab featuring deep slots in a regular pattern of columns and rows. Each slot accommodated a small bronze plaque, or *pinakion*, bearing a citizen's name and the name of his deme. A kleroterion for jury duty, for example, featured several dozen rows of slots arranged into ten columns, each column representing one of the ten tribes, or administrative divisions, into which the entire population was organized. On the morning of a trial, each citizen eligible for jury duty dropped his pinakion into a basket identified with his tribe's name. Once all the plaques had been deposited, the presiding magistrate took one of the baskets, pulled out a random pinakion, and inserted it into the first slot of the corresponding tribal column. He randomly pulled out a second pinakion and inserted it into the second slot, and he continued the process until he had emptied the basket and filled all the slots. He did the same for each of the remaining baskets. When he was done, each horizontal row on the kleroterion contained the plaques of ten citizens, one from each tribe, and it was only by chance that a particular plaque came to occupy a particular row.

At this point, another layer of randomness came into play. Along the side of the stone slab ran a hollow bronze tube with a funnel at the top and a crank at the bottom. Into this funnel the magistrate poured a large quantity of balls, some white and some black, and waited as they made their way down the tube. When the magistrate turned the crank at the bottom, a single ball rolled out. If the ball was white, the ten citizens with plaques in the first row were assigned to the jury; if the ball was black, those ten citizens were dismissed for the day. The magistrate continued the process until he reached the final row.

The number of rows and columns in a specific kleroterion varied according to the context, but the device functioned the same way for virtually all governmental appointments. Socrates found the method outrageous. He insisted, according to Xenophon, "that it was foolish to appoint political leaders by lot, and that nobody would employ a candidate chosen by lot as a pilot or a carpenter or a musician or for any other such post." As Socrates saw it, governing requires at least as much skill as other endeavors for which we never question the need for experts.

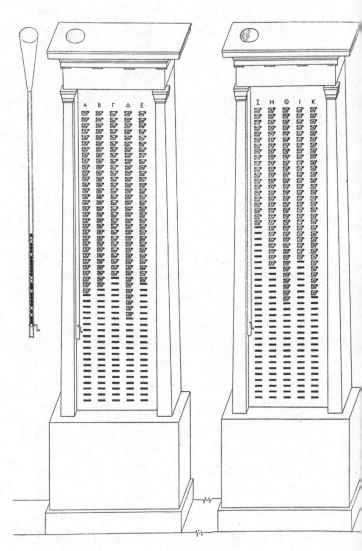

KLEROTERION: The pair of machines in this sketch provide a total of ten columns, one for each tribe. A tube for the black and white balls, depicted separately on the left for better viewing, was inserted into the hole at the top of each machine.

Restored drawing of allotment machines. S. Dow. American School of Classical Studies at Athens: Agora Excavations.

Different people do not possess such specialized skills in equal measure, and only a tiny minority possesses the specific skill of governing at all. Furthermore, as Socrates pointed out, in the cases of the pilot, carpenter, and musician, "if these posts are badly filled, they cause far less harm than bad political appointments." Poor governing devastates both the individual and the community. If people are careful to choose experts when the risk is low, they must be all the more careful when the risk is high.

Fifth-century Athens tended to cast political sympathies in either-or terms: one supported either the common people or the aristocracy. Since Socrates disparaged the general public, criticized the processes that gave them political voice and office, and kept company with a lot of wealthy young men, he was naturally cast as a proponent of aristocratic rule. In truth, Socrates did not support aristocratic rule any more than he supported democracy. As a qualification for leadership, the accident of being born into an upper-class family made as little sense as the accident of a white ball matching up with a citizen's row in the kleroterion. The only qualification that mattered was the ability to govern well. Xenophon recalled Socrates's absolute insistence on this point: "He said that it was not those who held the sceptre who were kings and rulers, nor those who were chosen by unauthorized persons, nor those who were appointed by lot, nor those who had gained their position by force or fraud, but those who knew how to rule."

Socrates's mistrust of democracy helps to explain why, despite his lifelong loyalty to Athens, he strongly admired a very different polis. This was Sparta, which had been the undisputed leader of Greece before Athens stole the limelight during the Persian Wars. Athens and Sparta were only 130 miles apart, a distance that a fleet-footed messenger covered in just two days, according to a celebrated legend, but the two city-states might just as well have inhabited two separate worlds.

Sparta organized all of life around a single, unwavering goal: the successful conduct of war. That goal was so comprehensive that it touched even the youngest members of Spartan society. Feeble newborns were left to die on hillsides as they were in the rest of Greece, but in Sparta, even healthy babies were denied any pampering. Children were raised to be hardy, with meager meals and only the barest clothing and footwear. Boys left home at the age of seven, when they were organized into groups that lived together, and until they became soldiers at the age of twenty, their education consisted of grueling athletic and military training. Girls benefited from state-run schooling as well—a notable advantage, since Athenians saw no need to offer their daughters any formal instruction. Like their male counterparts, Spartan girls engaged in rigorous physical exercise and participated in public sports competitions. Women did not fight in the army, but their role—breeding and raising the next generation of warriors—demanded physical and emotional discipline.

The Spartan army was the envy of all Greece, and Spartan soldiers developed an unsurpassed reputation for their dauntlessness. Military readiness was necessary to preserve the polis's way of life, which was constantly threatened by the risk of rebellion. Early in its history, Sparta had conquered large numbers of fellow Greeks in the Peloponnese and forced them and their descendants into servitude. These state-owned slaves, or *helots*, far outnumbered their masters and keenly resented their servile condition. "[H]e would be glad to eat them raw" was how a local described the attitude of the typical helot, among others, about fully entitled Spartans.

Although Sparta reaped the benefits of slave labor, the people lived in the stark simplicity evoked by the English word "spartan." It was impossible to accumulate wealth or possessions. Owning silver and gold was prohibited, and the land belonged to the state, which allocated a plot to each citizen and regulated the amount of produce each household could receive. Large-scale commerce was impossible. Spartan currency was made of iron, which was not favored by other city-states; foreigners were admitted to Sparta only on official business; and Spartans were restricted from traveling abroad. The polis's minimal trade with foreign markets was conducted by a class of residents who were barred from citizenship.

The Spartans' clarity of vision and disregard for material wealth or personal advancement struck a chord with Socrates, who bemoaned the absence of those qualities in his fellow Athenians. But he especially admired the Spartans for their government, which avoided the pitfalls he had identified in Athenian democracy. Sparta's government was a carefully orchestrated unity that included two hereditary kings who ruled simultaneously, along with elected magistrates, a council of elders, and an assembly of all the citizens. In effect, however, most power lay in the hands of an oligarchy, a small group of aristocrats who held political office. Socrates considered Sparta to be one of the best-governed city-states in Greece, and to the extent that a government's longevity and stability are signs of its success, history supports his assessment. Sparta was notably immune to the political turmoil that plagued other Greek city-states, including Athens even in its democratic heyday.

Socrates admired Sparta for a more surprising reason as well: he considered the Spartans especially good philosophers. "To be a Spartan," he declared, "is to be a philosopher much more than to be an athlete." For anyone who doubted his assertion, Socrates had a recommendation. "Pick any ordinary Spartan and talk with him for a while. At first you will find he can barely hold up his end of the conversation, but at some point he will pick his spot with deadly skill and shoot back a terse remark you'll never forget, something that will make the person he's talking with (in this case you) look like a child." Just about any

Greek already knew some examples of Spartan philosophy. The temple to Apollo at Delphi, a popular pilgrimage spot because of the oracle who resided there, bore several famous inscriptions, and two of them originated in Sparta: "Know thyself" and "Nothing in excess."

Only Socrates's distinctive understanding of philosophy could have led him to identify Sparta as a philosophical stronghold. In the five and a half centuries it existed as an independent city-state, Sparta never shone as an intellectual or cultural center, and as far as we can tell, the Spartans ignored the arts and sciences and produced virtually no written documents. It is even unclear whether Spartan children received any instruction in reading and writing. Obviously, Socrates was not thinking about philosophy as many of us do—that is, as an academic study of mostly esoteric topics in language that only experts can decipher. For Socrates, good philosophy was plainspoken, relevant, and wise, just like the Spartans' pithy advice.

Socrates was not alone in admiring Sparta, but others admired it for more superficial reasons. Many Athenians respected the Spartans for their toughness and embraced various fads to achieve it. Well-heeled parents hired no-nonsense Spartan nurses to care for their babies, and young men engaged in strenuous exercise and neglected the niceties of diet, hygiene, and attire. Socrates was not intentionally cultivating a Spartan look, but he did exhibit some of the same neglect, and it was easy to confuse him with the wannabes. His contemporary, the comic playwright Aristophanes, deliberately conflated the followers of Socrates and the followers of Sparta: "Why, men went mad with mimicry of Sokrates, / affected long hair, indifferent food, / rustic walking sticks, total bathlessness, / and led, in short, what I can only call / a Spartan existence."

The Athenian infatuation with Sparta was a mixed bag. The Spartans actively disapproved of Athenian democracy and opposed the rise of democracy in the rest of Greece; they feared a massive rebellion if their helots and other noncitizens caught wind of too much talk about political rights. Not surprisingly, Sparta's most wholehearted fans in Athens were aristocrats who still hoped to regain the power they had lost with the establishment of democracy. If their dream ever turned into a concrete plan, they anticipated Sparta's support—all the more so because the aristocracy in the two city-states shared ties of blood and marriage. To staunch democrats in Athens, Socrates's vocal support for Sparta's way of life, along with his apparent mimicry of Spartan behaviors, provided yet more proof that he sided with the aristocracy against the common people.

CHAPTER 10

ATHENS ON THE ASCENT

THE DIFFERENCES BETWEEN ATHENS AND
Sparta were inescapable. The Athenian state
existed to serve the citizen; the Spartan citizen
existed to serve the state. Athenians prized
material wealth; Spartans prized extreme
frugality. Athens looked outward and envisioned
a future of dynamic growth; Sparta looked
inward and worried about maintaining the
status quo. The two city-states could never
share a deep rapport, but the inevitable tensions
might have remained at a low simmer if Athens,
rather too confident in its special destiny, had
not stoked the flames. The war that broke out
between Athens and Sparta—the Peloponnesian
War—consumed the entire Greek world for
almost three decades. That devastating conflict

darkened the second half of Socrates's life and played a significant role in his death.

Conflicts began almost immediately after Persia's retreat from mainland Greece. Although relieved of any direct danger, Athens pressed on for the liberation of Greeks on the coast and islands of the northern and eastern Aegean, which were still under Persian control. Athens was motivated, at least in part, by a sense of cultural kinship. Ancient Greece was not a political entity but a conglomerate of settlements that were united by their shared language, customs, ancestors, and gods. These settlements fought almost constantly among themselves, but their conflicts faded into insignificance once non-Greeks entered the scene. The Greek name for a non-Greek was *barbaros*, a derisive reference to the incomprehensible "bar-bar" that such a vulgar person spoke. The English word "barbarian" conveys some of the haughty disdain that the ancient Greeks felt toward anyone who was not one of them.

And so the Athenians, outraged by the continuing submission of fellow Greeks, organized a formal alliance to combat the Persian barbarians. City-states joined voluntarily, but they were required either to provide their own navies or to pay tributes for the construction, upkeep, and staffing of ships by other members. The physical location of the members' joint treasury, on the Aegean island of Delos, has given the alliance its modern name, the Delian League, but at the time, people just referred to "Athens and her allies." The ancient designation was apt. Although member states were technically equals and voted jointly on all measures, in reality Athens, which controlled the largest fleet in the alliance, held the greatest sway over decisions and policies.

THE TRIREME: Named for its three tiers of rowers on each side, the trireme was the backbone of the Athenian navy. Fast, light, and easy to maneuver, it was a devastatingly effective battering ram at sea.

Model of a trireme. Aristoteles and George Rallis. American School of Classical Studies at Athens: Agora Excavations.

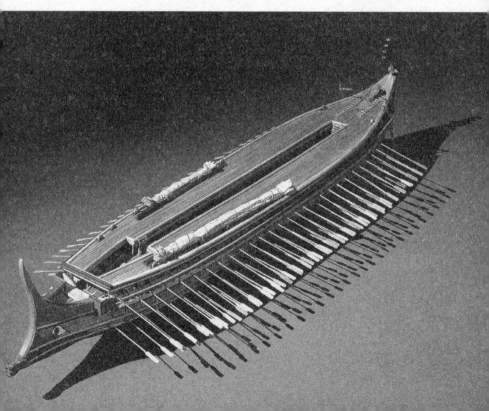

During the first two decades of its existence, the Delian League brought safety and prosperity to the Aegean, the heart of the Greek world. The League's policing weakened the Persian presence and diminished the threat of piracy, allowing trade routes to flourish. But gradually the alliance's character changed. Increasing numbers of allies, drained by the constant effort of waging war, opted to make payments to the treasury at Delos rather than provide their own ships and soldiers. Athens drew steadily on those funds to enhance its own navy, which soon became the largest and strongest maritime force in the history of Greece. The Athenian economy prospered as well. As the League's dominant military force, Athens appropriated the lion's share of spoils seized from Persian outposts, and abundant work for shipbuilders and rowers gave even the poorest Athenians an unprecedented ability to earn and spend money. Athens now had a vested interest in keeping the Delian League alive—and under Athenian control.

Sparta eyed these developments with profound suspicion. How long would it take before Athens interfered with Spartan interests in the Peloponnese? The concern was justified, and Sparta was not alone in its fears. With its

ATHENIAN TETRADRACHM: Merchants throughout the Aegean and beyond benefited from a common currency, the Athenian tetradrachm, a coin that was minted from the copious silver discovered in Attica. The coin bore unmistakable signs of its Athenian origins: Athena's head, crowned with olive leaves, on one side, and an owl, the bird most associated with the goddess, on the other. An olive sprig hangs above the owl's back, and on the bottom right, the letters AΘE stand for "ATHENAION," which means "of the Athenians." The coin in this photograph, which was discovered in a hoard on the Jordanian-Syrian border, testifies to the Athenian tetradrachm's widespread circulation.

Coin (tetradrachm) of Athens, 475–465 BCE. Created in Athens, Greece. Found near ancient Bostra, Hauran, Jordan. J. Paul Getty Museum. Image courtesy of the Getty's Open Content Program.

considerable success against the Persian threat, the Delian League had lost much of its relevance, and member states began to chafe at Athenian dominance. One ally tried to withdraw as early as 469 BCE, and other attempts soon followed. In each case, Athens crushed the rebellion, imposed harsh penalties, and forced the rebel state to remain in the League. Meanwhile, Athens steadily withdrew the allies' option of contributing ships and soldiers, rather than money, to the common effort; after a number of years, all but two of the Delian League's most powerful members were forced to make annual payments to the joint treasury—and to watch helplessly as Athens appropriated those funds to strengthen itself even further. The allies had begun to grasp some painful truths. The Delian League was neither voluntary nor equal, and if it still served a protective function at all, it was protecting Athens—not against the Persian barbarians, but against fellow Greeks. In short, Athens had transformed its allies into subjects and the Delian League into the Athenian Empire.

Indignant members of the Delian League were quick to find common cause with Sparta, and the situation was especially explosive because Sparta controlled its own alliance of city-states. We know little about that alliance's beginnings, which date back to the sixth century BCE, but the arrangement probably arose because Sparta needed the help of its neighbors to keep the helots in line. The alliance, which we now call the Peloponnesian League, posed a serious threat to any state that challenged any one of its members. The existence of both the Peloponnesian and Delian Leagues virtually guaranteed that a crisis between Athens and Sparta would reverberate far and wide.

Socrates was just a baby when the first rebellion broke out within the Delian League, and during his first decade of life, numerous battles laid bare the complex entanglements of the Greek world. When he was about ten, Athens embarked on fifteen years of intermittent fighting that historians now call the First Peloponnesian War. That conflict involved the Delian and Peloponnesian Leagues as well as unaffiliated states that were friendly to one side or the other. In the thick of the chaos, Athens transferred the Delian League's treasury from the island of Delos to the Acropolis. The Athenians claimed that the money would be safer in Athens, because Delos was vulnerable to attack, and perhaps they were right.

Nonetheless, the move inflamed their allies. Athens now wielded full control over funds that were meant to be held jointly.

The First Peloponnesian War ended in 446 or 445 BCE, when Socrates was about twenty-five, with an agreement called the Thirty Years' Peace. The treaty divided the Greek world into two by forbidding the members of either the Peloponnesian or Delian Leagues to change sides. The outcome was a significant boost for Athens, whose empire had received tacit recognition. Despite the discontent among its subjects and the tensions with Sparta, Athens was triumphant and thriving.

The most prominent politician during this period of Athenian history was Pericles, the same man who became Alcibiades's guardian when the young boy's father died. Pericles was repeatedly elected as one of the polis's strategoi, and though his vote counted for no more than any other citizen's, he was an outstanding orator whose opinions consistently carried weight in the Ekklesia. Although he came from an old aristocratic family, he aligned himself with the common people and believed profoundly in their right and ability to govern themselves. Pericles made such an impact on Athens that his contemporary, the historian Thucydides, described him as the polis's "first citizen," and many scholars of Athenian history now refer to the period from 461 to 429 BCE as the Age of Pericles.

It was especially under Pericles that Athens became the rich cultural center that could nurture a thinker like Socrates. Pericles was himself a man of considerable intellect who valued his friendships with thoughtful and knowledgeable individuals. One of his closest relationships was with a most unusual woman named Aspasia. Originally from Ionia, the cradle of natural philosophy, Aspasia stood out among Greek women for her high level of education. She became Pericles's partner after he divorced his first wife but never achieved the respectability of a proper Athenian wife. Her dubious status was not necessarily a disadvantage. As a foreigner and unmarried companion, she escaped the usual constraints on women and enjoyed the freedom to pursue her intellectual interests. She gave lessons in public speaking and may have opened a school for girls, and she was said to have taught Pericles his considerable skills at rhetoric. Socrates credited her with writing Pericles's most famous speech, his "Funeral Oration," a commemoration of the polis's fallen soldiers and one of history's most stirring tributes to democracy. Although it became fashionable to ridicule Aspasia as a way of belittling Pericles, Socrates expressed only the highest praise for her, and he gratefully acknowledged her as one of his own teachers.

Pericles also counted himself both a student and friend of Anaxagoras, the natural philosopher whose ideas about Mind briefly excited Socrates as a young man. Pericles and Anaxagoras were so closely connected in the public mind that a group of aristocrats who hoped to topple Pericles seized on the idea of putting Anaxagoras on trial. By discrediting the teacher, they hoped to discredit the student, and finding a pretext was simple. Anaxagoras's untraditional ideas about the natural world, especially his peculiar view that the sun, moon, and stars are fires and rocks rather than divinities, left him open to the charge of impiety. Anaxagoras was condemned to death but escaped his sentence by fleeing Athens. Pericles, the real target, emerged unscathed.

According to Plutarch, the Greek historian of the first century CE, Anaxagoras saved Pericles from the "superstitious terror" that results from ignorance of natural philosophy. Whether or not

Anaxagoras played such a role in the statesman's life, the Age of Pericles certainly gave vigorous expression to a rational, humanist spirit. In a variety of forms, the achievements of the period announced that people can take hold of the world and make sense of it on their own, without having to appeal to the gods. Perhaps nowhere was this message clearer than in the extensive construction program that Pericles oversaw. The precise proportions and symmetries of the new buildings communicated confidence in the ability of human beings to harness reason and impose order where none had existed before. The most famous of these structures was the Parthenon.

Before Pericles initiated the construction of that famous temple to Athena, little attempt had been made to hide the scars of the Persian attack on the Acropolis. Most of the debris had been cleared away, some of it incorporated into a war monument on the north side of the plateau, but for three decades the Athenians had conducted their worship in the charred remains of the grand temples that had once stood on the site. When the builders finally broke ground for the new temple, the location they chose was surprising. Although the Parthenon was meant to replace an older temple to Athena that the Persians had destroyed, the new structure was erected to the south of the older temple's foundation, not directly above it. The shift was deliberate. The Athenians preserved the old foundation, still visible as rubble, to recall their selfless heroism during the Persian Wars.

The inside of the temple proclaimed the Athenians' faith in themselves at least as loudly as their faith in Athena. Even though the building resembled other Greek temples—essentially a large hall, or *cella*, surrounded by a colonnaded portico—we have no indication that the building housed the altars or officiating priestesses that were standard in other temples. The revered wooden statue of Athena, the one that received a new peplos during the Great Panathenaea every four years, resided in a different building altogether. The new statue of the goddess that stood in the Parthenon's cella was less an object of religious devotion than a projection of the polis's strength. Fashioned of ivory and gold and towering forty-two feet tall, the Parthenon's Athena was fully decked out for battle with breastplate, helmet, shield, and spear; in her extended right palm she carried a six-foot-high statue of Nike, the goddess of victory. Athena's golden ornaments were designed to be removable

THE PARTHENON:
The subdued color of
the marble is deceptive,
since the Greeks painted
their buildings and
statues in vibrant colors.

so that they could be melted down if the polis needed extra cash, but for now such an exigency seemed farfetched. Behind the daunting statue, a room at the rear of the cella housed the polis's treasury, which swelled with the funds that Athens had commandeered from Delos.

Nowhere was the Athenians' civic pride clearer than in the temple's frieze, the sculptured band that decorated the outside of the cella's walls. The frieze depicted what most scholars identify as the procession of the Great Panathenaea: a cavalcade of horses, riders, and chariots, along with men and women on foot, some tending to sacrificial animals and others carrying musical instruments, water jugs, or trays. Several especially large characters represented gods, but they were far outnumbered by the human multitude, and they framed rather than occupied the focal point of the composition. That focal point, showcased right above the doorway into the cella, featured a small group of adults and children handling the peplos that was to be presented to the wooden statue of Athena. At a time when temple decoration drew predictably on the familiar myths, the Parthenon frieze focused on the flesh-and-blood people of Athens.

THE PARTHENON FRIEZE: This drawing depicts the central section, the focus of the procession that is the subject of the frieze as a whole. To the left, two girls carry stools whose legs are now mostly missing. The ceremonial role of these stools is disputed, but one of them is being taken by a woman who may be a priestess of Athena. On the right, a boy and a man, possibly the archon basileus (see chapter 18), handle the peplos that will soon adorn the wooden statue of Athena.

The Five Central Figures. Clara Erskine Clement Waters. *A History of Art for Beginners and Students: Painting, Sculpture, Architecture.* (Frederick A. Stokes, 1887) part 2, p. 44.

The Parthenon concretized in marble, gold, and ivory the same expansive spirit—or arrogance, in the view of Athens's critics—that animated Pericles's policies. Pericles masterminded the transformation of allies into subjects and the transfer of the treasury from Delos to Athens, a transfer that may well have bankrolled his ambitious building program. When Sparta demanded that Athens reconsider its policies, Pericles refused to budge. He explained his reasoning in a speech to the Ekklesia. Submitting to Sparta's demands would mean that Athens could no longer conduct its affairs as it pleased, and no self-respecting Athenian would tolerate that loss of freedom. But Pericles harbored no comforting illusions about the justice of his policies. When the Peloponnesian War finally erupted and Athenians wondered whether their empire was worth the cost, he spoke frankly. "[T]o recede is no longer possible," he told the people, "if indeed any of you in the alarm of the moment has become enamored of the honesty of such an unambitious part. For what you hold is, to speak somewhat plainly, a tyranny; to take it perhaps was wrong, but to let it go is unsafe."

With this cavalier attitude about justice, Pericles seems to have violated everything that Socrates held dear. Since the philosopher was never one to hold his tongue, we might expect to find abundant evidence that he denounced the statesman. But the closest we get is Socrates's response to Thrasymachus in the *Republic*. With his might-makes-right argument, Thrasymachus apparently supports the position of Pericles and the Athenian Empire—essentially, that a strong Athens can act precisely as it pleases. By countering that view with a noble vision of absolute justice, Socrates apparently censures his polis's behavior. In this context, it is perhaps significant that Plato sets the dialogue a few years after the outbreak of the Peloponnesian War. Perhaps Plato is implying that the two opposing views of justice are not just theoretical.

But this evidence is indirect at best. Neither Thrasymachus nor Socrates makes any reference to current affairs, even though any number of real-world applications of their ideas stare them in the face. Besides, other sources suggest that Socrates admired Pericles. In a different dialogue, Plato shows Socrates praising Pericles as a man of "magnificent wisdom" and "in all likelihood the greatest rhetorician of all," by which Socrates means not the slippery kind of public speaker that he disdains but an honorable teacher, one who supplies the soul with "the reasons and customary rules for conduct that will impart to it the convictions and virtues we want."

Perhaps the clearest evidence of Socrates's position comes from his actions, not his words. For at least ten years of his life, from 432 to 422 BCE, Socrates fought on behalf of the Athenian Empire. Since he was a citizen of military age, his service was compulsory. But Socrates never sank into the lackluster behavior of a man with no choice. He fulfilled his military duty with energy and distinction.

CHAPTER II

POTIDAEA AND THE WELCOME RETURN

THE SPARK THAT ULTIMATELY IGNITED THE Peloponnesian War was Potidaea, a polis in the northern Aegean. Although it was a subject of Athens, Potidaea had originally been founded as a colony by the northern Peloponnese polis of Corinth, an ally of Sparta. The mother and daughter city-states remained close, and Athens worried that Corinth planned to incite Potidaea to revolt against the Athenian Empire. The Athenians had no evidence of such a plot, but they did not want to be taken by surprise. In 432 BCE, they ordered Potidaea to tear down a section of its defensive walls, expel all Corinthian ambassadors, and hand over hostages. When the Potidaeans refused to comply, Athens sent in its troops, and a fierce battle left heavy losses on both sides.

The Potidaean survivors retreated behind their defensive walls, and the Athenian soldiers settled in for a long siege.

Socrates served at Potidaea as a *hoplite*, the heavily armed foot soldier that was the mainstay of the Athenian army. A fully outfitted hoplite carried approximately seventy pounds' worth of equipment, and he was required to supply it all himself. The expense ran as much as three hundred drachmas, the equivalent of a full year's salary for an average laborer. Since Socrates would not have had such a considerable sum, he probably settled for an incomplete set. At a minimum, he acquired a spear that measured eight to ten feet long and a shield that extended from his thigh to his cheekbone. If he could manage the additional expense, perhaps by relying on the generosity of friends or by accepting used gear on loan, he also procured a bronze helmet for his head, bronze greaves for his lower legs, and a breastplate made of bronze, leather, or thick layers of linen. When it was time to muster, he grasped his spear in his right hand and his shield in his left, and he took his assigned place in a densely packed line in which each soldier's shield covered the left side of his own body and the right side of the man to his left. Several of these lines in close succession formed a *phalanx*, a virtually impenetrable block that moved in unison, its soldiers brandishing their long spears above the daunting wall of their armor.

Alcibiades served in the same campaign and had many opportunities to observe Socrates as a soldier, far from the usual haunts of Athens. From Alcibiades's account, it is clear that Socrates broke the modern stereotype of the intellectual as a flabby weakling. Although Alcibiades was in his strapping twenties and Socrates was already close to forty, the older man dealt more easily with the hardships of military life. "When we were cut off from our supplies, as often happens in the field," Alcibiades recollected, "no one else stood up to hunger as well as he did." Socrates acquitted himself just as well in times of plenty. "[H]e was the one man who could really enjoy a feast; and though he didn't much want to drink, when he had to, he could drink the best of us under the table. Still, and most amazingly, no one ever saw him drunk."

Amazing, too, was Socrates's resilience to the unaccustomed cold of Potidaea—"the winter there is something awful," Alcibiades recalled. Other soldiers balked at leaving

HOPLITE ARMOR:
The style of protective gear changed over time. This helmet, which probably predates Socrates by a few decades, resembles the one that crowns the bust of Athena on page 8. The simple, anatomical style of the greaves suggests a later date, perhaps during Socrates's lifetime.

Helmet of the Corinthian Type and Pair of Greaves, early fifth century BCE. The Metropolitan Museum of Art, New York.

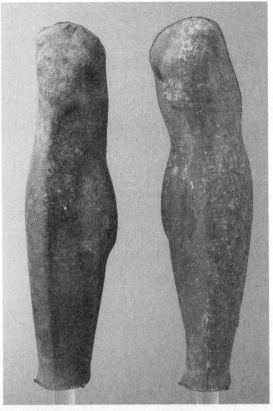

their tents, and when they had no choice, they bundled themselves up and took particular care to wrap layers of felt or sheepskin over their boots. Socrates dressed in just the lightweight peplos that he always wore, and much to the astonishment of his fellow soldiers, he put nothing on his feet at all. "[E]ven in bare feet he made better progress on the ice than the other soldiers did in their boots," Alcibiades recalled. "You should have seen the looks they gave him; they thought he was only doing it to spite them!"

Socrates proved himself in battle too. When Alcibiades was wounded during the campaign, Socrates single-handedly beat off the attackers who wanted to finish the job and rob the corpse of its valuable armor. Alcibiades was decorated for his bravery, but he believed Socrates was the one who really deserved the honor. "I told them right then that the decoration really belonged to you," he later told the philosopher. "But the generals, who seemed much more concerned with my social position, insisted on giving the decoration to me, and, I must say, you were more eager than the generals themselves for me to have it."

Socrates attracted attention at Potidaea for yet another reason. He stood outside early one morning, "thinking about some problem or other," as Alcibiades interpreted his friend's behavior. Unable to resolve the problem but unwilling to give up, Socrates remained frozen in place, oblivious to everything around him. As the hours passed, word spread, and in the evening, a group of fascinated soldiers dragged their bedding outside to see what would happen. Those who managed to stay awake saw no change at all. Socrates stood like a statue the entire night and moved again only at dawn, when he "made his prayers to the new day" and quietly left the spot, offering no explanation to his many observers. Apparently Socrates often exhibited this behavior, but presumably for much shorter stretches than in Potidaea, and some modern medical experts have theorized that he was epileptic. Nonetheless, Alcibiades's interpretation remains significant. Socrates's intellectual focus was so intense that Alcibiades saw nothing absurd in assuming that his friend wrestled with ideas for a full twenty-four hours in the inhospitable conditions of a military camp.

After more than two years under siege, the desperate Potidaeans were reduced to cannibalism. The wretched survivors surrendered in the winter of 430–429 BCE and braced themselves for lifelong exile. But Athens's triumph was far from clear. A chilling battle at the end of the siege, one in which Socrates participated, killed hundreds of Athenians, and the larger situation was bleak. At the beginning of the conflict, Corinth had appealed to Sparta for help over the Athenians' humiliation of Potidaea, and in a matter of weeks, the Peloponnesian League had declared Athens in violation of the Thirty Years' Peace. By the time Potidaea surrendered, the Peloponnesian War had been raging for nearly two years, and more than another twenty-five would elapse before it would end. It is no exaggeration to call the conflict an ancient world war. This was certainly the view of the historian Thucydides, who experienced many of the events firsthand as *strategos*, one of the Athenian generals. Using the Greeks' own name for themselves, which has entered English as "Hellenes," he described the Peloponnesian War as "the greatest movement yet known in history, not only of the Hellenes, but of a large part of the barbarian world—I had almost said of mankind."

For Socrates, at least, the end of the siege meant a welcome return to Athens, where he arrived in the spring of 429, after an absence of close to three years. In the dialogue *Charmides*, Plato depicts the philosopher's first day back. "[S]ince I was arriving after such a long absence I sought out my accustomed haunts with special pleasure," Socrates explains. He makes his way to a palaestra, where he is surrounded by a crowd seeking information about the recent battle. Once he has satisfied everyone's curiosity, he enjoys the opportunity to catch up on local news. "I in my turn began to question them with respect to affairs at home, about the present state of philosophy and about the young men, whether there were any who had become distinguished for wisdom or beauty or both."

In just a few moments, all attention turns to Charmides, a teenager who has just arrived at the palaestra. The newcomer is reputed to be "the handsomest young man of the day," and his entrance precipitates a humorous interlude. The bench where Socrates is sitting is crowded with men, each determined to have Charmides by his side. To make room, the men shove each other so hard that the people on either end of the bench fall off. The handsome teenager ultimately chooses to sit next to Socrates, who finds himself at an uncharacteristic loss for words. "I saw

inside his cloak and caught on fire and was quite
beside myself," the philosopher recalls.

Socrates recovers quickly. Charmides is
indeed handsome, but is his soul as beautiful as
his body? Since the teenager has "the reputation
of being the most temperate young man of the
day," Socrates makes temperance the subject of
his questions. Here modern English falls short
of the ancient Greek. Socrates's term, *sophrosune,*
designated not only the self-restraint implied
by the English word "temperance" but also a
broader awareness of one's duties toward oneself
and others. Socrates asks Charmides to share
what he knows about the subject. Surely the
young man can define the quality for which he
has won acclaim.

The dialogue follows the familiar pattern:
Socrates's interlocutors attempt various
definitions, and Socrates points out the
flaws in each suggestion. In a first attempt,
Charmides defines temperance as "a sort of
quietness," a trait that in the original Greek
connotes slowness as well. In response, Socrates
demonstrates that although temperance is
always desirable, quietness is sometimes
detrimental. When it comes to learning
academic subjects, participating in athletic

activities, and formulating a course of action, the quiet and slow achieve less than the bold and quick. Charmides tries again. Since temperance often makes people ashamed and bashful, perhaps temperance is the same as modesty. But Socrates refutes this idea too. No less an authority than Homer declared that "modesty is not a good mate for a needy man"—in other words, a beggar must be assertive, even impudent, to supply his needs. Since modesty is sometimes good and sometimes bad, it cannot be identical to temperance, which is always good. Charmides proposes a third possibility: temperance is "minding one's own business." But this definition fares no better. As Socrates points out, the activities that people regularly undertake—writing, healing, housebuilding, manufacturing, and governing, for example—all involve engagement in the business of others. In any well-governed city, people necessarily involve themselves in each other's lives.

At this point in the dialogue, Charmides's cousin and guardian, a man named Critias, shows obvious signs of unease, and it becomes clear that he, not Charmides, is the source of the third definition. Critias takes over with a spirited defense of his idea, but Socrates's unrelenting criticism eventually forces him to change course. After several attempts at a new definition, Critias settles on a final possibility: temperance is knowing what one knows and does not know.

This definition, too, falls apart. The main problem is that a knowledge of what one knows and does not know would be a knowledge of knowledge—a "science of science," Socrates calls it—rather than a knowledge of any particular subject. Socrates argues that this sort of knowledge is an impossibility because we gain knowledge only through study or practice in specific areas. We gain the knowledge of health through the study or practice of medicine, the knowledge of justice through the study or practice of politics, and the knowledge of harmony through the study or practice of music. How, then, can a science of science—in effect, a content-less form of knowledge—exist? How would we learn it, and what would it encompass? And even if we posit its existence, how helpful would a science of science actually be? At most it would enable people to know *that* they know or don't know. It would not help them know *what* they know or don't know, since the *what* is the content that the science of science lacks. Finally—and this is the most pressing problem for Socrates—the science of science would not include the knowledge of what is good and bad, the only knowledge that can bring us happiness.

The dialogue ends in the usual aporia, the participants' inability to resolve the problems that have arisen. Since Socrates is no closer to a definition of temperance than he was at the beginning of the discussion, he half-jokingly advises Charmides to dismiss him as "a babbler, incapable of finding out anything whatsoever by means of argument." But the young man rejects such a conclusion. He has been so enchanted by the exchange of ideas that he declares his intention of studying with Socrates on a daily basis. Since Critias heartily endorses the plan, the *Charmides* ends with the hope of better answers in the future.

CHAPTER 12

CRISIS AND CRUELTY

THE *CHARMIDES* SHOWS SOCRATES IMMERSED
in business as usual—focusing on the health of
the soul, selecting a particular virtue to define,
testing the definitions that other people propose,
and recognizing that the task requires further
effort. But in this case, business as usual is
almost unthinkable. Aside from having just
returned from a devastating battle, Socrates has
come home to a city in crisis.

At the outbreak of the Peloponnesian War,
Pericles based his strategy on the polis's network
of defensive walls. In addition to walls that
encircled the city proper, a set of newer defenses,
the Long Walls, connected Athens to its two
ports to the southwest. Since each port was
about five miles from the city center, the Long
Walls outlined two sides of a sizable triangular
region whose third side was formed by the coast.

The arrangement provided the landlocked city with the advantages of an island: isolation from surrounding territory and unfettered access to the sea. Athens would never suffer a siege like the one that destroyed Potidaea. As long as the Athenians could reach their ships, they would be able to secure food and supplies from abroad.

The protective walls inspired Pericles with an unconventional strategy: Athens would just wait out the conflict. The people in the countryside would send their livestock to nearby islands for safekeeping and then join the residents of the city within the protected triangular region. At the same time, the Athenian forces would remain largely dormant, undertaking only limited raids on the Peloponnesian coast. Soon enough, Pericles believed, the Athenians' imperviousness to attack and their carefully focused aggressions would discourage the enemy, and the war would come to a swift conclusion. The plan was unusual in the highly competitive Greek world, but it seemed reasonable enough. Since Greek battles were generally contained affairs that took place in the spring and summer, the refugees would be able to return home during the colder part of the year to deal with any damage their property had sustained.

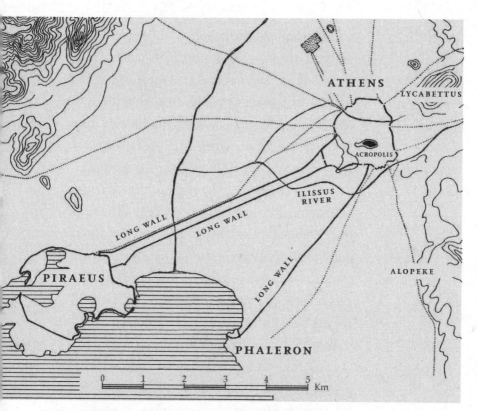

The Long Walls: The two outer walls, which connected Athens to its bustling ports, the Piraeus and Phaleron, were built under Pericles's predecessor in the early 450s BCE. About ten years later, Pericles added a middle wall to create a more secure corridor to the Piraeus, which was the more important port, not least because it was the base of the Athenian navy.

This map is a modified version of the following source: *Ancient Athens.* Napoleon Vier. Wikimedia Commons, https://commons.wikimedia.org/wiki/File:AtheneOudheid.JPG.

The people dutifully followed Pericles's instructions when the fighting began in the spring of 431. But Pericles had miscalculated the effect of so many people in such a small space. The refugees had such trouble finding a patch of ground on which to plant themselves that some took the desperate step of ignoring the oracle of Delphi, who had prohibited access to a sacred area just below the Acropolis. Soon the crush of people, the inadequate sanitation, and the stifling heat, especially at the height of the summer, merged into a toxic brew. In the second year of the war, when Socrates was still at Potidaea, the unsanitary conditions led to the outbreak of a deadly plague.

Thucydides was one of the plague's victims, and ever the historian, he scrupulously observed his own case to record the progression of the disease. After "violent heats" broke out in the head, the eyes became inflamed, the throat and tongue turned bloody and foul-smelling, and the patient suffered terrible bouts of sneezing and hoarseness. The disease next moved down to the chest, where it produced a hard cough, and then to the stomach, where it induced painful retching. Meanwhile, the skin turned red and broke out in pus-filled swellings and sores, and victims felt as if they were burning inside. Most refused even the thinnest clothing or covering, and the most wretched threw themselves into tanks of rainwater. If the disease descended all the way to the bowels, it produced violent inflammations and severe diarrhea. By that point, the chance of recovery was slim.

Modern scholars have identified the Athenian plague as measles, smallpox, typhoid, and pneumonic plague, among other diseases, but no single possibility accounts for all the symptoms. Thucydides himself survived, but huge numbers of people were not as lucky. By the time it ran its full course, according to some estimates, the epidemic had killed a third of the polis's population. Survivors often bore permanent scars on their genitals and extremities, and many victims lost their fingers, toes, and eyes. Some of the afflicted also lost their memories.

Overcome by fear and hopelessness, the people of Athens developed an inhumane indifference to one another. The sick were left to suffer and die alone, and streets filled with piles of corpses that were denied the customary funeral rites, an unthinkable omission under ordinary circumstances. Normal restraints gave way to crime, licentiousness, and sacrilege. As Thucydides observed, "No one was held back in awe, either by fear of the gods or by the laws of men: not by the gods, because men concluded it was all the same whether they worshipped or not, seeing that they all perished alike; and not by the laws, because no one expected to live till he was tried and punished for his crimes." In any case, punishment did not seem like much of a threat. How could any punishment be worse than the plague itself?

Athens was spinning out of control, and Pericles bore the brunt of the people's rage. Over his strenuous objections, the Ekklesia sought an immediate end to the nightmare by sending a peace mission to Sparta. The mission failed, and public fury went unabated. In the fall of 430 BCE, shortly before Potidaea's surrender, the people convicted Pericles of corruption, a common charge against leaders who had fallen out of favor, and stripped him of his command. But Athens had no good options at that point. The Spartans had rejected peace, and the plague-ridden polis was in no shape to undertake aggressive action. For the time being, Pericles's passive strategy was the only real possibility. He was reinstated as strategos the following year.

And so, when Socrates returned from Potidaea, he found a perilously overcrowded city, a raging plague, a breakdown of human attachments, a chilling lawlessness, and a stewing controversy over Pericles's leadership—certainly a meaty set of concerns for a thinker preoccupied with ethics. In the *Charmides*, however, Socrates does not address any of these issues. When he questions his fellow Athenians about the state of the city, he is not asking about Pericles or the plague. Instead, he wants to hear about the current intellectual scene and the up-and-coming stars among the young men. In the discussion about temperance, he focuses on logical abstractions, not on the real, tumultuous situation that he can hardly avoid seeing. Apparently, Potidaea was not the only place where Socrates could immerse himself in his own reflections, oblivious to the devastation around him.

Of course, in the *Charmides* as in the other dialogues, Plato is presenting a scenario that he has constructed himself, and we do not know what Socrates actually did or said the day after his return from Potidaea. But the portrayal is credible. Socrates did not hesitate to share what was on his mind, and if he habitually discussed current events, we might expect to find evidence of that interest in Plato, Xenophon, and other sources. Instead, we find mostly silence. Socrates seems to have been curiously detached from the social, political, and military transformations that were taking place all around him.

Socrates's detachment is even more perplexing in the context of subsequent events. Pericles enjoyed his political rehabilitation for less than a year. In the fall of 429, just a few months after Socrates's return home, the once formidable leader became the plague's latest fatality. Pericles's death invigorated the polis's militaristic faction, and the majority of the people, tired of huddling behind walls, were ready to listen. The plague was tapering off, and it was time to fight back. In short order, Athens exhibited a tolerance for cruelty that was shocking even by the brutal standards of ancient Greece.

One of the most dreadful incidents concerned Mytilene, a city on the northeastern Aegean island of Lesbos. The entire island was part of the Athenian Empire, but Mytilene was ruled by an aristocratic oligarchy that hated democracy and resented Athenian control. Mytilene fortified its navy, constructed defensive walls, and appealed to the Peloponnesian League for support. Athens retaliated with a siege in the winter of 428–427, and the starving city surrendered the following summer. The general in charge of the operation identified the most active rebels and sent them to Athens to await their sentence.

Hotheads prevailed when the Ekklesia took up the question of Mytilene's punishment. Cleon, the ringleader of the militaristic faction—a man whom Thucydides unceremoniously designates "the most violent man at Athens"—maintained that it was not enough to execute the rebels already in Athens. The entire city of Mytilene bore the guilt, and it was pointless to make fine distinctions between oligarchs and democrats or rebels and non-rebels. Instead, the city's entire population of adult males should be killed, and all the women and children should be sold into slavery. The proposal was shockingly harsh. Just two years earlier, when Potidaea had surrendered, the survivors had been exiled, not slaughtered. Nonetheless, Cleon's suggestion carried the day. A ship departed for Mytilene, bearing orders for the Athenian forces to execute the sentence without delay.

It took almost no time for Athens to regret, as Thucydides describes it, "the horrid cruelty of a decree, which condemned a whole city to the fate merited only by the guilty." The very next day, the Ekklesia held a special session to reconsider the question, and this time a more moderate proposal prevailed: only the rebels already in Athens would die. Since the first ship with the original orders was already on its way, a second ship set sail immediately with the revised sentence. The race was on. Boosted by plentiful rations and the promise of a generous reward for arriving in time, all provided by Mytilene's distraught ambassadors in Athens, the sailors on the second ship labored around the clock, eating as they rowed and sleeping in shifts. Their frantic efforts ended in a heart-pounding climax. As Thucydides describes it, the Athenian general in Mytilene "had only just had time to read the decree, and to prepare to execute the sentence, when the second [ship] put into port and prevented the massacre."

The Athenians had averted a tremendous atrocity, but even the revised sentence represented the harshest punishment of rebellious subjects to date. Over a thousand Mytilenean men had been imprisoned in Athens, and they were given no opportunity to stand trial before their execution. And four years later, brutality was the norm, not the exception. After quashing a rebellion in Torone, a subject city in the northern Aegean, Athens dispensed with any pretense of distinguishing the guilty from the innocent. All adult males were imprisoned, and all women and children were sold into slavery. They were lucky compared with the people of nearby Scione. Upon Scione's surrender, Athens destroyed the city and executed its entire adult male population. This time the Ekklesia expressed no misgivings at all.

It would be pleasant to imagine Socrates denouncing these atrocities and making an appeal at the Ekklesia for a more humane response to Mytilene, Torone, and Scione. If he genuinely wanted to improve the ethical health of Athens, what more relevant context could he have found? And yet we find no suggestion that he intervened in word or deed. Quite to the contrary, our best evidence indicates that he maintained a studious distance from the city's political life. "I'm not one of the politicians," he unapologetically declares in one of Plato's dialogues. "Last year I was elected to the Council [one of the Ekklesia's administrative committees] by lot, and when our tribe was presiding and

SLAVERY: It was a terrible fate to be a slave, but at least in Athens, alone among Greek city-states, slaves received the same wages as free day laborers. Slaves worked in households, farms, factories, shipyards, houses of prostitution, and mines. Slaves also composed the majority of medical workers, since it was considered inappropriate for citizens to touch the sick and injured. In the image on this wine jug, a young slave carries his master's belongings and holds a container to catch his urine.

Attic Red-Figure Oinochoe, Shape 3 (Chous), ca. 470 BCE. Oionokles Painter, Greek, Attic. J. Paul Getty Museum. Image courtesy of the Getty's Open Content Program.

I had to call for a vote, I came in for a laugh. I didn't know how to do it."

Did Socrates's silence about his polis's brutality make a mockery of his concern for ethics? He would have responded with a resounding no. Voters in the Ekklesia wanted quick answers and muscular certitudes, and Socrates was not in that line of work. With his exacting analyses and frequent admission of ignorance, he would never sway a crowd—especially when that crowd was hell-bent on injustice. As he told the jury at his trial, "[N]o man will survive who genuinely opposes you or any other crowd and prevents the occurrence of many unjust and illegal happenings in the city. A man who really fights for justice must lead a private, not a public, life if he is to survive for even a short time." Socrates was acting upon his ethical commitments in the only way he deemed practical: inviting individuals, one at a time, to examine their misguided assumptions.

Of course, since a city is made up of individuals, Socrates was having his own sort of impact on public policy. By engaging two generations of young men in serious thought about ethics, he was making the future leaders of the polis more mindful of the common good.

Nonetheless, Socrates was flying in the face of his community's norms. With its proud history of enhancing the power of its citizens, the polis had transformed political involvement from a right to a responsibility. An Athenian man who did not take an active part in his government was labeled, quite literally, an idiot: the Greek *idiotes* designated a person who did not engage in public affairs. Although the English word does not retain that original meaning, "idiot" still evokes the disdain that Athenians felt for someone with Socrates's mindset. Outside his immediate circle of followers, his polis had yet another reason to distrust him.

CHAPTER 13

DEFINITIONS
OF COURAGE

IN 424 BCE, JUST OVER FIVE YEARS AFTER HIS return from Potidaea, Socrates was back on the battlefield. With the aid of local sympathizers, Athens was attempting to establish democratic, pro-Athenian governments in Boeotia, a Spartan ally just to the northwest of Attica. Success would simultaneously weaken Sparta's influence in the region and secure the northwestern border of Attica against invasion. But success proved elusive. In a decisive battle at Delium, a town just across the border, the Boeotian army outmaneuvered the Athenian forces. The Athenians retreated in a panic-ridden stampede, and by the time the slaughter ended, one thousand of their hoplites, as well as their strategos, had fallen—the heaviest losses that Athens had suffered since the beginning of the war.

Socrates was a hoplite in that unlucky battle. Alcibiades participated too, but this time he fought with the cavalry, a division manned by wealthy citizens who could afford the purchase and upkeep of horses. The two men crossed paths during the frantic retreat, and from his relatively safe perch atop his horse, Alcibiades had an excellent opportunity to watch his friend. Despite the chaos around him, Socrates maintained his usual composure. "He was observing everything quite calmly," Alcibiades relates in Plato's *Symposium*, "looking out for friendly troops and keeping an eye on the enemy. Even from a great distance it was obvious that this was a very brave man, who would put up a terrible fight if anyone approached him." The philosopher's presence of mind put even Laches, a preeminent strategos, to shame. "[I]t was easy to see that he was remarkably more collected than Laches," Alcibiades remarks, and in the dialogue *Laches*, the general himself acknowledges Socrates's outstanding courage: "I can tell you that if the rest had been willing to behave in the same manner, our city would be safe and we would not then have suffered a disaster of that kind."

Plato sets the *Laches* shortly after the battle of Delium. Two men who want to educate their sons seek advice from Laches as well as Nicias, another prominent strategos. What studies or pursuits should be part of the sons' education? Soon it becomes clear that the two generals disagree about the value of teaching boys to fight in armor, and Lysimachus, one of the fathers, appeals to Socrates "to cast the deciding vote." Socrates responds with his characteristic disdain for majority rule. "What's that, Lysimachus? Do you intend to cast your vote for whatever position is approved by the majority of us?" Lysimachus sees no other option. "Why, what else could a person do, Socrates?"

Socrates turns to the second father, Melesias, to find out whether he, too, would follow the majority. To clarify the question, Socrates offers an analogy. "Suppose there should be a council to decide whether your son ought to practice a particular kind of gymnastic exercise, would you be persuaded by the greater number or by whoever has been educated and exercised under a good trainer?" As Socrates anticipates, Melesias responds that he would probably seek the advice of someone who has had the requisite training. "So I think it is by knowledge that one ought to make decisions, if one is to make them well, and not by majority rule," Socrates replies. He spells out what he means: "[I]t is necessary to investigate first of all whether any one of us is an expert in the subject we are debating, or not. And if one of us is, then we should listen to him even if he is only one, and disregard the others. But if no one of us is an expert, then we must look for someone who is."

First, however, the men must define the subject for which they require an expert. Is the issue really whether young boys should be trained to fight in armor? Socrates once again turns to analogy. People who consider using medicine for their eyes should focus on the health of their eyes, not on the medicine, and people who consider using a bridle for a horse should focus on the horse, not on the bridle. The medicine and the bridle are merely the means to the end, and the end is the only thing that really matters. The same approach should hold true for fathers who are considering armed fighting as a component of their sons' education—or, as Socrates pointedly rephrases the situation, fathers who "are considering a form of study for the sake of the souls of young men." For these fathers, the proper focus is the soul, not armed fighting. The expert that the group requires is not a master of the military arts, but a master of the soul, someone who is himself good and has successfully taught others to be good.

Although the care of the soul has long been Socrates's concern, he denies that he has the relevant knowledge. "Now I, Lysimachus and Melesias," he tells the two fathers, "am the first to say, concerning myself, that I have had no teacher in this subject . . . and I myself, on the other hand, am unable to discover the art even now." He defers to the generals, who undoubtedly possess the knowledge that he lacks. They are richer and older than he is, so they have been able to afford good teachers and have had the time to develop their understanding. They also have strong opinions about the value of teaching young boys to fight in armor. If the generals are so sure about this specific aspect of education, they must have a solid grasp of education in its entirety—in other words, they must be experts in the care of the soul. Socrates invites them to share their knowledge of virtue. More specifically, he asks them to define *andreia*, the part of virtue that relates most closely to fighting in armor. As is so often the case, no English word does justice to the original Greek. "Andreia," which literally means "manliness," designates staunchness in civic leadership as well as valor in military engagements. The usual translation is "courage."

Laches is quick to make the first attempt. "Good heavens, Socrates, there is no difficulty about that: if a man is willing to remain at his post and to defend himself against the enemy without running away, then you may rest assured that he is a man of courage." Socrates rejects that idea for its narrowness. What about a soldier who fights against the enemy while retreating—is he not courageous too? Socrates clarifies what he expects from a definition:

> I wanted to learn from you not only what constitutes courage for a hoplite but for a horseman as well and for every sort of warrior. And I wanted to include not only those who are courageous in warfare but also those who are brave in dangers at sea, and the ones who show courage in illness and poverty and affairs of state; and then again I wanted to include not only those who are brave in the face of pain and fear but also those who are clever at fighting

desire and pleasure, whether by standing
their ground or running away—because
there are some men, aren't there, Laches,
who are brave in matters like these?

Since no single courageous act captures the full
scope of courage, it is necessary to examine a
wide variety of courageous acts to determine
what they have in common. A satisfactory
definition will identify that commonality.
Laches tries again, this time defining courage
as "a sort of endurance of the soul." With some
prodding from Socrates, he adds an important
qualification: the endurance must be a wise
one, not a foolish one. But Socrates is still not
satisfied. First, some forms of wise endurance
have nothing to do with courage. An investor
might endure in spending money as a way to
achieve greater gains, and a doctor might endure
in denying food or drink to a patient as a way to
effect a cure. Both the investor and the doctor
endure wisely, but we would not consider their
behavior courageous. Second, some forms of
foolish endurance actually do seem to qualify
as courage. One example is a soldier's refusal
to give up, even when he faces a more sizable,
prepared, and fearsome enemy. The soldier's

persistence is an act of folly, but most people would call him courageous.

Now that both of Laches's attempts have failed, Nicias enters the fray and gradually works his way to his own definition: courage is "the knowledge of the fearful and the hopeful in war and every other situation." Nicias defends his definition against several attacks by both Laches and Socrates, but it finally collapses when Socrates shows the impossibility of distinguishing courage, according to Nicias's definition, from the entirety of virtue.

Socrates's argument has several steps. First, he establishes that the fearful and hopeful relate to the future: fearful things are the evil that we anticipate, and hopeful things are the good that we anticipate. If courage is indeed the knowledge of the fearful and hopeful, then courage must be a branch of knowledge that deals only with the future. Next, Socrates argues that no branch of knowledge concerns itself only with the past, only with the present, or only with the future. The study of medicine, for instance, encompasses what has already happened, what is currently happening, and what will probably happen in the field of health; the study of agriculture does the same for the products of the earth, and the study of generalship does the same for the conduct of war. If courage is indeed a branch of knowledge, then it, too, must concern itself with the past, the present, and the future. But if courage really is the understanding of good and evil at all times, whether past, present, or future, how is courage any different from virtue in its entirety? Like Laches, Nicias has failed to provide a good definition.

The philosopher has no better answers than the two generals, and the discussion ends in aporia. Socrates has nonetheless made a strong impression on Lysimachus, who is still looking for someone to teach his son. "Well, it would be a terrible thing, Lysimachus," the philosopher responds, "to be unwilling to join in assisting any man to become as good as possible." But Socrates is speaking in a general way; he has no intention of accepting the formal position. "If in the conversations we have just had I had seemed to be knowing and the other two had not, then it would be right to issue a special invitation to me to perform this task; but as the matter stands, we were all in the same difficulty. Why then should anybody choose one of us in preference to another?" Socrates has a better plan—"to join in searching for the best possible teacher, first for ourselves—we really need one—and then for the young men, sparing neither money nor anything else. What I don't advise is that we remain as we are." The dialogue closes with Socrates's promise to meet Lysimachus the next day to plan their further study. Aporia is never an excuse to stop looking for answers.

CHAPTER 14

THE *CLOUDS*

IN EARLY 423 BCE, AFTER EIGHT LONG YEARS OF war, Sparta and Athens agreed to a one-year truce. The hope of peace heightened the usual delights of spring. The harsh winter rains had ended, the worst of the summer's heat was still a few months away, and the City Dionysia was in full swing. This festival, second only to the Great Panathenaea in importance and extravagance, was an annual celebration of the dramatic arts in honor of Dionysus, the god of wine, fertility, and the theater. Like the Great Panathenaea, the City Dionysia included a lively procession—but with an interesting addition to the usual baskets of food and jugs of water and wine. In recognition of Dionysus's role as the god of fertility, joyful participants brandished wood or bronze *phalloi*—models of penises. One phallus was so large that it had to be pulled along in a cart.

The procession escorted an ancient wooden statue of Dionysus to the city's enormous outdoor theater, the Theater of Dionysus, which nestled into the southern slope of the Acropolis. Spectators sat on bleacher-like benches set into the hill; the seats curved around the *orchestra*, the flat, circular area where the actors performed. Despite the theater's capacity, space was tight. Athenian theater was not an idle entertainment for the privileged few but an essential part of civic and religious life, and the audience included women as well as Greek visitors from outside Athens. The spectators numbered a full fifteen thousand or more. Performances extended over several days and were competitive, with one contest for tragedies and another for comedies. The tragedies explored the familiar stories of Greek mythology, often as an indirect commentary on the issues of the day; the comedies focused more explicitly on current affairs. By 423 BCE, Socrates had become so famous—or notorious—that he was featured in two of the three entries in the comedy competition.

Socrates's strangeness provided splendid opportunities for any actor who portrayed him. Actors were male, even for female roles, and they all wore masks over their faces. While most masks were standard issue, the one for the actor who played Socrates may have been specially designed to capture the philosopher's distinctive ugliness. Since the mask prevented the actor from making dramatic use of his facial expressions, he compensated with gestures so exaggerated that even back-row spectators could see them. His short tunic revealed a large leather phallus, a staple of the costume for male characters.

Neither of the two comedies that featured Socrates won first place, but both give a sense of the reputation that Socrates had developed among his fellow Athenians. The play that finished second was *Commus* by the comic poet Ameipsias; the title was apparently the name of Socrates's music teacher. Only fragments of the text survive, but one of them pokes fun at Socrates's ragged apparel and describes him as "among few men the best, / And among many vainest." The play that finished third was the *Clouds* by the famous playwright Aristophanes. Fortunately, we have a slightly later version of that text in its entirety.

The main character of the *Clouds*, an old man named Strepsiades, is deep in debt because his son, Pheidippides, has developed an expensive

A COMIC ACTOR:
This delightful
statuette, just 3.5 inches
high, gives a sense
of how a comic actor
might have looked in
his costume.

*Terracotta statuette of
an actor*, late fifth to
early fourth century
BCE, Greek, Attic. The
Metropolitan Museum
of Art, New York.

passion for racehorses. Strepsiades has no intention of actually paying the money he owes, and to outsmart his debtors, he decides to enroll Pheidippides in a school that will teach him how to make weak arguments seem strong and strong arguments seem weak—in other words, a school run by a sophist. Strepsiades chooses an institution called the "Thinkery," which is under Socrates's direction. When Pheidippides refuses to attend the school, the old man decides to become a student there himself.

Socrates makes his first appearance hanging above the stage in a basket, where he has apparently been blending his rarified intellect with the rarified heavens. He meets his new student and promptly convinces him to abandon traditional beliefs. The only gods that Socrates recognizes are natural forces: "O Lord God Immeasurable Ether, You who envelop the world! / O Translucent Ozone! / And you, O lightningthundered holy Clouds!" After a chorus of clouds appears on stage in response to his invocation, Socrates announces, "These are the only gods there are. The rest are but figments."

It takes little time for Socrates to determine that Strepsiades is not bright enough for the Thinkery. But the old man must still find a way to elude his creditors, so he drags his reluctant son to the school. There, the same subject that opens Plato's *Laches*, the proper approach to a boy's education, becomes the subject of a debate between the characters Sophistry and Philosophy. Sophistry rails against those who criticize him for having "devised a Method for the Subversion of Established Social Beliefs / and the Undermining of Morality," but at the same time, he boasts that "this little invention of mine, / this knack of taking what might appear to be the worse argument / and nonetheless winning my case, has . . . proved to be / an *extremely* lucrative source of income."

Sophistry wins the debate and gains Pheidippides as a student. But the father's plan backfires. Although Strepsiades does manage to evade his creditors, he soon discovers that Pheidippides has learned his lessons all too well. Pheidippides brazenly disobeys his father, and when Strepsiades protests, the young man beats him with a stick—and then justifies the action with the sort of logic he has learned at the Thinkery. "[D]id you lick me when I was a little boy?" he asks his father, and then uses the old man's answer against him:

Strepsiades

*Of course I licked you. For your own
damn good. Because I loved you.*

Pheidippides

Then ipso facto, *since you yourself admit
that loving and lickings are synonymous, it's
only fair that I—for your own damn good,
you understand?—whip you in return.*

Too late, Strepsiades realizes that his situation
is worse than it was at the beginning. The old
man sets fire to the Thinkery and attacks its
occupants as they attempt to flee. "[W]hy did
you blaspheme the gods? / What made you spy
upon the Moon in heaven?" he yells just before
Socrates's school collapses into ruin.

Like all comic writers in ancient Athens,
Aristophanes filled his play with tomfoolery.
His Socrates ponders the momentous question
of whether gnats buzz through their mouths or
their rears, and after a student at the Thinkery
relates the philosopher's answer in technical detail,
Strepsiades offers an earthier rephrasing: "So the
gnat has a bugle up its ass!" Socrates's students
bend their heads to the ground because they are
"doing research on Hades"; they engage in study

with their rear ends too, which point upward
so that the students can complete "a minor in
Astronomy." Socrates is "cheated of an immense
discovery" because he is gaping at the moon when
a lizard discharges the contents of its bowels into
his mouth, and to feed his ragged, emaciated
students, he resorts to underhanded maneuvers.
He bends a skewer in the shape of a compass,
draws an arc to an unsuspecting victim, and hooks
the victim's cloak, which he then pawns for money.

The real Socrates was just as disgusted as
Aristophanes by the sophists' unscrupulous
behavior and slick talk. Was Aristophanes simply
following popular opinion? Was he aware that
Socrates was not just another unsavory sophist?
Interestingly, in the *Symposium* Plato depicts
the playwright and the philosopher dining side
by side, with no sign of tension between them.
But Aristophanes's opinion of Socrates as an
individual may not mean very much at all. It is
likely that the playwright never intended for the
head of the Thinkery to be a portrait of Socrates
himself. Aside from making heavy use of popular
stereotypes, Aristophanes drew on well-known
features of several different intellectuals in
Athens, not Socrates alone. The playwright may
have named this composite "Socrates" simply

because he wanted to have the character look like the real-life philosopher; for comic effect, Socrates's ugliness was too good to pass up.

If Aristophanes did take this artistic license, however, it was lost on the thousands who watched the *Clouds* on that spring day in 423 BCE. What those spectators saw was Socrates— perhaps a bit more absurd onstage than in real life, but the same man they knew from the streets of their city. If they had not realized it before, they knew it now: Socrates's natural philosophy threatened traditional religion, his sophistic rhetoric undermined honor and integrity, and his personal example taught young people to disrespect their elders.

How did the real Socrates respond to the drubbing he received in the *Clouds*? The stories that have come down to us date from much later times. One is told by the Roman author Aelian, who lived from the late second to the early third century CE. According to Aelian, Socrates knew in advance that he was to be the focus of Aristophanes's play and therefore went to the theater, even though he customarily avoided it, and found himself a good seat. During the performance, he observed the restless curiosity of the visitors from abroad, who were looking around for the real-life butt of all the onstage ridicule. Socrates obliged the strangers by standing and remaining on his feet for the rest of the performance—a sign, says Aelian, of the philosopher's utter contempt for comedy and his fellow Athenians.

Aelian's story is improbable. It is hard to imagine that other audience members would have tolerated Socrates's obstruction of their view; besides, Aelian's larger account of the history and reception of the play is fraught with glaring inaccuracies. But most telling of all is Aelian's description of Socrates as an embittered and contemptuous man. The people who knew the philosopher personally paint a completely different picture. In their writings, Socrates is unfailingly cheerful, playful, and quick to find amusement in absurdity.

A second story, traditionally but probably mistakenly attributed to Plutarch, is more consistent with the philosopher's good humor: "[W]hen Aristophanes brought out the *Clouds*, and heaped all manner of abuse upon Socrates in every possible way, one of those who had been present said to Socrates, 'Are you not indignant, Socrates, that he used you as he did in the play?' 'No indeed,' he replied; 'when they break a jest upon me in the theatre I feel as if I were at a big party of good friends.'" Socrates may indeed have chuckled along with everyone else at the wasted look of his students, the oddness of his appearance, the outrageous attacks on his character, and the wisecracks and sight gags that belittled his work as a philosopher. But one day Aristophanes's barbs would be no laughing matter.

DEPARTURE FOR BATTLE: A soldier, center, clasps his father's hand in farewell as a standing woman, possibly the soldier's mother, looks on. The man on the right is ready to hand over a helmet and shield. The ornate design at the top of the jug is ominous, since it resembles the decorations that often appeared on grave markers.

Terracotta neck-amphora (jar) with twisted handles, ca. 440 BCE. Attributed to the Lykaon Painter, Greek, Attic. The Metropolitan Museum of Art, New York.

CHAPTER 15

FAMILY AND DIVINE MISSION

IF SOCRATES ANTICIPATED A LONG STRETCH of calm for his philosophical mission, he was disappointed. The one-year truce between Athens and Sparta, shaky from the start, failed to produce a permanent peace. In the summer of 422 BCE, Socrates was called back into action, this time at Amphipolis, an Athenian colony that Sparta had seized shortly before the truce.

Amphipolis had strategic importance because it was the Athenians' major base in Thrace, a region rich in gold and silver as well as timber for shipbuilding. The city also overlooked the maritime route between Athens and the Black Sea, a passage that was vital to the Athenians' survival. Athenian farmers had long abandoned the struggle to grow an adequate supply of grain in Attica's unpromising soil. Olives and grapes were easier to coax from the rocky terrain, and when they were processed into oil and wine and marketed abroad, they drew handsome profits. This export-driven agriculture meant that the polis relied on other lands for much of its food, especially for grain, which came from the fertile fields of the Black Sea region. With a foothold in Amphipolis, Sparta could wreak significant damage on Athens.

Athens had been unable to recover Amphipolis from Sparta because of the truce, but when hostilities erupted again in 422 BCE, Socrates found himself on a hill outside the captured city. Along with his fellow hoplites, he awaited the orders of his strategos, Cleon, the fiery leader of Athens's militaristic faction, the man who five years earlier had urged the punishment of all Mytileneans whether innocent or guilty. On this occasion Cleon called for caution. After scouting the terrain and observing the placement of Spartan troops, he decided to wait for reinforcements, and he ordered his soldiers to withdraw. But something went terribly wrong in the complex maneuvering of the withdrawal, and Sparta seized the opportunity to mount a fierce attack. Unprepared and terrified, the Athenian soldiers broke ranks and fled in complete disorder. When it was all over, Athens had lost six hundred men. Sparta had lost seven.

The generals of both armies numbered among the casualties. Cleon and his Spartan counterpart, Brasidas, had been bold leaders, but their aggressive positions and popular followings had precluded the possibility of peace. Their deaths weakened the militaristic position on both sides, and in 421 BCE Athens and Sparta agreed to what is now known as the Peace of Nicias—a name that commemorates the moderate Athenian general who was instrumental in the negotiations, the same man who discusses courage with Socrates in Plato's *Laches*. According to the agreement, the two sides would return much of the territory that they had conquered, exchange the prisoners that they had captured, and resolve future disputes without resorting to combat.

The Peace of Nicias was meant to last for fifty years, but arrangements were doomed from the start. Sparta refused to restore Amphipolis to Athens, and several of Sparta's allies rejected the treaty altogether. The accord was formally abandoned in 414 BCE, only seven years after its hopeful beginning. Nonetheless, those seven years offered a respite to the war-weary combatants, and Socrates returned home to do what he enjoyed most, frequenting the public places of his city in search of stimulating conversation. His military career, as far as we know, ended with Amphipolis.

At around this point in his life, Socrates finally married. Although many husbands and wives undoubtedly grew to love one another, personal fulfillment and romance were almost never the reasons for a couple to wed in ancient Greece. The main goal of marriage was to produce the children who would ensure the survival of both the family and the state, and because this goal was so important, it was generally assumed that anyone who had reached the appropriate age would marry. A typical bride was a girl who had just reached puberty, while a typical bridegroom was a grown man of thirty or more. Socrates, now close to fifty, was older than the norm, but not excessively so. His close friend and age-mate Crito had married his own wife only about ten years earlier, when he was close to forty.

Crito had been an especially eligible bachelor. Although many farmers and ranchers had sustained huge losses during the Spartan raids, Crito's holdings, which were probably in Alopeke, benefited from their proximity to the protective Long Walls. He was rich and may well have married a woman of aristocratic birth. Socrates was poor, but now that the war had depleted the ranks of marriageable men, just about any unwed man was a good catch. He married a woman named Xanthippe, whose ability to bear children over the next fifteen years or so suggests that she was a good deal less than half his age. The couple had three boys, Lamprocles, Sophroniscus, and Menexenus.

The little we know about Xanthippe is contradictory. Plato depicts her as a sensitive and loving wife who appreciated her husband's philosophical mission, but Xenophon presents her as a shrew. Naturally, Xenophon's spicier version has taken hold of the popular imagination—so much so that the name Xanthippe has come to refer to any ill-tempered woman. In one of Xenophon's stories, Socrates is asked by his follower Antisthenes why he tolerates "a wife who is of all living women—and I believe of all that ever have been or will be—the most difficult to get on with." Socrates takes no offense. "[P]eople who want to become good horsemen keep not the most docile horses but ones that are high-spirited," he replies, "because they think that if they can control these, they will easily manage any other horses. In the same way, since I wish to deal and associate with people, I have provided myself with this wife, because I'm quite sure that, if I can put up with her, I shall find it easy to get on with any other human being."

Later sources embellish the caricature. In one famous account, Xanthippe viciously scolds Socrates and then drenches him with water, at which point the unruffled philosopher calmly observes, "Did I not say that Xanthippe was thundering now, and would soon rain?" Subsequent versions take the story a step further, replacing the water with more pungent liquids, like slops or the contents of a chamber pot.

Xenophon also offers a rare glimpse of Socrates as a father. Lamprocles, the oldest son, has apparently had a falling-out with his mother—ever the shrew, since this is Xenophon's account—and Socrates intervenes to set matters straight. Socrates begins by posing a question. "Look here, my boy, you know that there are some people who are called ungrateful?" The following exchange ensues:

"Yes, of course," said the boy.

"Are you clear about what it is that people do to earn this name?"

"Yes, I am," he said. "People are called ungrateful when they have been well treated and could show gratitude in return, but don't."

"Then you think that ingratitude is regarded as wrong?"

"Yes, I do."

The conversation continues at length. Socrates eventually equates ingratitude with injustice and establishes that "the greater the favours that a person receives without showing gratitude in return, the more unjust he is." From that point, it is a simple maneuver for Socrates to argue that individuals receive the greatest favors from their parents and then to drive home his conclusion: ingratitude toward a mother is especially unjust. Lamprocles is indignant—"But really, even if she has done all this and a great deal more besides, nobody could put up with her temper." Socrates, unfazed, responds with the same deliberate, step-by-step reasoning as before. "Which kind of ferocity do you think is harder to bear—a wild beast's or a mother's?" he asks, and the conversation continues.

Socrates's share in the exchange is almost comical. The situation is commonplace enough: an adolescent son, enraged by his mother, has expressed his discontent in words or deeds. But instead of offering the response we might expect of a father—a scolding, a threat, a demand for proper behavior, or even, if Xanthippe was really the shrew that some of our sources claim, a whispered expression of sympathy—Socrates plays the dispassionate reasoner. He asks for a definition of ingratitude, and he constructs a methodical argument, complete with analogies, to reach his logical conclusion. If this story has any basis in fact, Socrates must have been an exasperating father.

The Peace of Nicias was probably the occasion for another momentous development in Socrates's life. Aside from renewing the possibility of civilian travel, which had been difficult or downright impossible for many years, the treaty guaranteed the access of all Greeks to their commonly revered shrines.

One clause specifically established the independence of Apollo's temple at Delphi, which had become the object of a tug-of-war between Athens and Sparta. Once again, all of Greece could bring its urgent questions to the famous oracle. Among the people who took advantage of the opportunity was Socrates's childhood friend Chaerephon.

It is perhaps no surprise that Chaerephon's question concerned Socrates; Chaerephon was so famously devoted to the philosopher that Aristophanes depicted him as an avid scholar at the Thinkery in the *Clouds*. This devotion must have served Chaerephon well during the lengthy wait outside the temple of Apollo. The oracle answered questions only on the seventh day of each month during the spring, summer, and fall, and the line was always long. Supplicants were assigned a place in that line by lot, and anyone who did not get to see the oracle before sunset had to wait until the following month for another turn.

The oracle was a specially appointed priestess who prepared for consultations by purifying herself in a sacred stream, crowning her head with sprigs of laurel, and seating herself in the innermost sanctuary of the temple. She sat on a special seat right at the spot that ancient Greeks considered the earth's geographical center—the *omphalos*, or navel, of the world. A chasm just beneath her emitted vapors that sent her into a trance, a state that she intensified by chewing on laurel leaves and inhaling their smoke from a nearby fire. Chaerephon, too, engaged in a series of preparations. He participated in a purification ritual, took part in various sacrifices, and paid a hefty consultation fee. When his turn finally arrived, a priest conducted him to a spot from which the oracle could be heard but not seen.

The moment had come for Chaerephon to pose his question, and this is what it was: Did there exist any man wiser than Socrates? The oracle was the conduit of the god Apollo, so her answers were authoritative and true. Unfortunately, they were also famously unintelligible. The attending priest helpfully restated the oracle's words in more comprehensible language, but his restatements took the form of short poems that were often ambiguous. Chaerephon had the rare luck of a perfectly clear answer. No, no man was wiser than Socrates.

Chaerephon happily brought the good news back to Athens, but the oracle's answer left Socrates dissatisfied and perplexed. The philosopher was certain that he had no great knowledge of his own to share; almost all he did was to draw out and examine the ideas of others. "Whatever does the god mean?" Socrates asked. "What is his riddle? I am very conscious that I am not wise at all; what then does he mean by saying that I am the wisest?" The baffled philosopher devised a plan. He would find an individual who was undeniably wiser than himself and challenge the oracle with the evidence. Socrates knew just the person, a public figure who was widely reputed for his wisdom. But after speaking with that individual, Socrates was unimpressed: "I thought that he appeared wise to many people and especially to himself, but he was not. I then tried to show him that he thought himself wise, but that he was not."

So far, the oracle's words held true, but not because Socrates possessed a store of wisdom that his first candidate lacked. "[I]t is likely that neither of us knows anything worthwhile," Socrates mused. One thing, however, did set the two men apart. The public figure, said Socrates, "thinks he knows something when he does not, whereas when I do not know, neither do I think I know." The wisdom that tipped the scales in Socrates's favor was his awareness of his own ignorance.

Still hoping to find someone wiser than himself, Socrates approached another individual famed for his wisdom. But this man, too, believed he knew what he did not know. Now Socrates began to work more systematically. He went first to the politicians, then to the tragic and comic poets, and finally to the craftsmen. None of these fared any better than the first people he had examined. "[E]ach of them, because of his success at his craft, thought himself very wise in other most important pursuits, and this error of theirs overshadowed the wisdom they had." Socrates now recognized the truth of the oracle's answer, which he restated in his own words: "This man among you, mortals, is wisest who, like Socrates, understands that his wisdom is worthless."

Socrates had always probed the limits of other people's knowledge, but now the activity had Apollo's official endorsement. Many years later, the philosopher was still working at the same task and still describing it as a form of divine service: "So even now I continue this investigation as the god bade me—and I go around seeking out anyone, citizen or stranger, whom I think wise. Then if I do not think he is, I come to the assistance of the god and show him that he is not wise." Of course, Socrates's goal went beyond the exposure of ignorance, since he had not lost sight of his preoccupation with a life worth living. The tearing down of incorrect ideas was only a prelude to the construction of genuine knowledge on the firm ground of reason, and the ultimate objective was to use that genuine knowledge to make ethically sound decisions.

Socrates's goals were lofty, but most people resented his efforts to expose their ignorance. They already knew more than they cared to know about that insufferable man, and now he was prowling around Athens with the express purpose of showing them just how stupid they were—and what impudence to assert that his offensive little project was a service to the god! What was that service if not a way for him to show off? What was his claim to know nothing if not a sly device to ridicule everyone else?

TRIBUTE LIST:
This stone, part of a much larger record, lists the tribute payments that Athens expected six or seven years into the Peloponnesian War. The assessment for Melos, which appears toward the bottom, amounted to fifteen talents, enough to cover the wages of a trireme's crew for fifteen months. Melos refused to hand over the money.

Fragmentary marble inscription, ca. 425–424 BCE, Greek, Attic. The Metropolitan Museum of Art, New York.

CHAPTER 16

MELOS, ALCIBIADES, AND THE TEACHABILITY OF VIRTUE

IN 416 BCE, TWO YEARS BEFORE THE UNSTEADY Peace of Nicias was formally abandoned, Athens committed one of the worst atrocities of the Peloponnesian War. Melos, a small island off the southeastern coast of mainland Greece, had never joined Athens as an ally in the Delian League and was doing its best to remain neutral. This neutrality nettled Athens. Melos had long enjoyed the security and economic welfare that Athens had brought to the Aegean, but the island had never borne any of the costs. An attempt to subjugate Melos in 426 had failed, and ten years later, Athens decided to try again. Thirty-eight ships bearing some three thousand soldiers converged on the island.

The forces stood at the ready, awaiting their orders to attack, but Athens still hoped to avoid the expense, inconvenience, and inevitable losses of battle. Perhaps the Melians could be convinced that their situation was hopeless and that their only good option was a peaceful surrender. Athens invited Melos to a joint discussion now known as the Melian Dialogue, which Thucydides dramatically reconstructs in his history of the war. Athens appealed to Melos with the same might-makes-right argument that Thrasymachus presents in the *Republic*: "[Y]ou know as well as we do that right, as the world goes, is only in question between equals in power, while the strong do what they can and the weak suffer what they must." Whether Athens was acting unjustly was beside the point. Melos would suffer drastic consequences if it did not comply with Athenian demands.

The Melians rejected Athens's argument. A nobler justice indeed exists, they insisted, and it has real-world consequences. An attack against Melos would so grievously violate basic standards of fairness that it would provoke other neutrals, not to mention entrenched enemies of Athens, to act against the aggressors. "[W]e are just men fighting against unjust," the Melians affirmed, certain that both gods and humans would see the righteousness of their cause and come to their aid. Athens dismissed the Melians' position as naïve: "Of the gods we believe, and of men we know, that by a necessary law of their nature they rule wherever they can. . . . [W]e bless your simplicity but do not envy your folly."

Athens had the last laugh—a decidedly cruel one. Unable to achieve their goal through negotiation, the Athenians laid siege to the island, in effect imprisoning the Melians in their own city. The Melians made several attempts to break the siege, but to no avail, and after several months, they were forced to surrender. Athens summarily executed all the men, sold all the women and children into slavery, and sent five hundred of its own citizens to establish a colony on the island. The brutality exceeded the lamentable standards that Athens had already set at Mytilene, Scione, and Torone. This time Athens had butchered not a rebel state, but a neutral one that was merely trying to stay out of harm's way.

Despite Socrates's determined opposition to the might-makes-right position in the *Republic*, we still do not see him taking a public stand on Athenian policy. But his ability to avoid politics was about to end. The earliest trouble involved Alcibiades. In 415

BCE, the year after the massacre of Melos, Athens undertook a military campaign in Sicily, the large island at the base of Italy. Some of the cities in Sicily had aligned themselves with Athens while others had aligned themselves with Sparta, and growing tensions between these two groups had induced a couple of cities to appeal to Athens for military assistance. Athens responded favorably, but not out of any real concern for its friends. As Thucydides records, the Athenians were motivated by greed for land and power: they were "ambitious in real truth of conquering the whole."

Perhaps no one advocated the Sicilian campaign more passionately than Alcibiades. Although he was only in his midthirties, he was a celebrity. He had already served as strategos, which means that he must have been appointed when he was close to thirty, the lowest eligible age. That achievement was phenomenal. The strategoi were not only the most important public officials in Athens but also part of the tiny minority that was elected instead of chosen by lot. To have won the position at such a young age, Alcibiades must have made an extraordinary impression on his fellow citizens. Now, in masterful speeches in the Ekklesia, he held out the tantalizing promise of the richer and larger empire that would result from the conquest of Sicily, and he won the people's support. Late in the summer of 415, he and two other generals took their positions at the head of what Thucydides calls "by far the most costly and splendid Hellenic force that had ever been sent out by a single city up to that time." The launch, full of pomp and circumstance, inspired visions of glorious conquest. But the Sicilian campaign turned out to be a terrible mistake. Since Alcibiades played a pivotal role in the calamitous turn of events, Socrates did not escape the fallout.

The problems began just before the launch. The Athenians woke up one morning to discover that stone statues of the god Hermes had been desecrated throughout the city. These statues, called herms, depicted the god's face and phallus and customarily appeared in the doorways of homes and temples as boundary markers. Overnight, a group of people had swept through the city, mutilating all the herms they encountered. The situation was worrisome. The desecration of ritual objects always stirred fears of divine retribution, and the specifics of this case made matters worse. Hermes was the god of travel, and Athenian ships were about to set sail for Sicily. Could Athens hope for a positive outcome now?

The crime had a political dimension too, since the perpetrators undoubtedly anticipated the impact of their actions on the Sicilian campaign. The citizens had made a collective decision to undertake the Sicilian expedition, and now some conspirators were trying to undermine that decision. The desecration of the herms was no less than a plot against the democracy.

Alcibiades was unlikely to sabotage an expedition that he supported so strongly. But in the alarm unleashed by the desecration of the herms, all forms of ritual desecration fell under scrutiny. The investigation mushroomed, and Alcibiades was slapped with an accusation: he had recently profaned the Eleusinian Mysteries. The cult of Eleusis was a religion open to anyone, including women, slaves, and foreigners, but only individuals who had become formal initiates were entitled to learn its secret rituals. Alcibiades's violation probably amounted to mocking the sacred rites or performing them without the proper priests in attendance.

This time, suspicions against Alcibiades were credible. Alcibiades often caroused with troublemakers and exercised little self-restraint. In the *Symposium*, which depicts one of the formal banquets that went by that name, Plato

HERMS: It is rare to find a fully intact herm from Socrates's time. The head above would have originally topped a squared column, plain but for a depiction of the male genitals. Pictured to the left is a small but complete bronze herm from the Peloponnese.

Marble head from a herm, probably late fifth century BCE, Greek. The Metropolitan Museum of Art, New York.

Bronze herm, ca. 490 BCE, Greek, Arcadian. The Metropolitan Museum of Art, New York.

shows Alcibiades arriving late, "very drunk and very loud," and practically unable to stand without assistance. "I'm plastered," Alcibiades announces, but as soon as he spots a jar that can hold more than two quarts of wine, he orders his servants to fill it to the brim and guzzles down its contents. It is easy to imagine this man making light of rituals that other people revered, and Plato shows him doing just that. Just before recounting the racier parts of his attempt to seduce Socrates, Alcibiades describes his own introduction to philosophy as an initiation into the frenzies of a mystery religion. "As for the house slaves and for anyone else who is not an initiate," he facetiously announces, "my story's not for you: block your ears!"

Alcibiades staunchly denied any involvement in the profanation of the Eleusinian Mysteries, and he may have been telling the truth. Even so, he was trapped. First, it was a particularly inopportune time to fall under suspicion about ritual matters. The chaos of ongoing war was dealing a critical blow to the rational spirit of the Periclean period, and religious superstition was on the rise. Second, he stirred widespread resentment as an individual, since he was wealthy and arrogant. Third, he was an

THE SYMPOSIUM:
At the symposium, men enjoyed wine, song, poetry, and serious discussion. Women were not invited as guests, but they were often present as dancers and musicians, and some of them may have also offered their services as prostitutes. In this image, a woman plays the flute as one man holds a lyre and another man holds a cup of wine. The boots tucked under the couches emphasize the men's relaxation and well-being.

Terracotta bell-krater (bowl for mixing wine and water), mid-fifth century BCE. Attributed to the Painter of the Louvre Centauromachy, Greek, Attic. The Metropolitan Museum of Art, New York.

aristocrat, and the war had raised concerns about the many family ties between the Athenian and Spartan aristocracies.

Evidence linking Alcibiades to the enemy seemed especially damning. In addition to having a Spartan name, he had inherited the role of *proxenos* to Sparta. Greek city-states did not maintain permanent diplomatic representatives abroad, like modern-day ambassadors and consuls. Instead, each polis appointed a citizen of another city-state, a proxenos, to look after its interests in his local community. A proxenos provided hospitality, useful introductions, and legal guidance to delegates and other visitors from the polis that had appointed him, and because it was central to the conduct of foreign affairs, the arrangement usually weathered the tensions of a Greek world almost constantly at war. It was frankly accepted that the proxenos might have to fight against the polis that had appointed him; his first loyalty always belonged to the polis where he was a citizen. In Alcibiades's case, however, that primary loyalty was cast into doubt. Many Athenians were eager for any additional spur to their envy, hatred, or both, and his role as proxenos fit the bill.

Alcibiades pushed for his trial to take place immediately, before the departure of the fleet he was meant to co-command. If he were abroad with the charges still pending, his enemies in Athens would enjoy free rein as they rallied public sentiment against him. That scenario obviously appealed to his enemies, and since they prevailed in postponing the trial, he had no choice but to set sail under a cloud of suspicion. The cloud grew darker in his absence, and within three months, a ship was dispatched from Athens to bring him home for his trial. A guilty verdict would carry the death penalty.

Alcibiades promised to return to Athens in a ship of his own, but he broke his word and made for Sparta instead. Tried in absentia by his fellow Athenians, he was found guilty, stripped of his property, and sentenced to death. In the meantime, he shared with the Spartans his intimate knowledge of Athens's military affairs and undercut the Athenian campaign in Sicily. But soon he fell out of favor in Sparta too. The details are murky, but according to an intriguing rumor, he fathered a child with the wife of one of Sparta's two ruling kings. When Alcibiades caught wind of a Spartan plot to assassinate him, he fled to Asia Minor. There he became an advisor to an influential Persian satrap, or regional governor, who had formed an alliance with Sparta in an effort to reconquer the Ionian cities that had fallen under Athenian influence at the end of the Persian Wars. Alcibiades now convinced the satrap to minimize his support of Sparta and concentrate instead on prolonging the fight between Athens and Sparta. The more those enemies wore each other down, Alcibiades argued, the more easily Persia could swoop in at the end of the war to conquer the entire region. Alcibiades was betraying all of Greece to the Persians.

As Thucydides interprets these maneuverings, Alcibiades's real goal was to return to Athens. Now that he could flaunt his influence with the Persians, Alcibiades had some useful leverage. He contacted a number Athenian generals and proposed a mutually beneficial deal. He would procure Persian money and perhaps even the Persian fleet to aid the Athenian war effort, and they would help him topple the Athenian democracy and replace it with an oligarchy. That government would expand the generals' powers and pave the way for Alcibiades's return to the polis.

The plan met with success in 411 BCE, when the conspirators brought down the democracy that had existed for over a century. Although the oligarchy they established lasted for less than a year and Alcibiades failed to secure the Persian assistance he had promised, he was already well on his way to his rehabilitation in Athens. First the Athenian forces, managed by the generals who were sympathetic to Alcibiades, invited him to join them and restored him as strategos. Then, after leading a series of impressive military campaigns over a number of years, he persuaded the polis to suspend all charges against him. He finally made it back to Athens in 407 BCE, when the jubilant Athenians proclaimed him "general-in-chief with absolute authority." But public feeling soured the following year, when the polis's fleet suffered heavy losses on his watch. Alcibiades escaped the fallout by moving to Thrace, along the northern Aegean coast. Even then, he had a final scene to play before the war ended.

To his fellow Athenians, Alcibiades was an object of fascination and revulsion, often simultaneously. As late as 405, some in Athens still hoped that he would return from Thrace to revive the faltering war effort; in a comedy produced that year, Aristophanes made fun of the polis's fluctuating moods: "It longs for him, it hates him, and it wants him back." For many

Athenians, however, Alcibiades's significance was unequivocal. Trampling on every principle but self-interest, Alcibiades represented the most abject treachery.

The intimate connection between Socrates and Alcibiades was no secret, and Socrates could not escape the implications. If Athens wanted hard evidence to support its longstanding distrust of the philosopher, Alcibiades provided it in ample measure. Now the people understood that the peril was even greater than they had previously imagined. Socrates had actively nurtured a traitor. What other enemies of the polis would Socrates produce next?

From our perspective it may seem absurd to imagine that Socrates, so constant in his commitment to virtue, could have had any direct connection with Alcibiades's shameless behavior. How could the Athenians have understood so little of what the philosopher represented? Clearly, popular misconceptions proved to be stronger than the truth; based on hearsay or caricatures like Aristophanes's, most people already thought they knew everything they needed to know. But we are still left with an inescapable question. Alcibiades had been an avid disciple, eager to elevate himself through his attachment to Socrates, and Socrates had a proven track record of inspiring young men. Why didn't the relationship make Alcibiades a better person?

Xenophon and Plato both blame Alcibiades. Xenophon claims that Alcibiades was flawed from the very beginning by his boundless ambition. The young man never considered Socrates a serious role model but attached himself to the philosopher simply to gain the rhetorical skills and habits that would pave his way to power. Plato gives Alcibiades a bit more credit. In the *Symposium*, Plato shows Alcibiades frankly acknowledging his own failings: "Socrates is the only man in the world who has made me feel shame—ah, you didn't think I had it in me, did you?" Unfortunately, Alcibiades's self-awareness did not produce long-lasting results: "I know perfectly well that I can't prove he's wrong when he tells me what I should do; yet, the moment I leave his side, I go back to my old ways: I cave in to my desire to please the crowd." Alcibiades had good intentions, Plato suggests, but was too weak to act on them in Socrates's absence.

We do not know where Socrates himself pinned the blame, but he would have surely examined the assumption that he—or anyone else, for that matter—could have made Alcibiades a better man. Socrates returned to the same question again and again: Is virtue at all teachable? Plato's *Protagoras* explores the question at length. The renowned sophist Protagoras claims to teach his students virtue, but Socrates questions whether such a thing is possible. Socrates shares two reasons for his doubt. The first arises from proceedings at the Ekklesia. Whenever the city undertakes a project that requires special expertise, the citizens expect to hear the advice of individuals who possess that expertise. If the plan is to construct buildings, the citizens want to hear from builders; if the plan is to craft ships, the citizens want to hear from shipwrights. Advice from anyone who has not mastered the relevant subject, "no matter how handsome and rich and well-born he might be," is irrelevant; the crowd just laughs at him or shouts down his recommendations. On the other hand, whenever the Ekklesia deliberates on city management—which Socrates considers to be a matter of justice, itself an essential component of virtue—"anyone can stand up and advise them, carpenter, blacksmith, shoemaker, merchant, ship-captain, rich man, poor man, well-born, low-born—it doesn't matter—and nobody blasts him for presuming to give counsel without any prior training under a teacher." It seems, then, that people generally consider the sense of justice to be innate rather than acquired. Education cannot produce that sense in individuals who lack it.

Socrates's second reason for doubting the teachability of virtue is the lack of evidence that teaching virtue actually works. "[T]he wisest and best of our citizens," he observes, "are unable to transmit to others the virtues that they possess." Scanning the crowd that is watching his debate with Protagoras, he identifies the sons of Pericles and other children of notable men. Seemingly unconcerned—or perhaps just mischievously amused—by the embarrassment he must be causing, he describes how the fathers of those individuals failed to educate them properly. Since virtuous teachers and role models have so little impact, virtue must not be teachable.

Protagoras vigorously objects to Socrates's conclusion, and his reaction comes as no surprise; the sophist's profession, reputation, and income all depend on the premise that virtue is teachable. First Protagoras addresses Socrates's observation that everyone feels qualified to speak about city management at the Ekklesia. This is the case, Protagoras claims, because everyone who lives in a human community possesses at least a modicum of the political art, by which Protagoras means a fundamental sense of justice and the basic ability to feel shame. Without that basic endowment, human beings would not be able to live together at all; its importance is so widely recognized that even individuals known to be unjust make every effort to make themselves look just. Unjust people would be considered insane if they publicly announced their injustice in the same way that they might, for instance, publicly announce their inability to construct buildings or ships. "[I]t is madness not to pretend to justice, since one must have some trace of it or not be human."

But this basic sense of virtue, Protagoras argues, is insufficient on its own and must be developed through education. All human societies recognize this truth. Penal systems, for instance, assume that criminals can be reformed and that the prospect of punishment deters other people from wrongdoing—in other words, that virtue is teachable. If it were not grounded on this assumption, the infliction of punishment would amount to no more than the "mindless vindictiveness of a beast." The raising of children is grounded on the same premise. "As soon as a child understands what is said to him, the nurse, mother, tutor, and the father himself fight for him to be as good as he possibly can, seizing on every action and word to teach him and show him that this is just, that is unjust, this is noble, that is ugly, this is pious, that is impious, he should do this, he should not do that." Children continue to learn proper attitudes and behaviors in school, and when their formal instruction ends because they have grown into adults, the state takes over by compelling them to learn and obey the laws.

Protagoras can also explain why many good fathers fail to produce equally good children. Individuals vary in their abilities. If all people were instructed in flute-playing, we would not expect every single one of them to achieve the same level of mastery. At the same time, however, we would undoubtedly expect an individual who has undergone flute lessons to play more skillfully than an individual who has never been instructed at all. In the same way, some people will naturally make more progress in their moral development than others, but by no means do these varying results prove that it is impossible to teach virtue. Any father who educates his children in virtue most certainly enhances their basic moral sense.

The subsequent debate between Socrates and Protagoras takes several detours, and by the end of the dialogue, the two men have reversed positions. Protagoras concludes that courage, which the two men have defined as one of the parts of virtue, cannot in fact be taught, while Socrates concludes that all of virtue is indeed teachable. Socrates changes his mind because of his belief that we choose our course of action by weighing prospective pleasures and pains—good and bad—on a figurative balance scale. The act of weighing is the essential point: "Since it has turned out that our salvation in life depends on the right choice of pleasures and pains, be they more or fewer, greater or lesser, farther or nearer, doesn't our salvation seem, first of all, to be measurement, which is the study of relative excess and deficiency and equality? . . . And since it is measurement,

it must definitely be an art, and knowledge."
Virtue is not an amorphous goodness that we
either possess or lack but a body of knowledge
and a set of specific skills that we can acquire
through education.

But even this conclusion is provisional.
After chuckling at the irony of having switched
positions with Protagoras, Socrates remarks,
"Now, Protagoras, seeing that we have gotten
this topsy-turvy and terribly confused, I am
most eager to clear it all up." He points out that
he and Protagoras have not adequately defined
virtue, and only once they manage to do so can
they legitimately conclude whether virtue can be
taught. Socrates offers to continue the discussion
at some future meeting, and Protagoras
graciously accepts the invitation.

Socrates revisits the teachability of virtue
in the *Meno*, a dialogue that Plato sets more
than thirty years after the *Protagoras*. But
even as a man in his late sixties, Socrates
has no clear answer. Like the *Protagoras*, the
Meno ends with the usual aporia, along with
the familiar commitment to continue seeking
answers; no conclusion is complete or absolute
enough to preclude ongoing scrutiny. At this
point in Socrates's life, however, the open-

endedness is surprising. Socrates had already spent more than four decades trying to awaken others to their ethical responsibilities. Didn't his mission depend on the certainty that virtue is teachable?

Obviously Socrates carried on without that certainty. His ability to do so probably grew out of the way that he understood the process of education and his own role as an educator. Instead of considering himself a teacher, he imagined that he was following his mother's profession; after her second marriage and the birth of Socrates's half brother, Phaenarete had begun to work as a midwife. Like a midwife, Socrates tended to individuals in labor. This labor was not the physical exertion of women about to deliver babies, but the intellectual exertion of people about to deliver thoughts— "the labor of their souls," as Socrates called it. His followers were not empty receptacles, passively waiting to be stuffed with whatever it was that he supposedly knew; instead, they brought forth the ideas that they already carried within themselves. Socrates could assist in that process, but ultimately, like a midwife, he stood at the sidelines.

The metaphor had an additional implication in ancient Greece, where many newborns lacked the hardihood to survive and part of the midwife's job was to judge their fitness to live. Brand-new ideas are similarly fragile, and Socrates needed to assess their viability—in other words, to engage in his familiar work of ensuring that ignorance did not pass as knowledge. "[T]he most important thing about my art," he declared, "is the ability to apply all possible tests to the offspring, to determine whether the young mind is being delivered of a phantom, that is, an error, or a fertile truth."

The role that Socrates had carved out for himself was not nearly as flattering as the more common one, then as well as now: the teacher as sage, several notches above the students whom he or she graces with tidy bits of wisdom. Socrates had no use for that gratifying image. He believed instead that every single person must labor actively in pursuit of knowledge. Like childbirth, that pursuit is often long, messy, and painful. The results can be momentous, but they come with no guarantee.

FALLEN SOLDIERS:
This grave marker,
erected by the family
of a soldier who died
in battle, depicts two
enemy combatants
about to kill one
another. The Athenians
were careful to bring
home the ashes of fallen
soldiers, which they
buried in a cemetery
just outside the walls in
the northwestern corner
of the city.

*Grave stele with hoplite
battle scene,* ca. 390
BCE, Greek, Attic. The
Metropolitan Museum
of Art, New York.

CHAPTER 17

THE CONSCIENTIOUS OBJECTOR

THE EXPEDITION TO SICILY ENDED DISASTROUSLY in 413 BCE, two years after the festive launch of the Athenian fleet. Thucydides offers an unsparing assessment: "They were beaten at all points and altogether; all that they suffered was great; they were destroyed, as the saying is, with a total destruction, their fleet, their army—everything was destroyed, and few out of many returned home." To make matters worse, rebellion was surging among the subjects of Athens, Persia was entering the war on the side of Sparta, and the Athenian economy was falling into a tailspin. The labor force had dwindled as a result of fighting, disease, and privation, and the production of marketable goods had plummeted. Enemy incursions had ravaged farms and livestock, unsafe waters had thrown trade routes into disarray, and rebellious subjects refused to pay their tributes. In the meantime, Athens continued to shoulder the heavy costs of waging war. By 406 BCE, the treasury was so depleted that the polis was forced to melt down some golden statues of Nike that had once adorned the Acropolis. Still, the Athenians showed remarkable spirit and resiliency. The polis held on until 405, eight years after the Sicilian fiasco, before its final defeat.

Although Socrates was no longer a soldier, he played a role in one of the most dramatic events of that period. In 406, the Spartan navy blockaded the Athenian fleet at Mytilene, and Athens needed to rescue its trapped ships and soldiers. By that point the Athenian navy had been sorely weakened, but in an extraordinary effort over the course of a single month, the feisty polis constructed new ships and recruited new rowers, even promising citizenship to slaves and foreign residents who took up oars. With some additional ships from its allies, Athens patched together a more sizable force than Sparta's.

But most of the fresh recruits had never rowed before, and for the first time in the war, the Athenian crews were less skilled than those of the enemy. To compensate for this inexperience, the eight strategoi who led the mission wisely organized their ships in a special new formation, and when the two sides finally joined battle at the Arginusae Islands, between the island of Lesbos and the mainland of Asia Minor, Athens pulled off a magnificent victory. Sparta lost 77 of its 120 ships; Athens lost only 25 of 155. The Athenians were euphoric.

The jubilation faded quickly. Twelve of the damaged Athenian ships still floated, with perhaps a thousand men clinging to the wreckage in waters that teemed with the bodies of the drowned. A victorious fleet typically regrouped after a battle to rescue survivors and recover the dead, but this time something went terribly wrong. The thousand or so survivors were left to drown, and none of the bodies were ever recovered. Despite their apparent negligence, the eight generals had acted properly. They had sailed elsewhere to prevent the dangerous remobilization of the Spartan fleet, and they had left behind an adequate number of ships and appointed specific captains to handle the rescue. A terrifying storm had thwarted the operation, and to free themselves of blame, the captains who had been left in charge scurried back to Athens and denounced the generals.

Public furor broke out when the news reached Athens. The Ekklesia ordered the generals back to the city to stand trial immediately, but two of their number fled into exile. The remaining six argued their case before the assembly and had almost convinced the people to drop the charges when the sun set. Because it was too dark to count a show of hands, the vote had to wait, and the postponement proved fatal. First, it gave the inevitable hotheads more time to ignite public rage, and second, it meant that the vote could not take place until after the Apaturia, a three-day festival when children officially became members of their family clans. The Apaturia was normally a time for joyful family reunions, but that year it became an occasion to mourn the men who had been abandoned at sea. Eager to keep the spotlight on the generals, the captains magnified the tragedy by hiring people to pose as grieving relatives. The public's anger flared, and the fate of the generals became inescapable.

The five hundred members of the Boule, the executive council that set the Ekklesia's agenda, had the task of determining the trial's procedure. Their proposal practically guaranteed a guilty verdict. The vote would take place with no further debate, and the question would be phrased in language that was heavily prejudiced against the generals: Were they guilty "for not picking up the men who won the victory in the naval battle"? Furthermore, all the generals would be tried together, with a single vote in the Ekklesia determining the verdict for all of them. A guilty verdict would mean the death sentence and the confiscation of all the generals' property.

The Boule's proposal was highly unusual, and its legality was questionable. Especially problematic was the decision to try the generals as a group; normally, every defendant was entitled to a trial of his own and an opportunity to speak in his own defense. A few individuals attempted to raise objections on the floor of the Ekklesia, but they were swiftly silenced by the threat that they would be charged along with the generals. Some members of the prytany, the subgroup of the Boule that was responsible for executing the people's decisions, pressed on with the protest. By then, however, the people had lost their ability to think rationally. Without bothering to address the legal arguments, they clamored for any objectors to stand trial alongside the generals. The prytany backed down and agreed to hold the vote.

But the prytany's decision was not unanimous. The prytany's presiding officer stood firm in his objection, and that officer was Socrates. Although Socrates avoided politics, he dutifully fulfilled the obligations that came his way. That year, he happened to be chosen by lot to serve on the

Boule; that month, the administrative tribe to which he belonged happened to be serving on the prytany; and that day, he happened to hold the position of presiding officer. At his trial seven years later, Socrates described the situation to a jury composed of his fellow citizens: "I was the only member of the presiding committee to oppose your doing something contrary to the laws, and I voted against it. The orators were ready to prosecute me and take me away, and your shouts were egging them on, but I thought I should run any risk on the side of law and justice rather than join you, for fear of prison or death, when you were engaged in an unjust course."

As a lone objector, Socrates was powerless to change the course of events. The generals were tried as a group, found guilty, and sentenced to death. Reason eventually prevailed, but only after the men had been executed. In a flagrant denial of their own responsibility, the repentant citizens voted "that complaints be brought against any who had deceived the people." These were not mere complaints, but official charges of offense against the state. Five individuals were identified and arrested, and all five exercised their right to leave the city rather than stand trial. The episode had followed the familiar, sickening pattern: a difficult

THE THOLOS:
A round building on the west side of the Agora, the Tholos served as the meeting place and dining hall of the fifty members of the prytany. At least seventeen members slept in the building each night so that they could be available for emergencies. Because the roof reminded people of a sunhat, the structure was commonly known by the nickname *skias*, or "sunshade."

Model of the Tholos, ca. 470–460 BCE. Petros Demetriades and Kostas Papoulias. American School of Classical Studies at Athens: Agora Excavations.

situation roiled the polis, a few rabble-rousers inflamed the mood, the body of citizens lost all restraint, and any semblance of justice broke down. Socrates had more reason than ever to distrust a government that empowered an unthinking public.

Aside from its damage to the social and political fabric of Athens, the affair deprived the polis of its best military talent at an especially inopportune time. Now the weary, understaffed forces were being led by men without the experience and skill of the generals at Arginusae, and these new leaders, unnerved by the fate of their predecessors, shied away from bold action. The final defeat came one year later. Sparta had conquered Lampsacus, a city on the water route between the Black and Aegean Seas, and could now block the passage of grain-bearing ships to Athens. Since the polis would starve if the enemy stayed in that location, the Athenians moved their fleet to Aegospotami, across the strait and about three miles from Lampsacus. For several days, the Athenians sailed over to the Spartan side, attempting to provoke a battle that would dislodge the enemy ships. But each day the Spartan fleet refused to react, and the dispirited Athenians rowed back to their base.

Against this backdrop Alcibiades made his final appearance. Having observed the standoff from his neighboring Thracian estate, he mounted his horse and rode down to the Athenian camp. There he offered his advice and promised the military assistance of his most recent friends, the kings of local city-states. His help would come at a price: a share in the Athenian command. Could Alcibiades have made good on his promises and led Athens to victory? We will never know. Unwilling to take the risk, the Athenian generals sent him away.

Meanwhile, the futile exercise of rowing between Aegospotami and Lampsacus had demoralized the Athenian troops, and they began to neglect their usual precautions. The men scurried off to find food and water as soon as they returned to base, and their generals failed to take them to task. When Sparta finally attacked, the Athenians were so unprepared that many of their ships were perched on the beach, completely unmanned. Panic and confusion reigned as soldiers fled in all directions, and by the time the disaster had run its course, three to four thousand Athenian soldiers had been captured and executed. Only ten ships remained of the once daunting Athenian navy. It was the spring of 405 BCE, twenty-seven years after the start of the war, and Sparta's victory was complete.

When the news reached Athens, the people were terrified, and with good reason. What would prevent them from suffering the same fate they had inflicted on Scione, Torone, Melos, and other Greek cities, many of which had cast their lot with Sparta? Ultimately, Athens fared much better than its victims. The population was not exiled, enslaved, or slaughtered; the city was not razed or occupied by foreigners; and all of Attica remained under Athenian control. Nonetheless, the terms of the peace established a painful new reality. The Athenians were forced to give up their Long Walls, cede their rule over foreign cities, and relinquish control over the size of their fleet. They were obliged to readmit their exiles, who were mostly pro-Spartan aristocrats and oligarchs, and they were required to maintain the same friends and enemies as Sparta— essentially, to surrender authority over their own foreign policy. The Athenian Empire was gone.

Gone, too, was the democracy. Under Spartan supervision, the Ekklesia and its executive committees gave way to a group of thirty oligarchs commonly called the "Thirty" or, in later decades, the "Thirty Tyrants." These rulers wasted no time in murdering the polis's most prominent democrats and seizing their property, and before long, the Thirty targeted other groups as well: men of means, political moderates, and sometimes even members of their own ranks. No one in Athens felt safe.

The Thirty knew that their comeuppance would be terrible if they ever lost their power, so they did their best to spread the guilt. The larger the group they could get to do their dirty work, the less likely they would be singled out for retribution. One day they caught Socrates in their net. They ordered him, along with four others, to arrest Leon, a prominent citizen from Salamis. Leon had committed no crimes, and he had faithfully served the polis as strategos during the Peloponnesian War. But he was also a staunch supporter of democracy, and in the eyes of the Thirty he deserved to die. Alone of the men charged with the job, Socrates refused to comply. While the others proceeded to Salamis to make the arrest, he returned to his home.

For the second time in recent memory, Socrates was defying his government; the affair of the generals at Arginusae had occurred only about two years earlier. This time, however, chance had not thrown the philosopher into the political spotlight, and his resistance was private. He could have tried, perhaps, to stop the other men from following their orders, to warn Leon of the forthcoming arrest, or to raise a public outcry against the Thirty's atrocities. But Socrates took none of these steps. He simply followed his own principles and withdrew from the scene, leaving events to unfold as they would.

This modest resistance may seem grossly inadequate, but Leon of Salamis was doomed no matter what Socrates did or did not do. Furthermore, even Socrates's refusal to cooperate demanded bravery, since the Thirty might well have executed him for his disobedience. As he recalled later, "I showed again, not in words but in action, that, if it were not rather vulgar to say so, death is something I couldn't care less about, but that my whole concern is not to do anything unjust or impious. That government, powerful as it was, did not frighten me into any wrongdoing." Socrates probably escaped punishment only because the Thirty ran out of time. The polis's most stalwart democrats had fled to Phyle, about nine miles northwest of Athens, to form a resistance army, and in 403 BCE, after a brutal civil war, they restored the democracy.

Socrates had taken a stand against injustice under two different forms of government. He had defied a democracy over the Arginusae affair and an oligarchy over the arrest of Leon of Salamis. No matter who was in power, he maintained the same principles. But the democrats, flush with their return to power, cared little for such fine details. They already knew quite enough about the philosopher. He was a critic of democracy and a friend of aristocrats, and during the reign of the Thirty, he had remained in Athens instead of joining the resistance in Phyle. Most damning of all, he associated with the worst sorts of people. Aside from his connection with the infamous Alcibiades, he had enjoyed the company of Critias and Charmides, the same individuals with whom he discusses temperance in the *Charmides*. Critias and Charmides had died during the recent civil war, but not before gaining well-deserved notoriety for their cruelty. Critias had been one of the Thirty, and Charmides had been part of an affiliated group that governed the Piraeus, Athens's major port city.

The savagery of Critias and Charmides raises the same questions as the tumultuous career of Alcibiades. How could individuals who engaged in Socrates's philosophic endeavor turn out so bad? Is virtue teachable? Do the complexities of education make questions of blame altogether off-target? The people of Athens, battered by years of hardship, had no patience for these considerations. From their perspective, the situation was perfectly clear. The polis's most notorious villains and traitors had all shared the same teacher.

PART THREE

The Last Days

THE WORKINGS OF DEMOCRACY: Pictured on this wine cup is a vote to determine who will receive the armor of the hero Achilles, a recent casualty of the Trojan War. The dots on the two ends of the pedestal are pebbles that represent votes for either Odysseus or Ajax, the two claimants for the prize. Although the story is the stuff of legend, the artist introduced into his image a real-life artifact of the democracy he knew. During the fifth century, Athenian jurors used pebbles or similar small objects to register their votes.

Attic Red-Figured Kylix, 490–480 BCE. Attributed to the Brygos Painter, Greek, Attic. J. Paul Getty Museum. Digital image courtesy of the Getty's Open Content Program.

CHAPTER 18

THE CHARGES AND THE QUESTION OF PIETY

IT TOOK A WHILE FOR THE ANIMOSITY AGAINST Socrates to break into a full boil. Hoping to put a quick end to the unrest, the restored democracy wisely looked to the future instead of dwelling on the past. Rather than hunt down the guilty, the people declared an amnesty: no individual would be prosecuted for crimes committed during the reign of the Thirty. Many years later, the *Constitution of the Athenians*, a political treatise written by Aristotle or one of his students, praised the polis for its remarkable restraint: "[T]he Athenians appear both in private and public to have behaved towards the past disasters in the most completely honorable and statesmanlike manner of any people in history."

In reality, however, the amnesty fell short of its promise. Although the remaining oligarchs had received official permission to settle in Eleusis, about twelve miles from Athens, it did not take long before a militant group of democrats rounded them up and murdered them. And although it was technically illegal to accuse anyone of crimes related to the Thirty, it was easy enough to snag an individual on other charges. A handy accusation was impiety, a lack of respect for the gods in either thought or action—the same charge that Pericles's enemies had leveled against his close associate, the natural philosopher Anaxagoras, for denying the divinity of the heavenly bodies. The fact that the real target was Pericles demonstrates that the charge of impiety had long had its political uses. The accusation gained a special potency during the postwar period, when the bold rationalism of the Age of Pericles had given way to anxious superstition. The gods had unleashed one disaster after another, and the only way to end the nightmare was for the people to stamp out any impiety in their midst.

As usual, architecture provides a vivid illustration of the people's frame of mind. The Erechtheion, a temple on the northern side of the Acropolis, was completed in 406 BCE, just two years before the end of the Peloponnesian

War. It was a peculiar jumble, with porches of
different sizes, elevations, and styles jutting out
from the central cella. The roof of the larger and
taller porch was supported by typical columns,
but the roof of the smaller and shorter porch
was supported by six *caryatids*, or statues of
draped and virtually identical female figures.
The odd mishmash continued on the inside.
The building sheltered the hallowed wooden
statue of Athena, the original olive tree that the
goddess had given the city, and the trident marks
and saltwater spring of Poseidon. Nearby were
the burial sites of the polis's mythical founders
as well as spots dedicated to the daughters of
one of those founders, to a local hero who had
been a priest of Athena and Poseidon, and to the
smith-god Hephaestus. Furnishings included
a wooden image of Hermes, a chair crafted by
Daedalus, and a golden lamp that fed the fire
of Hephaestus with the olive oil of Athena. The
temple may have also housed a sacred serpent,
an animal closely associated with Athena, which
was fed honey cakes and revered as a guardian of
the city.

It would be hard to imagine a greater contrast
to the Parthenon, with its stately symmetry,
clean lines, and single, imposing statue of

Athena. The Parthenon celebrated a proud, self-assured city where people took charge of their destiny and imposed order on chaos, while the jumbled Erechtheion reflected a submission to unnerving forces that might be appeased but never controlled. The Peloponnesian War had dealt a catastrophic blow to the Athenian psyche, and in this new, uneasy environment, the suspicion of impiety triggered mass hysteria.

Socrates found himself in the crosshairs in the spring of 399, when he was close to seventy years old. A young man named Meletus formally leveled the charges: "Socrates is a malefactor, firstly, in that he does not recognize the gods recognized by the State, but introduces new deities; secondly, in that he corrupts the young." It was easy enough to imagine some of the specific, supposed evils that Meletus had in mind: Socrates's youthful involvement in natural philosophy; his scant philosophical attention to the gods; his relationship with Alcibiades; his obedience to his daimonion. In the highly charged atmosphere of the polis, however, these allegations were probably just a cover for the real issue, Socrates's objections to democracy and his connections to the Thirty. We do not know much about Meletus, but two other citizens who joined

him as plaintiffs, Lycon and Anytus, definitely had a score to settle with the deposed oligarchy. The Thirty had banished Anytus from Athens and stripped him of his property, and worse, they had executed Lycon's son. The two men must have felt some satisfaction in going after Socrates despite the amnesty.

Socrates learned of the charges within a few days of the official complaint, when he received a summons to appear at the Stoa Basileios, the Stoa of the King Archon or the King's Porch, in the northwestern part of the Agora. That stoa featured a display of the Athenian legal code and a stone platform where government officials took their oaths of office, but it served mainly as the headquarters of the *archon basileus*, or king archon. The archons were a group of nine officials who were appointed by lot to oversee the polis's religious and judicial affairs, and one of the specific responsibilities of the archon basileus was to handle all charges of impiety. On the day indicated in Socrates's summons, the archon basileus would conduct the preliminary hearing that was required by law. Meletus, Anytus, and Lycon would spell out their claim, and the archon would determine whether the plaintiffs had sufficient grounds for a trial.

Model of the Royal Stoa at the end of 5th c. BCE with the addition of the annexes. Petros Demetriades and Kostas Papoulias. American School of Classical Studies at Athens: Agora Excavations.

Plato stages one of his most entertaining dialogues, the *Euthyphro*, on the day of Socrates's preliminary hearing. While Socrates is standing outside the Stoa Basileios, he encounters a middle-aged man named Euthyphro who has come to the same place. Euthyphro is prosecuting his elderly father for murder, a crime that Athenian law considered a form of impiety, and he is eager to share his story. Not long before, the hired hand of Euthyphro's father was provoked into killing a household slave. In response, Euthyphro's father bound the killer hand and foot, threw him into a ditch, and sent a messenger to ask a priest what to do next. But the father neglected to make adequate provisions for the bound man, who died of hunger and cold before the messenger returned with the priest's instructions. In Euthyphro's opinion, his father is guilty of murder through negligence.

Socrates is surprised that Euthyphro would prosecute his father under these circumstances, and Euthyphro admits that he has made his family angry. His father had not actively murdered the hired hand, and even if he had, the dead man was a killer who had deserved to die. Furthermore, Euthyphro's relatives believe that it is an act of impiety for a son to prosecute his father. But Euthyphro will not relent. "[T]heir ideas of the divine attitude to piety and impiety are wrong," he declares.

Socrates cannot resist the temptation. On the one hand, if Euthyphro is indeed the expert on piety that he considers himself to be, Socrates wants him to define that quality. The philosopher has more reason than ever for seeking a definition: a solid grasp of piety will help him understand why he has himself been accused of impiety and what he might do to refute that accusation. On the other hand, if Euthyphro overestimates his own expertise, Socrates wants him to recognize his own ignorance.

Without any hesitation, Euthyphro provides a definition: "[T]he pious is to do what I am doing now, to prosecute the wrongdoer, be it about murder or temple robbery or anything else, whether the wrongdoer is your father or your mother or anyone else; not to prosecute is impious." Euthyphro invokes the gods to support his position. Zeus punished his father, Cronus, for an act of injustice, just as Cronus had previously punished his own father, Uranus, for a different misdeed. Socrates expresses skepticism. "Indeed, Euthyphro, this is the reason why I am a defendant in the case, because

I find it hard to accept things like that being said about the gods, and it is likely to be the reason why I shall be told I do wrong." But Euthyphro will not be shaken. He fancies himself an authority on the gods and is so impervious to doubt about the myths that Socrates drops the subject. Socrates still wants a definition of the pious, and Euthyphro has not provided one. Instead of a definition—an account of what the pious is in itself—Euthyphro has offered only an example of behavior he considers pious.

Among Euthyphro's further attempts, one that sparks an especially interesting discussion is that "the pious is what all the gods love, and the opposite, what all the gods hate, is the impious." His point, more succinctly, is that "pious" is another way of saying "beloved-of-god." Socrates responds with a chicken-and-egg question. Do the gods love a thing *because* that thing is pious, or does the love of the gods *make* that thing pious? Euthyphro takes the first approach: the gods love a thing *because* that thing is pious.

If Euthyphro's assertion is true, Socrates replies, it makes no sense to define the pious as the beloved-of-god. To explain why this is the case, Socrates starts with the more general relationship between a state of being and the act that results in

that state of being. The act of carrying an object
makes that object a carried thing; the act of seeing
an object makes that object a seen thing. Those
relationships do not work the other way around: the
state of being a carried thing does not engender the
act of carrying, and the state of being a seen thing
does not engender the act of seeing. The situation
is the same with love. In the case under discussion,
the gods' act of loving a thing makes that thing
beloved-of-god; a thing's being beloved-of-god does
not make the gods love that thing. More simply,
being beloved-of-god is an *effect* of the gods' love.
And yet Euthyphro has just claimed that the pious
quality of a thing is what *makes* the gods love it—in
other words, that the pious is a *cause* of the gods'
love. Since Euthyphro has characterized the pious
as a cause of the gods' love, but the beloved-of-god is
necessarily an effect of the gods' love, the pious and
the beloved-of-god cannot be one and the same.

Socrates's argument may seem like a
technical diversion rather than a serious look
at the real issue. But historically, his cause-and-
effect question has been one of the thorniest
problems in religious thought—a problem
that has become known, suitably enough, as
the Euthyphro dilemma. A monotheist might
rephrase the question like this: Is a thing good

only because God declares it to be good, or does God declare a thing good because it is already good in itself? Either option creates difficulties. The first option turns all of morality into a product of divine whim. God happens to determine that helping orphans is good and torturing them is bad, but God could just as easily determine that helping orphans is bad and torturing them is good. The second option, that God declares a thing good because it is already good in itself, avoids the distasteful arbitrariness of the first option but at a tremendous price. If right and wrong exist apart from God, then God no longer holds supreme authority; clearly, some force other than God has had to determine what is right and what is wrong. A God who merely rubber-stamps what some other force has decided is obviously unacceptable to monotheistic religions that posit an all-powerful deity. Besides, we are still left with our original problem, because we can ask the same chicken-and-egg question of the higher authority to which God is beholden. And even if we somehow find a way around these problems, why would God be necessary to morality at all?

The dialogue does not offer an answer to the Euthyphro dilemma; Socrates raises the question only to refute Euthyphro's equation of the pious with the beloved-of-god. After a final attempt at a definition fails as well, Socrates urges Euthyphro not to give up. After all, a man in Euthyphro's position must be an expert on ethics: "If you had no clear knowledge of piety and impiety you would never have ventured to prosecute your old father for murder on behalf of a servant. For fear of the gods you would have been afraid to take the risk lest you should not be acting rightly, and would have been ashamed before men." Socrates's words are more barb than praise. Euthyphro lacks the knowledge he claims to possess, and in his ignorance, he is likely to behave unethically. But thick-headed Euthyphro hears only the praise. Claiming to be in a hurry, he abruptly ends the discussion, and he exhibits no awareness that he must give more thought to the issues that Socrates has raised. The dialogue ends in aporia, but only the philosopher feels the loss.

The *Euthyphro* is actually the second of two dialogues that Plato sets on the day of Socrates's preliminary hearing. The first one, the *Theaetetus*, takes place a few hours earlier, when Socrates, indulging his lively interest in the promising youth of Athens, visits a gymnasium. There he meets a brilliant young man named Theaetetus, and the two engage in a long and intricate discussion about the nature of knowledge. Only at the very end does the philosopher mention the momentous appointment that he must keep that day. "And now I must go to the King's Porch to meet the indictment that Meletus has brought against me," he says, and then, addressing the friend who has introduced him to Theaetetus, continues, "but let us meet here again in the morning, Theodorus."

Socrates's behavior in both the *Euthyphro* and *Theaetetus* is remarkable. The charge of impiety carried serious consequences. Anaxagoras and Alcibiades had both been sentenced to death for that crime, and each of them had survived only by fleeing Athens. If the preliminary hearing resulted in an actual trial, Socrates had no reason to believe that he would fare any better. And yet he went about business as usual, with hardly any acknowledgment of his fateful appointment at the Stoa Basileios. Of course, the usual caveats apply here. The *Euthyphro* and *Theaetetus* are dialogues, not historical records, and we have no idea what Socrates actually did on the day of his hearing. Even if Socrates did, in fact, spend some of that day with Euthyphro and Theaetetus, Plato did not transcribe their actual words. Nonetheless, it remains certain that Plato respected the broad outlines of Socrates's personality; the earliest readers of the dialogues knew Socrates as a real human being and would have objected to any blatant distortion of his character. To Plato and his audience, it seemed perfectly reasonable for Socrates to ignore the personal urgency of the day.

Even more remarkable is that Plato shows Socrates keeping his promise to meet Theaetetus and Theodorus the next day. Together with several others, the three men engage in a conversation that Plato depicts in two additional dialogues. Socrates is not the main speaker in either one, but in both cases he establishes the subject of the discussion and displays his usual enthusiasm. His composure is altogether astonishing. He makes no reference to the day before, and an uninitiated reader would have no idea that anything unusual has taken place. But Socrates's world has already begun to collapse around him. The archon basileus had ruled against him, and his case was going to court.

MONUMENT OF THE EPONYMOUS HEROES: Although the ruins of this structure date from the century after Socrates, literary references indicate that it existed in some form as early as 425 BCE. The monument stood in the Agora, where it served as the public's main notice board. The statues represented the ten mythical heroes after whom the ten tribes were named, and information that pertained to each tribe was posted beneath the relevant statue.

Perspective view of the Peribolos of the Eponymous Heroes. W.B. Dinsmoor, Jr. American School of Classical Studies at Athens: Agora Excavations.

WDD. Jr. – 1969

CHAPTER 19

THE TRIAL

THE NEXT STEPS WENT SWIFTLY. SHORTLY AFTER the preliminary hearing, details of the charges were posted in the Agora, a court was assigned to the case, and the trial was scheduled. Socrates does not seem to have dragged out the process with the delays and appeals that citizens were entitled to file, so he had perhaps only two months before his court date. The proceedings themselves would begin and end on a single day, and if the jury returned a guilty verdict and no unusual circumstances arose, punishment would follow almost immediately.

During the brief period before their day in court, Socrates and his accusers had the opportunity to prepare their speeches. Although they often enlisted the help of professional speechwriters, litigants did the actual speaking at their trials; the Athenian legal system featured no lawyers of the modern sort. The litigants addressed their words directly to the jury, and that assemblage would have fully vindicated Socrates's long-standing mistrust of unthinking crowds. Most jurors never bothered to master the laws inscribed on stone blocks in the Agora, and the trial provided no opportunity for the ignorant to become better informed. The prosecution and defense presented or misrepresented the laws as they pleased, and there was no presiding judge to set the record straight. In many cases, the most successful litigants were not the ones with justice on their side, but the ones who manipulated their audience's emotions most skillfully.

Socrates had never appeared in court before, but he did not seem especially concerned about his preparations. According to Xenophon, the philosopher's companions began to worry that he was not composing his speech for the jury. "Really, Socrates, ought you not to be considering your defence?" one of them asked. Socrates had a ready answer: "Don't you think that my whole life has been a preparation for my defence?" The friend asked for clarification, and Socrates explained: "Because I have consistently done no wrong, and this, I think, is the finest preparation for a defence." Socrates then revealed that he had, in fact, tried to compose his speech, but his daimonion had opposed his efforts. He thought he knew why: it was time for him to die. He had enjoyed a blameless and fulfilling life, and if he died now, he would not have to endure the intellectual and physical decline of old age. His death would bring him little discomfort, and his friends would remember him as he wanted to be remembered—full of joy, with a sound body and mind.

The end of Xenophon's account does not sit well with Plato's characterization of the philosopher. The Socrates that Plato depicts does not seek death at all, and he is too intent on his mission to worry about sparing himself or his friends the discomforts of his old age. But no matter whose characterization is correct, Socrates's days were indeed numbered. On an early morning in 399 BCE, in the rising heat of an Athenian summer, he made his way, as required, to the judicial district. His trial was one of several scheduled for that day, and potential jurors swarmed near the kleroterion, where an official was setting their pinakia into the grid. Jurors were drawn from an annually assembled list of six thousand volunteers, each of whom had reached the age of thirty and sworn to fulfill his duties faithfully. Many of these men were retirees who enjoyed the spectacle of the courtroom and gratefully accepted the modest payment that they received for their services.

Once the black and white balls had determined who would serve on the juries, the crowds sorted themselves out. Plaintiffs, defendants, and an enormous number of jurymen proceeded to their designated courtrooms. Socrates's case probably called for five hundred jurors, and that number was not especially large by Athenian standards. They were joined by throngs of spectators—friends and enemies of the litigants as well as hangers-on who simply sought a few hours of entertainment. The courtroom was standing room only, and the crowds posed a considerable challenge to the plaintiffs and defendants. Aside from coping with the inevitable noises produced by such a large group, litigants had to contend with the cheers and hoots that frequently interrupted their speeches. The magistrate in charge, selected by lot, had no authority to punish or expel unruly jurors or spectators.

Both sides were entitled to speak for the same amount of time. To regulate the length of speeches, court officials used a simple but ingenious clock called a *klepsydra*. The device consisted of two pots. The first, with a hole near its base, stood on a raised platform; the second, lower down, caught whatever came out of the hole in the first pot. When the plaintiff or the defendant got up to address the jury, an official filled the upper pot with water. The liquid flowed into the lower pot during the course of the speech, and once the upper pot was empty, the speaker's turn was over. If a speech needed to be interrupted for the reading of legal documents or laws, the official paused the flow of water by inserting a plug into the hole.

The prosecution always spoke first. We have no record of Meletus's address to the jury, but we can infer some of what he said from the way that Socrates responded. As usual, Plato provides much of our information. Plato attended the trial and later reconstructed Socrates's speech in a work called the *Apology*, which many scholars consider one of our most historically reliable sources on Socrates. The *Apology* has nothing to do with remorse or regret. In fact, it is almost precisely the opposite. In Greek, an *apologia* was a speech made in one's own defense.

Meletus apparently spent some time emphasizing the prosecution's patriotism and good character. Since he was quite young, he must have focused mainly on the credentials of Anytus and Lycon, who were older. These were more than conventional assurances. The amnesty barred any direct mention of Socrates's connections to the Thirty or his failure to join the democratic resistance in Phyle, but by highlighting the prosecution's patriotism, Meletus could indirectly cast aspersions on Socrates's loyalties. Meletus also denounced Socrates's character more explicitly. He ridiculed the philosopher's daimonion and warned that Socrates was a master of manipulative speech. But Meletus spoke most about his formal accusations: Socrates corrupted the young, denied the gods of the polis, and introduced new objects of worship. At some point Anytus took over with a rabble-rousing argument. Now that Socrates had already landed in court, Anytus contended, the jurors were duty-bound to execute him. If the jurors neglected to do so, their sons would "practice the teachings of Socrates and all be thoroughly corrupted."

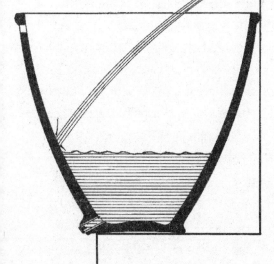

KLEPSYDRA: This
sketch illustrates the
operation of the water
clock. The holes that are
depicted in the upper
left wall of each pot
ensured that the water
was filled to the same
level for each speaker.

*Restored profile drawing
of a klepsydra, showing
two water clocks in
action.* Piet de Jong.
American School
of Classical Studies
at Athens: Agora
Excavations.

Socrates knew that it would be difficult to undo the effect of his accusers' words. At the beginning of his speech, he acknowledged the challenge with resigned humor: "I do not know, men of Athens, how my accusers affected you; as for me, I was almost carried away in spite of myself, so persuasively did they speak." But Socrates believed that his reputation had suffered a greater blow long before the current court case. For many years, popular opinion had associated him with the myth-defying natural philosophy that he had abandoned as a young man and with the unprincipled behavior of the sophists whom he deplored. As he told the jury, his detractors "got hold of most of you from childhood, persuaded you and accused me quite falsely, saying that there is a man called Socrates, a wise man, a student of all things in the sky and below the earth, who makes the worse argument the stronger." Contending with the impact of that earlier slander was virtually impossible. The rumors had been circulating for a long time, and with the exception of Aristophanes, who had maligned Socrates in the *Clouds* and other plays, it was difficult to identify the individuals who spread them. Refuting those rumormongers was like trying to "fight with shadows" or to "cross-examine when no one answers."

Nonetheless, Socrates endeavored to set the record straight. He was neither a natural philosopher nor a sophist; he charged no fees, and he had no formal students. How, then, did he occupy himself? It was time to explain his mission, and he embarked on the story of Chaerephon's visit to Delphi. He recounted Chaerephon's question, the oracle's answer, and his own disbelief when he heard Chaerephon's account. He recalled his search for someone wiser than himself and his gradual realization that he alone recognized his own ignorance. He described the result: his conviction that the god had called upon him to show others the limits of their wisdom. He pursued that mission wholeheartedly, despite the personal costs. He had no time to engage in public affairs or earn a good living, and he had become distinctly unpopular, especially when his young followers imitated him by challenging their elders.

Socrates knew that the story of Chaerephon's visit to Delphi would irritate the jurors. As he began to tell it, he implored them, "Do not create a disturbance, gentlemen, even if you think I am boasting." Why, then, did he use the story as part of his defense? Obviously, he wanted to convey the urgency of the philosophical mission to which he had devoted his life. But he probably had at least two strategic reasons as well. First, although Chaerephon was dead, he had been a well-known democrat who had joined the resistance in Phyle, and the story might arouse fellow feeling among the mostly democratic jurymen. Second, the story conveyed Apollo's favorable view of Socrates, and the jurors might worry that a vote for the prosecution would anger the god.

In any case, Socrates hoped that the story, and especially the image of his obedience to the god despite the personal costs, would put the older rumors to rest. He now turned to the current charges. Were his accusers acting in genuinely good faith? Socrates was skeptical. If Meletus were really so worried about the corruption of young Athenians, why had he never shown any prior interest in their upbringing and education? To demonstrate how little attention Meletus had given the matter, Socrates grilled him before the jury. "Tell me, my good sir, who improves our young men?" Meletus's first response—the laws—completely missed the mark. "That is not what I am asking," Socrates shot back, "but what person who has knowledge of the laws to begin with?" Meletus's next answer was sure to please his audience: "These jurymen." Socrates pushed for clarification. Did *all* the members of the jury improve the young? Meletus counted on the jury's support and could hardly suggest that any of them fell short. Yes, he answered, all of the jurors had a positive effect on the young.

The answer was patently absurd. In any group that consists of hundreds of people, some stand out for their principles and others do not; it was unrealistic for Meletus to claim that every one of the jurors, without exception, was a good role model. And if Meletus could make such a blanket statement about the jurors, how could he differentiate between them and any of the other large groups that regularly assembled in Athens? Socrates seized his advantage with another set of questions. What about the other spectators in the courtroom? What about members of the Boule? What about members of the Ekklesia? Did every single member of every single one of those groups improve the young too? Yes, Meletus replied, all those people improved the young. Socrates summarized his accuser's position: "All the Athenians, it seems, make the young into fine good men, except me, and I alone corrupt them. Is that what you mean?" Yes, said Meletus, that was indeed what he meant.

Socrates countered with a tactic familiar to anyone who had spent any time talking with him: he drew an analogy. In the case of horses, only a small group of specially trained experts knows how to effect improvement; the majority of people harm rather than help their horses. The same is true of other animals as well. How, then, could Meletus claim the opposite for human beings? "It would be a very happy state of affairs if only one person corrupted our youth, while the others improved them," Socrates mused.

Next, Socrates invoked one of the major implications of his bedrock belief that we all seek happiness: no one intentionally commits a wrong, because no one willingly seeks harm. He had already developed this idea in relation to the balance scale of decision-making, when he had argued that wrongdoing always results from a misreading of the pleasure to be derived from each option on the scale. Now Socrates spelled out the ramifications for his present situation. He stood accused of corrupting the youth of Athens, but if he had indeed committed that wrong, he could not have done so on purpose.

Intentionally corrupting the youth with whom he associated would have amounted to intentionally surrounding himself with wicked individuals. Why would he have knowingly sought the company of people who would be likely to harm him? If he had indeed corrupted anyone, his offense was inadvertent. His crime, then, was ignorance, and ignorance calls for education, not punishment. "[T]he law does not require you to bring people to court for such unwilling wrongdoings," he admonished Meletus, "but to get hold of them privately, to instruct them and exhort them; for clearly, if I learn better, I shall cease to do what I am doing unwillingly."

At any rate, Socrates wanted a better understanding of the charges he was facing, especially his alleged rejection of the polis's gods. Was he being accused of favoring gods that the polis did not recognize, or was he being accused of downright atheism? The charge, Meletus replied, was atheism. "My dear Meletus," Socrates exclaimed, "do you think you are prosecuting Anaxagoras?" Unlike that natural philosopher, who was found guilty of denying the gods, Socrates affirmed that he did indeed believe in the gods, and for proof he referred to Meletus's own words. Meletus had officially charged Socrates with introducing "new spiritual things" through his philosophy. Now, a person who believes in human-related matters necessarily believes in humans, a person who believes in horse-related matters necessarily believes in horses, and a person who believes in flute-playing matters necessarily believes in flute players. Similarly, said Socrates, a person who believes in spiritual matters necessarily believes in spirits, and spirits are by definition either gods or agents related to the gods. Meletus was therefore contradicting himself. It was impossible for Socrates to be both an atheist and a believer in spirits.

This quibbling over vocabulary sounds more like an evasion than an honest assertion of belief. Why didn't Socrates give an explicit account of his religious views? A great deal of evidence points to his genuine belief in the gods. Most notably, he thought of his daimonion as a divine sign, and after the visit of Chaerephon to the oracle of Apollo at Delphi, he regarded his philosophical work as a divine service. It is evident as well, from Socrates's later time in prison, that he believed his dreams carried messages from the gods. Ancient sources also show that he performed rituals and took part in holidays and other aspects of Greek religion; at the beginning of the *Republic*, for instance, he has just visited the Piraeus to pray to the goddess Bendis at a newly inaugurated festival. This last type of evidence, however, goes only so far. Participation in rites was required by law, so Socrates's compliance may not have reflected his actual views.

Yet other evidence suggests that Socrates, if not a complete atheist, at least harbored atheistic notions. The character that Aristophanes called Socrates in the *Clouds* describes traditional religion as "just nonsense" and pins his faith on natural forces, not gods. While it is true that the caricature may bear only a loose connection to the real Socrates, Plato's more sober portrait touches on the same tendencies. In the *Euthyphro*, Socrates denies the literal truth of the myths and raises questions about the gods' justice, power, and relevance. In the *Phaedrus*, Socrates explains how a specific myth might have grown out of perfectly natural circumstances. As he walks between Alopeke and the city of Athens along the Ilissus River, where Boreas, the god of the north wind, was said to have abducted the human princess Oreithyia, he remarks, "I could claim that a gust of the North Wind blew her over the rocks where she was playing with [the nymph] Pharmaceia; and once she was killed that way people said she had been carried off by Boreas." The example is not intended as an outlier. Socrates declares that he could find similar explanations for all the myths, but the effort would leave him with too little time for his ethical concerns. Perhaps the strongest indication of Socrates's atheism comes from those concerns themselves. In his ethical system, the ultimate arbiter of right and wrong is precise knowledge, and that knowledge derives not from traditional sources but from the proper use of human reason.

All told, then, we have no simple answer about what Socrates believed, but it seems fair to say that Meletus had some basis for his accusation. In any case, when Socrates denied that he was an atheist, the crowd broke into an uproar. With his slippery arguments, how was he any different from the sophists he supposedly disdained? Battling the clamor, Socrates declared that he had no intention of ceasing the activity that now imperiled his life. If his accusers offered to drop the charges on condition that he forsake his philosophical activity, he would choose conviction and death instead. Most people fear death as the greatest of evils, but that fear is based on sheer ignorance; for all we know, death may be the greatest of blessings. By contrast, abandoning philosophy would be unequivocally evil. Socrates would not only be disobeying the god who had assigned him his mission but also shirking his duty to improve the people of Athens. On the two sides of the balance scale were the great unknown of death and the certain evil of abandoning philosophy. Death was clearly the better option.

Once again, Socrates's words unleashed an uproar. "I think it will be to your advantage to listen," he exhorted the crowd, adding, "and I am about to say other things at which you will perhaps cry out." His next assertion was sure to provoke the crowd. "Indeed, men of Athens," he declared, "I am far from making a defense now on my own behalf, as might be thought, but on yours, to prevent you from wrongdoing by mistreating the god's gift to you by condemning me; for if you kill me you will not easily find another like me." The jurors must have wondered how Socrates had the gall to speak to them that way. That impious philosopher was a gift of the god? That self-important meddler was irreplaceable? Athens was just fine, thank you, without a suspected criminal looking after its interests.

But Socrates pressed on. He explained that he had pursued his mission on a private basis because politics clashed with his commitment to justice. After describing his objection to the trial of the generals and his refusal to arrest Leon of Salamis, he asked, "Do you think I would have survived all these years if I were engaged in public affairs, and, acting as a good man must, came to the help of justice and considered this the most important thing?" The question may have been legitimate, but it was ill-advised in a polis that considered political engagement to be the duty of every citizen. And within the context of the courtroom, the question was downright reckless. The citizens whom Socrates addressed had gone out of their way to volunteer for jury duty. This was a population that saw civil service as a duty, a pleasure, or both—certainly not a task to be avoided at all cost by good men. What was Socrates insinuating about the jurors?

Socrates now returned to the accusation that he had corrupted the youth of Athens. If he had indeed harmed many young men for many years, the passage of time must have enabled at least some of them to recognize the injury he

had done them. Why had the prosecution failed
to produce any of those individuals as witnesses?
If the men themselves were reluctant to come
forward, surely their outraged fathers and
brothers would be willing to speak out. Socrates
noted that the present audience included
relatives of Critobulus, Apollodorus, Plato, and
several others who had been his followers. If
Meletus wished to call up any of those relatives
as witnesses for the prosecution, Socrates would
happily sacrifice some of the time allotted for
his own speech. When no one came forward,
Socrates gave his blunt assessment of the
situation: "[T]hey know that Meletus is lying and
that I am telling the truth."

Finally, Socrates emphasized that he
was seeking justice, not pity. Unlike other
defendants, he would not shed tears, beg for
mercy, or parade grief-stricken relatives into
the courtroom. Those "pitiful dramatics," as he
called them, wrongfully influenced jurors and
induced them to break their oath to uphold the
law—an oath that they had solemnly sworn to
the gods. Socrates respected the gods too much
to engage in that kind of behavior; indeed,
if he did attempt any of the usual tricks, his
accusers would be fully justified in accusing

him of atheism. "This is far from being the case, gentlemen, for I do believe in them as none of my accusers do." This final plea was perhaps Socrates's most explicit statement about his religious beliefs. Authentic religion is a commitment to being as good as we can possibly be, and we achieve that goodness when we ground ourselves in knowledge. By dedicating his life to philosophy, Socrates expressed belief in its deepest and truest form. And here he ended. "I leave it to you and the god to judge me in the way that will be best for me and for you."

The last drops trickled out of the water clock, and Socrates fell silent. The hush promptly gave way to the brisk business of reaching a verdict. Jurors cast their votes individually, with no opportunity to confer as a group. Each juror held a ballot, most likely a pebble or a mussel shell, which he cast into one of two urns, one for votes in favor of the prosecution and the other for votes in favor of the defense. Some sort of contraption kept the votes hidden from prying eyes, perhaps a wicker funnel that fit wide-side down over the mouths of the two urns; at the top, the narrower opening allowed jurors to reach in and drop their ballots, sight unseen, into the urn of their choice.

Just before inserting his hand, each juror needed to show that he was holding only one ballot.

Once the last juror had cast his vote, officials set to work on the tally. The atmosphere was tense. If Meletus failed to receive a fifth of the votes, he would be fined a thousand drachmas—a significant sum, since a drachma was the standard daily wage of an average laborer. The stakes for Socrates were higher. If a simple majority voted against him, his sentencing would begin immediately.

The wait gave Socrates an opportunity to assess his recent performance, and he might have done so with satisfaction. He had rebutted the past and present accusations against him, and he had clarified his life's work. He had woven together some of his most important ideas: the balance scale of ethical choices, the impossibility of intentional wrongdoing, the supreme importance of the soul's health. He had demonstrated some of the methods by which we arrive at the truth: recognizing our ignorance, engaging in dialogue, examining analogies, testing our thoughts for contradictions or absurd ramifications. Most importantly, he had discussed the nature of a good life and described his efforts to awaken his beloved

Athens to that ideal. He had given his audience a comprehensive and even moving introduction to his ideas, methods, and mission.

Whether his friends could share that satisfaction is a different question. They loved the man but recognized his excesses, and they knew that some of his unappealing qualities and irresolvable incongruities had been on display just a few minutes earlier. Socrates's speech had soared with his fervent convictions, indefatigable quest for knowledge, and winsome modesty, but it had floundered with his defiance of convention, slippery argumentation, and exasperating self-importance. Socrates had implored the jurors to use their power of reason as they considered his case, but their votes were more likely to hinge on their instincts and emotions. Which side of Socrates would prevail, the inspiring thinker or the infuriating know-it-all?

The verdict was not long in coming. Socrates was guilty.

CHAPTER 20

SENTENCING AND IMPRISONMENT

THE GOOD NEWS WAS THAT THE PROSECUTION had won by only a slim margin. Had only thirty votes gone the other way, Socrates would have been acquitted. That fact did not change the guilty verdict, but it could have a significant impact on the sentencing. Perhaps Socrates would escape the death penalty after all. The prosecution and defense now had the opportunity to propose the punishment they each deemed appropriate; after this second round of speeches, the jury would select one of the two options.

Meletus spoke first, and although we have no record of his words, we know the upshot: Socrates deserved to die. The philosopher expressed neither anger nor surprise. "So be it," he calmly replied before turning to his own proposal. "What counter-assessment should I propose to you, men of Athens?" he began. "Clearly it should be a penalty I deserve." And here Socrates's self-importance got the better of him. He reminded the audience that he was a gift to the city, that he had avoided public life because of his honesty, and that he had neglected his own affairs because of his selfless devotion to his mission. His noble work had left him penniless. And now he recast his question in a way that was sure to inflame the jury: "What is suitable for a poor benefactor who needs leisure to exhort you?" Not only was Socrates defining himself as the Athenians' protector and supporter, but he was also calling on them to finance his efforts. He had a specific suggestion about how they could do so: "Nothing is more suitable, gentlemen, than for such a man to be fed in the Prytaneum." The fifty members of the prytany, the executive committee of the Ekklesia that Socrates had headed during the Arginusae affair, dined at the public's expense in the Tholos, their administrative center in the Agora.

The jurors must have been flabbergasted. A man they had just convicted was asking them, as punishment for his crime, to fund his continuing criminal activity. Was Socrates mocking them? Undoubtedly he was, at least to some extent. How could he fail to recognize that his proposal would madden his audience? And yet, as always, Socrates revealed a heartfelt urgency. He really did consider himself a benefactor to his city, and in that light his proposal made perfect sense. Successful Olympian athletes ate at the public's expense, and Socrates's contribution to the public's welfare—at least as he saw it—was far more valuable than theirs. He cut right to the point: "The Olympian victor makes you think yourself happy; I make you be happy." Besides, Socrates's commitment to virtue barred him from proposing any harm to himself. "Since I am convinced that I wrong no one, I am not likely to wrong myself, to say that I deserve some evil and to make some such assessment against myself." Any of the usual alternatives to execution would constitute such an injustice. Imprisonment would mean a loss of mastery over his own life, and exile would mean a future of expulsion from one city after another. As he explained in one of his more endearing, self-deprecating moments, "I should have to be inordinately fond of life, men of Athens, to be so unreasonable as to suppose that other men will easily tolerate my company and conversation when you, my fellow citizens, have been unable to endure them."

Ultimately, Socrates did manage to come up with a more reasonable alternative to free meals in the prytany's headquarters. Since material wealth meant nothing to him, he would not be wronging himself if he proposed a monetary fine. He would be able to scrape together one silver mina, roughly equivalent to a laborer's wages for a hundred days of work. Would the jury be satisfied with that amount? At this point, four of Socrates's good friends—Crito, Critobulus, Apollodorus, and Plato—offered to stand surety for the more substantial fee of thirty mina. "Well, then, that is my assessment," said Socrates, turning back to the jury, "and they will be sufficient guarantee of payment."

Thirty mina was an impressive sum, but Socrates had already done himself considerable damage. Couldn't he have restrained himself for once? Didn't he understand that his life was on the line? Such questions must have been running through the minds of his friends. But it was too late. The jurors were already registering their votes, this time by scratching their fingernails on wax tablets. A long line meant a vote for the death penalty, and a short line meant a vote for the thirty-mina fine.

The death penalty won—and by a wide margin. Eighty people who had originally voted against the conviction turned around and voted for the harsher penalty. Why would a person who had decided, just minutes before, that Socrates was innocent now condemn him to death? Some of those eighty jurors must have reconsidered the evidence; with his latest display of arrogance, Socrates indeed seemed the sort who would scorn the gods and corrupt the young. Others feared for the city. Surely it would anger the gods if a man convicted of impiety were allowed to continue living. A third group was probably just expressing its disgust. If a convicted man could speak so flippantly to the jury that was considering his sentence, well, then, he deserved to die.

Socrates took a final opportunity to speak after his sentencing. Athens, he warned, would come to regret its decision. Whether or not he was actually wise, the polis's critics would assert that he was so, and they would blame the Athenians for executing him. And even though his accusers had found a way to silence him, others would take his place to reproach Athens for its faults. Would the polis do away with those people too? "[I]t is best and easiest not to discredit others," he admonished his audience, "but to prepare oneself to be as good as possible."

As the jurors were filing out of the courtroom and the officers of the court were taking care of final administrative matters, Socrates invited the men who had voted for his acquittal to remain behind. "[S]tay with me awhile," he urged them, "for nothing prevents us from talking to each other while it is allowed." The philosopher wanted to reveal "a surprising thing" that had happened to him that day: his inner voice had shown no opposition to anything he had done. The daimonion had not objected when he left home at dawn, when he entered the courtroom, or when he spoke to the jury.

As Socrates saw it, the daimonion's silence cleared up any doubt about the nature of death: "[T]hose of us who believe death to be an evil are certainly mistaken." Death, Socrates conjectured, is either a complete lack of perception, like an endless, dreamless sleep, or a relocation of the soul from this world to another place. Neither possibility is a cause for alarm. If death is an endless, dreamless sleep, it promises the tranquility we all appreciate when we have spent a restful night in bed. If death is the relocation of the soul to another place—and for Greeks, this place was Hades, the realm of the dead—Socrates anticipated several benefits. First, he would enjoy his encounter with the "true jurymen who are said to sit in judgment there," mythological figures such as Minos and Rhadamanthus "who have been upright in their own life." Such judges would be a welcome change from the jurymen at his trial, whose character and discernment he trusted much less. Second, he would be able to share his experience with others who had been wrongfully convicted. Third—and most wonderfully—he would be able to carry on his mission in the afterlife. "I could spend my time testing and examining people there, as I do here, as to who among them is wise, and who thinks he is, but is not." At least some of the people who had lingered in the courtroom must have wondered whether the inhabitants of the underworld would appreciate the meddling philosopher any more than the Athenians had done. Socrates seems to have asked himself the same question. "In any case, they would certainly not put one to death for doing so," he wryly added.

Because death could not be evil, those who had hoped to injure Socrates had failed. The philosopher bore those people no ill will. If they needed a new outlet for their hostility, he had a suggestion:

> [W]hen my sons grow up, avenge yourselves by causing them the same kind of grief that I caused you, if you think they care for money or anything else more than they care for virtue, or if they think they are somebody when they are nobody. Reproach them as I reproach you, that they do not care for the right things and think they are worthy when they are not worthy of anything. If you do this, I shall have been justly treated by you, and my sons also.

It remained only for Socrates to bid his fellow Athenians farewell. "Now the hour to part has come. I go to die, you go to live. Which of us goes to the better lot is known to no one, except the god."

Socrates left the courtroom in the custody of the Eleven, the officials responsible for maintaining public order and overseeing the penal system. He made his way through the

Agora for the last time, past the places where he had engaged his fellow Athenians in countless discussions—the temples and altars, the administrative buildings and stoas, the statues and fountains, the open plazas and grand thoroughfares. His southwesterly route led past one of the no-nonsense border markers that declared, "I am the boundary of the Agora." Just on the other side of that inscribed stone was the familiar workshop of Simon the shoemaker. From there, it was a walk of only a few minutes to the three rocky outcroppings that embodied his polis's history and identity. Straight ahead was the Pnyx, the hilltop meeting place of the Ekklesia, the heart of Athenian democracy. To his left stood the Areopagus, the faded seat of aristocratic rule. And still farther left soared the sacred hill of the Acropolis, whose transformations he had witnessed—the rubble of the Persian Wars giving way to the splendors of the Age of Pericles, and then the confidence of the Parthenon degenerating into the confusion of the Erechtheion. In the distance, against the horizon, the massive, incomplete Temple of Olympian Zeus celebrated the people's resolute rejection of tyranny.

The state prison stood along the path between the Agora and the Pnyx, in a neighborhood where metalworkers, sculptors, and makers of terracotta figures plied their trades. The complex consisted of a two-story administrative building, eight cells on either side of a central passageway, and a walled, open-air courtyard. Under normal circumstances, this would have been Socrates's home for only a few days before his death. A quirk of the calendar, however, delayed his execution for several weeks.

Socrates owed his reprieve to one of his polis's founding myths. Long before, in the vague past of legend, Athens had been subservient to Minos, the king of Crete—the same king who had imprisoned Daedalus, Socrates's legendary ancestor, and who later became one of the judges in the underworld. Minos kept the Minotaur, a terrifying man-eating monster, in a labyrinth under his palace, and to feed the beast, he periodically demanded a ghastly tribute. At his command, Athens was required to send seven young men and seven young women to Crete, where they were thrown into the labyrinth and devoured. The dreadful practice ended only when the hero Theseus joined one of the ill-fated groups. Theseus found his way through the

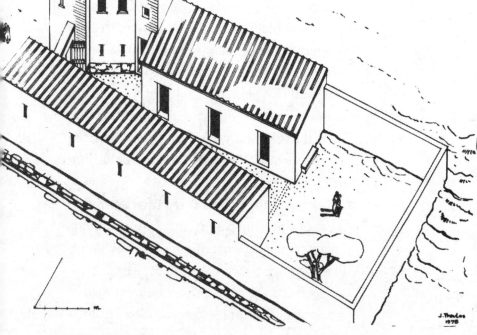

THE PRISON:
Archeologists believe that the ruins of the Athenian state prison have been found to the southwest of the Agora. This sketch evokes how the structure might have looked in Socrates's day.

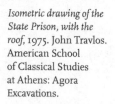

Isometric drawing of the State Prison, with the roof, 1975. John Travlos. American School of Classical Studies at Athens: Agora Excavations.

labyrinth, killed the Minotaur, and triumphantly sailed home with the other would-be victims.

The Athenians attributed Theseus's success to the assistance of Apollo, and to express their gratitude, they sent an annual religious mission to the island of Delos, which was sacred to that god. The tradition was very much alive in Socrates's day; even the ship that Athens dispatched to Delos each year was thought to be the one that had originally carried Theseus. A priest of Apollo inaugurated the mission by crowning the ship's prow with garlands, and from that point until the vessel's return to Athens, no executions were allowed. In 399 BCE, the garlanding of the ship took place the day before Socrates's trial, and the voyage lasted thirty-one days.

Because Athens considered imprisonment more of a holding pattern than a punishment, Socrates enjoyed what might otherwise seem like a strange benefit. During the several weeks he stayed at the prison, he welcomed a seemingly unlimited flow of visitors from the outside. Every day a dozen or more guests, some from out of town, came to see him. The visitors quickly developed a routine. At daybreak they gathered at the court where Socrates had

**THESEUS AND
THE MINOTAUR:**
Theseus's victory over
the Minotaur was a
favorite subject of
Athenian vase painters;
this photograph shows
the back of the storage
jug that is pictured
on page 109. In the
center of the image,
Theseus grasps the
Minotaur's horn and is
about to deal the fatal
blow. On the left and
right are some of the
Athenian youths whose
fate depends on the
outcome of the struggle.

*Terracotta amphora
(jar)*, ca. 540–530
BCE. Taleides as
potter, attributed to the
Taleides Painter, Greek,
Attic. The Metropolitan
Museum of Art, New
York.

been tried, where they spoke quietly among themselves until the start of visiting hours. Then they walked as a group to the prison and spent most of the day conversing with their friend. Socrates maintained the same interests and lively spirits he had always exhibited, and he treated his prison cell as simply the latest venue for his philosophical discussions. Crito, who frequently visited, expressed his amazement at Socrates's peace of mind. "Often in the past throughout my life," he told Socrates, "I have considered the way you live happy, and especially so now that you bear your present misfortune so easily and lightly."

Some of Socrates's visitors apparently used this time to have him review their records of his ideas, an endeavor that may have begun in the period between the formal accusation and the trial. At the beginning of Plato's *Theaetetus*, a man named Euclides describes how he arrived at a written version of one of the philosopher's discussions. Euclides himself had not been a party to the event, but after hearing Socrates describe it in detail, he went home and jotted down some notes. Then, as Euclides found the time, he expanded those notes into a full written text whose accuracy he verified in the weeks before the philosopher's death. "I used to ask Socrates about the points I couldn't remember, and correct my version when I got home." Although the philosopher did not leave behind any writings of his own, he seems to have authorized the contents of at least some of the dialogues in which he appears.

Socrates also took advantage of the opportunity to learn a new skill. For a long time, his dreams had urged him, "Socrates, practice and cultivate the arts." He had always interpreted these dreams as a kind of divine cheerleading—the gods' endorsement of his pursuit of philosophy, which he knew to be "the highest kind of art." But now, in his final days, he had begun to question his interpretation. Might his dreams be instructing him to take up the more popular art of writing poetry? With his typical enthusiasm, he decided to give the idea a try. He began by composing a hymn to Apollo, to whom he owed his extra month of life. His next project was to set Aesop's fables into verse.

Socrates's good cheer could not make his visitors forget the depressing situation. Each day that passed brought the ship closer to its return from Delos, and soon there would be no time left. But the philosopher's friends knew of a way out. Although their own comings and goings were monitored by a guard and though Socrates himself was bound in heavy chains, escape was possible. It was not especially rare for prisoners to slip out with their visitors or tunnel through the compound's dirt floor or mud walls. Besides, the prison staff was bribable. Socrates's friends rounded up plenty of money and begged him to accept their offer, but day after day he refused.

Soon enough, Crito arrived with the dreaded news. The ship from Delos was expected that same day, and the day after that, Socrates would die. Socrates felt certain, based on a dream, that he still had two more days to live, but the point was immaterial. If he wanted to escape, now was the time. Crito pleaded with his friend to act right away.

In the dialogue *Crito*, Plato dramatizes the discussion between the two men. Crito describes his despair. He will not only lose a dear friend "the like of whom I shall never find again," but also face public censure for failing to prevent the tragedy. "Surely there can be no worse reputation than to be thought to value money more highly than one's friends," Crito argues, "for the majority will not believe that you yourself were not willing to leave prison while we were eager for you to do so." Socrates must dismiss any concerns about the cost. Guards and informers are cheaply bought, and Crito and other friends have no shortage of money. Furthermore, if Socrates refuses to escape, he will be guilty of two acts of injustice. First, he will be surrendering his life before his time, and second, he will be depriving his three young sons of their father. If Socrates truly cherishes virtue, he must make his getaway before it is too late.

Socrates is unmoved. First, why should anyone care about the slander of the foolish majority? Crito should pay attention only to the views of reasonable people, and anyone reasonable will understand what actually happened in the prison. Crito objects. Even a foolish majority must not be ignored. "Your present situation makes clear," Crito points out, "that the majority can inflict not the least but pretty well the greatest evils if one is slandered among them."

But Socrates stands his ground. "Would that the majority could inflict the greatest evils," he sighs, "for they would then be capable of the greatest good, and that would be fine, but now they cannot do either. They cannot make a man either wise or foolish, but they inflict things haphazardly." Crito is focusing on an extraneous concern, and Socrates will have none of that. The two friends have only one matter to consider, and that is the health of their souls. Is the proposed escape just or unjust? Socrates has no doubt about the answer. Yes, he has himself been treated unjustly, but even when it seems justified as a form of retaliation, an unjust act remains unjust.

But why would his escape be unjust to begin with? To answer that question, Socrates pretends that he is speaking with the laws of Athens about his plans to break out of prison. "Tell me, Socrates, what are you intending to do?" he imagines the laws asking. With keen indignation, they demand to know why Socrates would destroy not just them but the entire polis, for no society can survive if its members flaunt its laws. "Or do you think it is possible," they ask, "for a city not to be destroyed if the verdicts of its courts have no force but are nullified and set at naught by private individuals?"

The laws have good reason for their anger. As they point out, they have made possible Socrates's entire way of life, including his very existence. He came into the world because the laws regulated his parents' marriage, he was nurtured and educated because the laws established his parents' duties, and he has enjoyed the benefits of citizenship because the laws have governed his polis. The claim of the laws runs deep. How does Socrates have the insolence to undermine them?

And here the laws make an especially significant point: no one ever forced Socrates into his relationship with them. Yes, Socrates was born an Athenian, and over that he had no control. But as an adult he always had the option of moving elsewhere, and at no point did he exercise that option. Indeed, he had never felt the allure of foreign cities, not even to visit friends or attend festivals, and he had chosen to marry and raise his children in Athens. Clearly Socrates found his polis a congenial place. His free decision to spend his life there amounted to an unspoken agreement to obey the local laws.

Socrates does not use this terminology, but the argument that he puts into the mouth of the laws is now known as social contract theory. According to this theory, people freely accept or reject membership in any specific society. They may express their acceptance by establishing the society themselves, entering one already in existence, or simply continuing to live in the one where they find themselves. The essential point in each of these scenarios is that the decision is voluntary. Now, since the fundamental decision to join a society is voluntary, so is the decision to obey any society's laws. But this freedom extends only so far. Once people do accept membership in a specific society, they signify their agreement to obey that specific society's laws. This agreement does not usually involve explicit declarations, documents, or signatures, but it has the binding force of a contract—the social contract. This basic set of ideas still surfaces among political thinkers today, but social contract theory is especially associated with the Enlightenment philosophers Thomas Hobbes, John Locke, and Jean-Jacques Rousseau. Socrates is often credited with its first articulation.

With his own version of social contract theory, Socrates did not mean to disallow all opposition to the laws. To the contrary, he believed that an individual who finds a law unjust must instruct the polis where it has gone wrong and attempt to remedy the situation through persuasion. But if this effort fails—as it has for Socrates himself—disobedience is not an option. As he has already established, it is never appropriate to return a wrong for a wrong; retaliation does not magically transform a bad deed into a good one. The only honorable course is for him to stay in prison and accept the death penalty that the laws of the polis have imposed.

Socrates adds several more reasons for his decision. First, everyone involved in the proposed escape will suffer. Crito and other accomplices will expose themselves to the risk of exile, disenfranchisement, and the loss of property, and Socrates will see his own reputation tarnished beyond repair, "for anyone who destroys the laws could easily be thought to corrupt the young and the ignorant." Second, Socrates has no place to go. He will be unable to flee to a well-governed city, because its people will distrust him, and he has no desire to live in the sort of poorly governed city that will take him in. The unrestrained inhabitants of a poorly governed city are incapable of civilized discourse, and even if Socrates entertained hopes of improving them, he could not do so without hypocrisy. "[W]hat will you say," he imagines the laws asking him, "the same as you did here, that virtue and justice are man's most precious possession, along with lawful behavior and the laws?" Furthermore, Socrates cannot wish to raise his family in a poorly governed city.

He is aware, he assures Crito, that his friends will take good care of his children if he leaves them behind in Athens—but surely his friends will perform that service just as faithfully if he is dead. Finally, Socrates imagines that he will suffer in the underworld for having broken his agreement with the laws.

Socrates ends his arguments in a kind of rapture. He compares himself to the Corybants, men who celebrated their religious devotion with ecstatic dancing. "Crito, my dear friend," he says, "be assured that these are the words I seem to hear, as the Corybants seem to hear the music of their flutes, and the echo of these words resounds in me, and makes it impossible for me to hear anything else." Socrates faces death with exhilaration rather than anguish. He invites Crito's reactions but warns that any attempt to oppose him will be pointless.

"I have nothing to say, Socrates," the heartbroken Crito replies.

"Let it be then, Crito, and let us act in this way, since this is the way the god is leading us," Socrates concludes.

CHAPTER 21

THE FATAL DRINK

THE ATHENIANS WERE PROUD OF THEIR LEGAL system. To differentiate between orderly deaths decreed by law and chaotic deaths resulting from warfare, they made sure that capital punishment involved no spilling of blood. The standard approach was a sort of bloodless crucifixion. After being shackled to a board by the wrists, ankles, and neck, the convict was strangled by the steady tightening of the collar around his throat.

Another option was death by hemlock, a highly toxic plant with lacy, umbrella-like flowers. The poison attacks the peripheral nervous system, causing a paralysis that begins in the extremities and spreads to the respiratory muscles. As the body loses its ability to supply oxygen to the heart and brain, victims feel a growing sluggishness but no pain. They remain conscious until almost the very end, when they experience a seizure that seems mild, at least to observers. By that point the paralyzed muscles are incapable of strong convulsions.

Hemlock was administered as a drink made of the plant's crushed leaves. The convict was handed a carefully measured dose, left to swallow it on his own, and told to lie down when he began to feel a numbness in his feet. This relatively gentle execution was preferable to the standard shackling and strangling, but most convicts did not have a choice. Hemlock was not grown locally, and it was extremely expensive. Only wealthy prisoners—or those lucky enough, like Socrates, to have wealthy friends—could afford it.

On the day of his death, Socrates was scheduled to drink the poison at dusk. About fifteen friends crowded into his cell for a final visit. Crito, of course, was in attendance, along with the steadfast Critobulus and Apollodorus. They were joined by Phaedo, the former sex slave whose freedom Socrates may have arranged; Antisthenes, the devoted student who had walked to Athens each day from his home in the Piraeus; and several admirers from the more distant cities of Megara and Thebes. Notably

Conium maculatum.

HEMLOCK: *Conium maculatum,* or hemlock, belongs to the same family as carrots, celery, dill, parsley, and parsnips. The plant's delicate appearance belies its lethal properties.

Curtis, William, *Flora Londinensis,* vol. 1. (London: Printed for and sold by the author and B. White, 1777). Pdf. Retrieved from the Biodiversity Heritage Library, https://www.biodiversitylibrary.org/bibliography/62570. A detail of this image appears on page 242.

absent were Xenophon and Plato. Xenophon was far away, fighting as a mercenary soldier on behalf of a Persian prince, and Plato was ill. Fortunately, Plato gathered enough secondhand information to compose the *Phaedo*, an account of Socrates's last day.

Hoping for as much time as possible with their doomed friend, the visitors arrived at the prison earlier than usual. The gatekeeper instructed them to wait. Socrates was in the middle of a meeting with the Eleven, who were explaining the logistics of his execution and, in a small concession for his last day, releasing him from his chains. When the visitors were finally admitted to the cell, they found Socrates sitting with his wife. Xanthippe was holding the couple's youngest son, just an infant, in her arms. "Socrates, this is the last time your friends will talk to you and you to them," she lamented. Socrates asked Crito to arrange for someone to take her home, and she left, beating her breast and wailing.

Socrates had only a few hours left to speak with his friends, and he wasted no time. Rubbing his leg where it had been relieved of its chain, he reflected on the inextricable link between pleasure and pain—"two creatures with one head," he called them, imagining how Aesop might have based a fable on the idea. Soon enough, the talk gave way to the subject that pressed on everyone's minds, the philosopher's imminent death. In ancient times, the *Phaedo* was also known as *On the Soul*, a title that aptly conveys the dialogue's philosophical focus. What awaited Socrates after drinking the poison that evening? Does the soul survive the death of the body?

It is unclear how much of the *Phaedo* reflects Socrates's own views. In Plato's depiction, Socrates offers four different proofs for the immortality of the soul, and during the course of his various arguments, he upholds Plato's theory of the Forms and expresses belief in the impurity of the body, the purity of the soul, and the notion of reincarnation. A man on the verge of death might well feel the attraction of these ideas, but in Socrates's case, the shift seems rather abrupt. He had always focused on the ethical concerns of this world, not on unprovable assertions about what may lie beyond it, and in his speech to the jury just a month earlier, he had explicitly denied knowing whether death is a complete lack of perception or a relocation of the soul to another place.

More convincing is the *Phaedo*'s portrait of Socrates himself during his final hours. Socrates conducted himself as he always had—after all, why would he have allowed his imminent death to interfere with a good philosophical discussion? He became so absorbed that he ignored Crito's repeated attempts to interrupt him. But at last Crito managed to break through with a warning he had received from the prison's expert on poisons. "People get heated when they talk . . . and one should not be heated when taking the poison, as those who do must sometimes drink it two or three times."

Socrates, of course, dismissed the advice. He would speak just as much as he chose. "[L]et him be prepared to administer it twice or, if necessary, three times."

"I was rather sure you would say that," Crito replied, "but he has been bothering me for some time."

Socrates ended up conversing with his friends the entire day. "I had a strange feeling," Phaedo later recalled, "an unaccustomed mixture of pleasure and pain at the same time as I reflected that he was just about to die. All of us present were affected in much the same way, sometimes laughing, then weeping." The discussion ended only as the sun neared the western horizon, when Socrates took a bath to lighten the burden of the women charged with tending his corpse. Crito accompanied Socrates to the bathing room while the other visitors remained behind, already overcome by their loss. They felt, as Phaedo put it, "as if we had lost a father and would be orphaned for the rest of our lives."

After his bath, Socrates met with his children, his wife, and the other women of his household for one last time. We do not know the identity of these other women, but because women were generally unable to achieve financial or social independence, female relatives often clustered into the same household, where they shared the work. Socrates gave the women and children his final instructions and sent them away. He wanted to spend his last moments with the men who had been his companions in philosophy— and who, he believed, were less likely to break down into unseemly emotion.

The sun had almost set by the time the philosopher rejoined his friends, and soon after his return, an officer of the Eleven entered the cell. "I shall not reproach you as I do the others, Socrates," he remarked, explaining that he usually endured a barrage of curses when he ordered prisoners to drink the poison. The officer was confident that this time he would be spared. He had come to know Socrates as "the noblest, the gentlest and the best man who has ever come here." But still, it was time to issue the order, and the officer performed his duty as delicately as he could. "You know what message I bring. Fare you well, and try to endure what you must as easily as possible." The officer wept as he left the room.

Socrates asked for the poison to be brought to him right away, despite Crito's observation that many prisoners waited until it was much darker. "I do not expect any benefit from drinking the poison a little later," replied Socrates, "except to become ridiculous in my own eyes for clinging to life, and be sparing of it when there is none left." Crito knew better than to argue. He silently nodded to the slave who stood nearby, and the slave went out to summon the official in charge of the poison. That individual soon arrived, bearing a small cup. "Well, my good man," Socrates addressed him, "you are an expert in this; what must one do?"

"Just drink it and walk around until your legs feel heavy, and then lie down and it will act of itself."

Socrates took the cup "quite cheerfully," according to Phaedo, and asked whether he might pour out some of its contents as a libation to the gods.

"We only mix as much as we believe will suffice," the official replied.

"I understand," said Socrates. He offered instead a brief prayer and then calmly drained the cup. At that, his friends lost any of the composure they had managed during the day. They broke into sobs, and Apollodorus cried out, loudly and bitterly. Socrates rebuked them. "I am told one should die in good omened silence. So keep quiet and control yourselves." Ashamed, the men choked back their tears and watched as Socrates walked around the room. When his legs felt heavy, he moved to his bed, where he lay on his back and covered his head. The official began to press different parts of Socrates's body to gauge the poison's effect. Did Socrates feel the pressure on his feet? On his calves? On his thighs? The paralysis spread upward, swiftly and inexorably.

As the poison reached his stomach, Socrates uncovered his head and made a curious comment. "Crito, we owe a cock to Asclepius; make this offering to him and do not forget." Asclepius was the god of medicine and healing, and sick people hoping for a cure customarily slept in his temples and offered him a rooster as a sacrifice. Had Socrates recently recovered from an illness but forgotten to fulfill his ritual obligation? This is perhaps the simplest interpretation, but it falls short of the momentousness we might expect from the deathbed of a great man. Another possibility is to understand Socrates's words metaphorically. Since death was curing him of the ills of life, he wished to express his gratitude to the god of healing. But this explanation is problematic too. Would a man who had always taken such a robust pleasure in life really have considered his earthly existence a sort of disease?

Crito, ever attentive, promised that the cock would be offered and asked whether Socrates had any further requests. But the philosopher had uttered his last words. A few moments later, his body shuddered abruptly, and the official conducted his final examination. The hemlock had done its irrevocable work.

Phaedo closes his account with poignant simplicity: "Such was the end of our comrade, a man who, we would say, was of all those we have known the best, and also the wisest and the most upright."

Epilogue

TO STUDY SOCRATES IS TO AIM AT AN ELUSIVE target. The man emerges as a bundle of contradictions: modest but arrogant, ugly but alluring, sensuous but ascetic, mocking but earnest. He disavowed superstition but obeyed his daimonion, lived in poverty but socialized with aristocrats, treasured Athens but denounced its values. He was passionate about life but almost blithely let it go.

This bewildering portrait is itself based on problematic sources. Some of the ancient manuscripts have disappeared over time, and others exist only in fragments. The surviving texts were never intended as history—or certainly not history as we understand it today—and many of them were composed long after

Socrates's death. To make matters worse, these sources sometimes disagree with one another. The crux of the problem is that we have no direct access to the man himself. Socrates left us no written record of his life and thought.

As one might expect of Socrates, this omission was not a question of laziness or negligence. Socrates mistrusted the ability of written texts to communicate effectively. He explains his position in Plato's *Phaedrus*:

> *[W]riting shares a strange feature with painting. The offsprings of painting stand there as if they are alive, but if anyone asks them anything, they remain most solemnly silent. The same is true of written words. You'd think they were speaking as if they had some understanding, but if you question anything that has been said because you want to learn more, it continues to signify just that very same thing forever.*

The written word, to Socrates, was static. Inked onto paper or inscribed into stone, ideas become inanimate objects, unresponsive to questions or challenges and incapable of transformation in the light of new understandings.

The absence of a written record is the bane of a biographer, but that void is precisely where Socrates comes into sharpest focus. Socrates's legacy is both simpler and grander than the specific facts of his days or the ins and outs of his thought. His most enduring contribution is his model of an ethically mindful life. For Socrates, that was a life based on philosophy— not dead words on a page, but a vital quest for what is good and true. He understood that quest to be dynamic, unending, and collaborative— dynamic because knowledge is not a commodity that one individual can simply hand over to another, unending because the answers often lie just beyond our reach, and collaborative because we think best when we engage with those who disagree with us.

Ultimately, we are not very different from the people that Socrates invited on that quest close to two and a half thousand years ago. We imagine ourselves happy in many of the same ways that they did. We pile up material possessions and seek influence and recognition. We pursue well-worn paths to success and curate the images we present to the public. We rally around charismatic leaders and look for reassuringly simple answers to complicated questions in an

uncertain world. Socrates would urge us, as
he urged his fellow Athenians, to stop, think,
and discuss the choices that we make each day.
Living meaningfully means making morally
sound decisions about every aspect of life—
about how to educate our children, behave
toward our parents, nurture our friendships,
shape our careers, select our leaders, enact our
laws, choose our heroes, deal with our criminals.

Perhaps no one more than Socrates knew
the dangers of the quest. Asking real questions
and seeking real answers can threaten a public
that would rather not think, and an indignant,
irrational public is a perilous force. But even
without anything quite as dramatic as Socrates's
trial and execution, the quest is unsettling. If we
take the effort seriously, we will encounter people
and ideas we deplore, endure assaults on beliefs
we hold dear, and—if we are honest and humble
enough—discover that some of our convictions
have been wrong all along. But the stakes are too
high for us to walk away. "An unexamined life is
not worth living," Socrates famously declared at
his trial. He invites us all to become philosophers
in the original sense of the word—lovers of
wisdom—because only that pursuit enables us to
shape lives of goodness and meaning.

Notes

Prologue

xv. *"Well, my good man," Socrates said, "you are an expert in this": Phaedo* 117a.

PART ONE: *The Path to the Questions*

Chapter 1: The City of Gods and Humans

3. *Phaenarete had given birth to a boy:* We do not know whether Socrates had a sister, but if he had one, Sophroniscus and Phaenarete would have announced her birth differently. Parents of a newborn girl decorated their doorway with wool, a symbol of the spinning, weaving, and other domestic tasks that awaited her when she grew up.

THE WORK OF WOMEN: One of the most important and time-consuming tasks for women was the making of cloth. The series of images on this flask shows women weighing the wool, spinning it into yarn, weaving the yarn on a loom, and folding the finished fabric.

Terracotta lekythos (oil flask), ca. 550–530 BCE. Attributed to the Amasis Painter, Greek, Attic. The Metropolitan Museum of Art, New York.

5. *his family descended from Daedalus: Euthyphro* 11b, *Alcibiades* 121a. It is possible that Socrates was speaking figuratively rather than literally when he traced his ancestry to Daedalus. Since Daedalus was a craftsman, stone-cutters like Socrates's father recognized him as their patron. The same reasoning may explain the idea that Hephaestus was Daedalus's ancestor: Hephaestus was a craftsman too.

7. *a genuine ship gliding through the city streets:* The vessel was apparently mounted on wheels for its journey through the city. Although the ship may have been introduced after Socrates's time, several scholars argue that it was part of the festival from the very beginning. (Wachsmann, Shelley. "Panathenaic Ships: The Iconographic Evidence." *Hesperia: The Journal of the American School of Classical Studies at Athens*, vol. 81, no. 2 [2012]: pp. 237–266.)

9. *that hallowed statue had fallen, fully fashioned, directly from the heavens:* Pausanias 1.26.6.

9. *They had returned with a crushing force on both land and sea:* Socrates's contemporary, the historian Herodotus, calculated the number of fighters at 2,641,610 and the total number, including support staff, at a staggering 5,283,220 (Herodotus 7.186). Today historians doubt these figures, but it is certain that the enemy spared no expense or effort in its renewed offensive.

10. *"Safe shall the wooden wall continue for thee and thy children":* Herodotus 7.141.

13. *all citizens had a chance of holding public office at some point in their lives:* This chance was increased by short terms of office and limits on how many times a person could hold the same position. In the Boule, the Ekklesia's main administrative committee, for instance, a citizen could serve no more than two one-year terms.

13. *a freeborn male over seventeen years of age:* Athenian law indicated that a candidate for citizenship was examined "in his eighteenth year." But the Greeks did not calculate age as we do. Their mathematics had no zero, so from the moment of birth, an infant was already "one"—in other words, in its first year of life. Also, Athenians marked birth *years*, not birth*days*, so all children born in a single calendar year moved to the next phase of their lives at the same time.

15. *"[F]reedom is an excellent thing":* Herodotus 5.78.

Chapter 2: The Way to Citizenship

19. *and then described himself as having "disgraced" his teacher, "who is still trying to teach me to play":* Euthydemus 272c.

19. *"breaking the laws of music," as he put it—led inevitably to a "general disregard for the law":* Laws 700e–701a.

21. *artistic contests, recitations of literary works, and spontaneous presentations by poets:* The *Iliad* and the *Odyssey* are actually collections of songs—poems set to music—that were performed at these sorts of

events. The musical competitions of the sixth century helped to shape the versions of those epics that we know today.

24. *the child was so impressive that he required no schooling at all:* Plutarch, *Moralia* 589e, *On Socrates' Divine Sign* 20.

25. *a sort of internal voice that warned him against taking specific actions:* Socrates gives his fullest description of the daimonion in Plato's *Apology* 31c.

26. *War, not peace, was the natural state of affairs in the Greek world:* Between 497 and 338 BCE, Athens was at war for three years out of four (JACT, p. 250).

27. *a government district, religious zone, marketplace, and social center rolled into one:* A wonderful quotation attributed to the comic poet Euboulos, who lived a century after Socrates, offers a peek into the energetic mishmash of the Agora: "You will find everything sold together in the same place at Athens: figs, witnesses to summonses, bunches of grapes, turnips, pears, apples, givers of evidence, roses, medlars, porridge, honeycombs, chick-peas, lawsuits, milk-puddings, myrtle, allotment-machines [for random jury-selection], irises, lambs, water-clocks [for timing law-court speeches], laws, indictments" (JACT, p. 76). The original passage appears in Athenaeus's *Deipnosophistae* (14.640 b–c), an early third-century CE work that is sometimes called the world's oldest cookbook.

28. *"more public and private lawsuits and judicial investigations":* "Xenophon," *Constitution of the Athenians* 3.2; translation from http://www.agathe.gr/democracy/the_popular_courts.html. "Xenophon" is in quotation marks because, although the text is traditionally ascribed to him, most scholars question his authorship.

29. *which met on a nearby hilltop called the Pnyx:* The Pnyx raises the interesting question of the degree to which the climate of Athens shaped its democracy. In contrast to the citizens of most of today's democracies, the Athenians did not elect a small body of representatives but participated directly in the affairs of government themselves. Six thousand citizens might have gathered at a well-attended session of the Ekklesia. Since ancient architects lacked the know-how to build structures large enough for such enormous crowds, only a region with favorable weather could have developed such a political system.

30. *a long rope dipped in red dye:* Aristophanes, *Ecclesiazusae* 376–379, *Acharnians* 17–22.

31. *"wild man"; "impulsive in any course of action":* *Charmides* 153b, *Apology* 21a. In Plato's *Gorgias*, by contrast, Chaerephon appears to be perfectly calm and coherent.

Chapter 3: The Young Intellectual

36. *"already quite venerable, very gray but of distinguished appearance, about sixty-five years old"; "close to forty, a tall, handsome man":* Parmenides 127b.

36. *they met a day or two before, presumably at a similar gathering:* Parmenides 135c–d.

36. *I understand that Zeno wants to be on intimate terms with you:*
Parmenides 128a–b.

38. *"kept from moment to moment"; "often glanced at each other"; "[Y]ou are much to be admired for your keenness for argument!":* Parmenides 130a–b.

39. *"[W]hen I get bogged down in that"; "That's because you are still young, Socrates":* Parmenides 130d–e.

Chapter 4: The Nature of Reality

42. *In the* Parmenides, *Zeno presents his reason for supporting this notion:* Zeno's most famous defense of a unitary, unchanging reality is a set of paradoxes that do not appear in this dialogue. One of these paradoxes is the Dichotomy, which I will present for both clarity and sentiment in the way my father taught it to me when I was seven years old. My father had me stand four feet away from a wall and then instructed me to step halfway to the wall. After I had done so, he told me to step half the remaining two feet to the wall. I took that step, and he told me to go half the remaining foot. He continued in the same way, insisting that even if we went on forever I'd never reach the wall. Of course, our little demonstration quickly broke down. I could no longer manage the minuscule steps he required, and my indignant common sense interfered—"Of course I'll reach the wall. Can't you see that I'm already touching it?" Obviously the point is more sophisticated than I realized at the time. Since any distance between two points can be divided into an infinite number of finite distances, it should be impossible to get from one point to another. Parmenides is right, then, to consider at least one type of change, motion, an illusion.

44. *"It was the others who made them separate":* Aristotle, *Metaphysics* 13.1078b; I have used the translation in Ferguson, p. 181.

48. *These particles, which they called atoms, come in many different shapes:* It is tempting to think that these thinkers shared our current understanding of matter, but their theories about atoms were pure speculations.

49. *"Natural philosophy" is the name we now give to this early scientific approach to the universe:* It may seem strange to apply the word "philosophy" to an essentially scientific endeavor, but for most of history, thinkers did not differentiate between science and philosophy. Both branches of knowledge explored the fundamental truths of reality, and both looked for answers in the same way. Until the Enlightenment of the seventeenth and eighteenth centuries, science was based less on the gathering and testing of evidence from the real world than on *a priori* reasoning—reasoning that is independent of (or "prior to") sensory experience.

50. *"Nous has control over all things that have soul, both the larger and the smaller":* DK59b12, *A Presocratics Reader.*

51. *We have no evidence that Socrates met him in person:* Diogenes Laertius (2.5.19) records the view that Socrates studied with

Anaxagoras and/or Archelaus, one of Anaxagoras's followers, but if that information were true, it seems likely that Plato would have mentioned it in the *Phaedo*, where he shows Socrates discussing his early interest in natural philosophy.

51. *"When I was a young man, I was wonderfully keen on that wisdom which they call natural science":* The quotations in this paragraph and the two that follow come from *Phaedo* 96a–98d.

54. *"things in the sky and below the earth"; "I do not speak in contempt of such knowledge":* Apology 19b–c.

Chapter 5: Questions for an Age of Humanism

57. *Aristotle sheds light on this neglect:* Politics 5.11.

62. *"was the first to call philosophy down from the heavens":* Cicero, *Tusculan Disputations* 5.4 (Cicero, Marcus Tullius. *Tusculan Disputations.* Translated by J. E. King. Harvard University Press, Loeb Classical Library, 2007.)

PART TWO: *Asking the Questions*

Chapter 6: The Growth of a Following

65. *"How many things are there which I do not want":* Diogenes Laertius 2.5.24.

66. *a slave who had never studied math could solve a problem in geometry:* Meno 82b–85b. The slave initially believes that to double the area of a square, one would need to double the length of each side. Socrates helps him realize that doubling the length of each side would produce a square whose area is not twice but four times that of the original. The slave ultimately recognizes that the square he seeks would need sides that are equal in length to the diagonal of the original square.

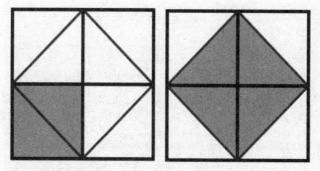

DOUBLING THE AREA OF A SQUARE: These diagrams present the essence of what the slave in the *Meno* gradually understood. The original square is shaded in the diagram to the left; doubling its sides creates a new square that is four times, not two times, the area of the original. When the square is divided into two triangles that are equal in area, it becomes easy to see that using the diagonal as a side would result in a square composed of four of those triangles—in other words, a square double in area to the original.

66. *one who taught him about the art of love:* In Plato's *Symposium*, we learn that Diotima, a woman from the Peloponnesian city of Mantinea, taught Socrates to view love as a bridge between our imperfect sensory existence and the perfect realm of abstraction. First we love beautiful things, then we recognize the features that all beautiful things share, and finally we understand beauty in its abstract, absolute form.

66. *and the other who instructed him in the skill of persuasive speaking:* This was Aspasia, whom I discuss in chapter 10.

66. *"Good Sir," he said to anyone who stayed long enough to listen, "you are an Athenian":* Apology 29d–e.

68. *a shoemaker named Simon kept a workshop:* None of the dialogues attributed to Simon survive. We know about him mainly from Diogenes Laertius (2.13.122–123); the closest we get to contemporaneous evidence is Xenophon's description of what may have been Simon's workshop (*Memorabilia* 4.2.1). Nonetheless, archeology has provided tantalizing support for the shoemaker's existence. In the rooms of a ruined house just outside the boundary of the Agora, archeologists discovered bone eyelets and iron hobnails, materials commonly used by shoemakers. In the roadway just outside the house, archeologists found the base of a drinking cup marked with the Greek for "of Simon."

69. *"You fancy yourself the tallest and best-looking man around":* Alcibiades 104a.

69. *both the adults and the adolescents expected sexual relationships to develop:* The relationship was governed by strict rules. The boy was eligible from around the time of puberty until the first appearance of a beard, roughly between the ages of twelve and eighteen, and was considered most desirable when he had fuzz on his cheeks. He was expected to lie still during the sexual encounter, and although he was meant to feel gratitude and admiration for his partner, he was not supposed to express or experience any passionate desire. The adult was usually between twenty and thirty years old and not yet married, but since it was socially acceptable to have a wife and a boy-lover simultaneously, older married men were common too.

70. *"What I thought at the time was that what he really wanted was me":* Alcibiades describes his failed attempts to seduce Socrates in the *Symposium* 217a–219e.

74. *"What's this?" said Socrates. "You're bragging as if you were more beautiful than I am":* Xenophon, *Symposium* 4.19.

75. *"Nothing is more important to me than becoming the best man I can be":* Symposium 218d.

78. *"They say that Socrates met him in a narrow lane":* Diogenes Laertius 2.6.48.

78. *once again, Diogenes Laertius provides a description of a fateful first encounter:* Diogenes Laertius 3.5. This story is preceded by one that is just as engaging but much less likely. The night before he first met Plato, who would one day flourish as a philosopher in his own right, Socrates dreamed that he held a young swan in his lap. The swan suddenly developed mature feathers and flew off with a musical call. Upon meeting Plato the next day, Socrates realized that he had found the bird from his dream.

79. *"At last I came to the conclusion that all existing states are badly governed": Sixth Letter* 326a.

Chapter 7: The Sophists

81. *"That I am the kind of person to be a gift of the god to the city": Apology* 31a–c.

82. *"[A] student pays the full price only if he wishes to": Protagoras* 328c.

83. *"a kind of merchant who peddles provisions upon which the soul is nourished": Protagoras* 313c.

84. *"Not a single man can stand up to them": Euthydemus* 272a–b.

85. *"Tell me, have you got a dog?": Euthydemus* 298d–e.

88. *"Everyone believes his own customs to be by far and away the best":* Herodotus 3.38. (Herodotus. *The Histories.* Edited by Paul Cartledge. Translated by Tom Holland. New York: Penguin Books, 2015.)

89. *"Concerning the gods," he said, "I am unable to know":* DK80b4, *A Presocratics Reader.*

90. *"A person is the measure of all things":* DK80b1, *A Presocratics Reader.*

91. *"speaking the truth and paying whatever debts one has incurred": Republic* 331c.

91. *"to give to each what is owed to him": Republic* 331e.

92. *"to treat friends well and enemies badly": Republic* 335a.

93. *"He coiled himself up like a wild beast": Republic* 336b.

93. *"Justice is nothing other than the advantage of the stronger": Republic* 338c.

94. *justice is really "very high-minded simplicity" and injustice is really "good judgment": Republic* 348c–d.

94. But truly knowledgeable people do not compete against one another; instead, they strive to emulate one another's words and deeds: Does this claim ring true? It does not take much to imagine a medical researcher who conceals her preliminary findings so that she can beat her peers to an important discovery, a teacher who refuses to share his lesson plans so that he can maintain his reputation as the "best" teacher at his school, or a software developer who refuses to share a technological breakthrough so that he can reap all the profits himself. But Socrates would argue that these cases prove his point. True knowledge seeks the benefits to which it is directly devoted; in these cases, the benefits are the health of human beings, the education of children, and the enhancement of people's productivity. Concerns like fame or reputation or money are extraneous, and when they engender competition that prevents knowledge from achieving its true end, they constitute ignorance.

96. *"It profits no one to be wretched but to be happy"; "And so, Thrasymachus, injustice is never more profitable than justice"*: Republic 354a.

96. *"Thrasymachus agreed to all this"*: Republic 350c–d.

97. *"[Y]ou became gentle and ceased to give me rough treatment"*: Republic 354a.

98. *"Isn't the person most able to land a blow"*: Republic 333e–334a.

Chapter 8: Knowledge and Morality

102. *"Aren't you capable of remembering that I asked for the fine itself?"*: Greater Hippias 292c–d.

103. *"How will you know whose speech—or any other action—is finely presented or not"*: Greater Hippias 304d–e.

104. *he offered a compelling argument for his position:* An especially clear and succinct formulation of Socrates's argument appears in *Meno* 87e–89a.

105. *"[I]f someone were to know what is good and bad"*: Protagoras 352c.

107. *"so long as he lived having taken pleasure in honorable things"; "Surely you don't, like most people"*: Protagoras 351c.

108. *"Weighing is a good analogy"*: Protagoras 356b.

Chapter 9: The Democracy and the Spartan Alternative

111. *"Are they the ones who know the truth—ordinary people?"*: Greater Hippias 284e.

113. *"[T]he very rocks and surroundings echo the din of their praise or blame and double it"; "What private training can hold out"*: Republic 6.492b–c.

114. *one of the ten tribes, or administrative divisions, into which the entire population was organized:* The ten tribes were established at the end of the sixth century BCE as part of the democratic reforms. Each of the polis's 139 demes was categorized into one of three groups—urban, coastal, and inland—and every tribe was composed of an assortment of demes from each group. Each tribe appointed its own political representatives, formed its own military regiment under a general it chose itself, and had its own sanctuaries and holidays.

115, 117. *"that it was foolish to appoint political leaders by lot"; "if these posts are badly filled"*: Xenophon, Memorabilia 1.2.9.

118. *"He said that it was not those who held the sceptre who were kings and rulers"*: Xenophon, Memorabilia 3.9.10.

118. *a distance that a fleet-footed messenger covered in just two days:* The specially trained runner Philippides (sometimes called Pheidippides) was sent to Sparta to ask for help in the Battle of Marathon, which in 490 BCE ended the Persians' first invasion of mainland Greece. Philippides reached Sparta the day after his departure from Athens, but by the time the Spartan troops reached Marathon, Athens had already defeated the

Persians (Herodotus 6.105–106).

The details of the tale evolved over time and many retellings. By the second century CE, Philippides made his furious run not from Athens to Sparta but from Marathon to Athens, a distance of about twenty-six miles, and his goal was not to secure Sparta's help but to bring Athens news of its amazing victory at Marathon. "Joy to you, we've won," Philippides breathlessly announces to the Athenian magistrates just before he drops dead (Lucian. *A Slip of the Tongue in Greeting* 3. *Lucian*, vol. 6. Translated by K. Kilburn. Harvard University Press, Loeb Classical Library: 1959, p. 177). The modern marathon derives its name as well as its length from this dramatic but apocryphal later version.

118. *children were raised to be hardy, with meager meals:* Plutarch claims that youngsters were so undernourished that they needed to scrounge around for additional food. A favorite children's story told of a boy who captured a fox that he planned to eat. When he saw a group of Spartan soldiers coming his way, he concealed the fox beneath his clothing rather than confess what he had done, and he betrayed no sign of pain even as the animal began to chew at his stomach. (Plutarch, *Moralia, Sayings of Spartans* 35).

119. *breeding and raising the next generation of warriors:* To rear children who conformed to the Spartan ideal, mothers are said to have suppressed their natural affection. One Spartan mother, according to Plutarch, handed her son his shield and sent him off to battle with the words "Either this or upon this"—in other words, if he did not return triumphantly with his shield in his hand, he should come back as a corpse laid out upon his shield (Plutarch, *Moralia, Sayings of Spartan Women, Other Spartan Women to Fame Unknown* 16).

119. *"[H]e would be glad to eat them raw":* Xenophon, *Hellenica* 3.3.6.

121. *Socrates considered Sparta to be one of the best-governed city-states in Greece: Crito* 53a.

121. *"To be a Spartan," he declared, "is to be a philosopher"; "Pick any ordinary Spartan and talk with him for a while": Protagoras* 342e–343b.

122. *produced virtually no written documents:* It is worth keeping in mind that since the Spartans left almost no written record of their own, our understanding of their lives is based on the accounts of outsiders. Some of these outsiders were enemies of Sparta, and most of them had never visited the polis they so vividly described. Their accounts may shed more light on their own prejudices than on the reality of Spartan life.

123. *"Why, men went mad with mimicry of Sokrates":* Aristophanes, *The Birds* 1280–83 (Arrowsmith, p. 105).

Chapter 10: Athens on the Ascent

126. *Conflicts began almost immediately after Persia's retreat from mainland Greece:* The earliest conflict, which concerned the Athenians' plan to rebuild their ravaged city walls, nicely illustrates the difference between the two city states. Sparta objected to the plan. Their own soldiers, the Spartans boasted, provided all the protection that their polis needed.

Besides, a walled city north of the Peloponnese endangered all of Greece. If Persia invaded again, it could easily turn such a city into an impregnable fortress.

Athens simply ignored Sparta's opposition and resolved to keep the construction a secret until the walls were high enough to serve their defensive function. Suspecting that they were being tricked, the Spartans sent delegates to Athens to see what was really going on. The Athenians, unfazed, imprisoned the delegates and released them only once the walls had reached a suitable height (Thucydides 1.1.90–1.1.91).

126. *Ancient Greece was not a political entity but a conglomerate of settlements:* According to recent estimates, Greeks established 1,035 settlements throughout the Mediterranean basin, from the Iberian Peninsula in the west to Asia Minor in the east, including not only southern Europe but also the northern coast of Africa (JACT, p. 58).

128. *Sparta eyed these developments with profound suspicion:* Thucydides details the many points of contention that led the two sides to war, but his more general pronouncement is this: "The real cause I consider to be the one which was formally most kept out of sight. The growth of the power of Athens, and the alarm which this inspired in Lacedaemon [Sparta], made war inevitable" (1.23.6).

133. *his contemporary, the historian Thucydides, described him as the polis's "first citizen":* Thucydides 2.65.9.

133. *Socrates credited her with writing Pericles's most famous speech, his "Funeral Oration":* The speech appears in Thucydides 2.34.8–2.46.2. Socrates's claim that Aspasia was its author appears in *Menexenus* 236b.

134. *it became fashionable to ridicule Aspasia as a way of belittling Pericles:* Pericles's enemies maligned Aspasia as a seductress who exercised undue influence over her partner. Her alleged contribution to his public speaking was part of the fodder, since having a woman as a teacher would have been seen as a sign of Pericles's deficiency.

134. *he gratefully acknowledged her as one of his own teachers: Menexenus* 235e–236a.

134. *Anaxagoras saved Pericles from the "superstitious terror" that results from ignorance of natural philosophy:* Plutarch, *Lives, Pericles* 6. Plutarch relates that in the middle of a struggle against the polis's aristocratic faction, Pericles received the head of a one-horned ram from his country estate. A soothsayer who examined the natural curiosity declared it a good omen. Just as the ram's two horns had resolved themselves into one, so too would the two dominant parties in Athens, the democratic and aristocratic, unite under Pericles. The prediction would have been welcome to Pericles, but Anaxagoras dismissed it outright. The natural philosopher ordered a dissection of the ram's head and soon discovered the reason for the single horn. The ram's brain, which should have filled the entire cavity of the skull, was abnormally contracted into the small area from which the one horn had sprouted.

135. *some of it incorporated into a war monument on the north side of the plateau:* Recycled pieces of old buildings, or *spolia*, were common in the ancient world. The spolia on the north side of the Acropolis are especially prominent, and they were deliberately positioned to face the heart of the city. The statement was powerful: despite the trauma of the Persian invasion, Athens had emerged victorious.

136. *Athena's golden ornaments were designed to be removable:* Thucydides 2.13.5.

140. *a transfer that may well have bankrolled his ambitious building program:* Plutarch, *Lives, Pericles* 12. Modern scholars debate whether Pericles actually used Delian League money to pay for the project, and if so, to what extent. But even if all the funding came from more legitimate sources, Athens could bear the staggering construction costs only because of the economic benefits of its imperialist policies.

140. *He explained his reasoning in a speech to the Ekklesia:* Thucydides 1.140–144.

140. *"[T]o recede is no longer possible":* Thucydides 2.63.2.

141. *But the closest we get is Socrates's response to Thrasymachus in the* Republic: Book 2 of the *Republic* may provide additional evidence that Socrates opposed Pericles's policies. Socrates describes a healthy city as one in which only the most basic needs of its members are satisfied; by contrast, the "city with a fever" indulges in unnecessary luxuries and requires many additional workers. To grow the necessary food for its bloated population, the city with a fever must seize its neighbors' territory, and the inevitable result is war. Socrates does not mention Athens explicitly, but the suggestion is unmistakable. The policies that Pericles pursued—empire-building, lavish construction, and the relentless march to war—were harmful to the polis.

141. *Plato shows Socrates praising Pericles as a man of "magnificent wisdom":* Meno 94b. In context, this praise is double-edged. Socrates's larger point is that despite Pericles's wisdom and accomplishments, he has failed to make his sons virtuous. I return to this point in chapter 16.

141, 142. *"in all likelihood the greatest rhetorician of all"; "the reasons and customary rules for conduct":* Phaedrus 269e–270b. Plutarch recounts an amusing story that attests to Pericles's powers of persuasion. One of Pericles's political opponents was an aristocrat named Thucydides—not the historian, but one of the boys whose education is under discussion in the *Laches* (see chapter 13). According to Plutarch, one of the Spartan kings asked Thucydides who was the better wrestler, Pericles or Thucydides himself. Thucydides replied, "Whenever I throw him at wrestling, he beats me by arguing that he was never down, and he can even make the spectators believe it" (*Lives, Pericles* 8).

Chapter 11: Potidaea and the Welcome Return

145. *"When we were cut off from our supplies":* Alcibiades's account of Socrates at Potidaea appears in the *Symposium* 219e–220e.

148. *Apparently Socrates often exhibited this behavior: Symposium* 174d–175c.

148. *some modern medical experts have theorized that he was epileptic:* Englert, Walter G. and Osamu Muramoto. "Socrates and temporal lobe epilepsy: a pathographic diagnosis 2,400 years later." *Epilepsia,* vol. 47, no. 3 (Mar. 2006): pp. 652–654.

149. *Using the Greeks' own name for themselves, which has entered English as "Hellenes":* The words "Greek" and "Greece" come from Latin. The Greeks believed that they were descendants of the mythical figure Hellen, whose paternal grandfather was Prometheus and maternal grandparents were Epimetheus and Pandora. The Greeks therefore called themselves Hellenes and referred to their land as Hellas.

149. *"the greatest movement yet known in history, not only of the Hellenes":* Thucydides 1.1.2.

150. *"[S]ince I was arriving after such a long absence":* This quotation, along with the ones in the next two paragraphs, appears in *Charmides* 153a–159a.

151. *"a sort of quietness": Charmides* 159b.

152. *"modesty is not a good mate for a needy man": Charmides* 161a.

152. *"minding one's own business": Charmides* 161b.

153. *"science of science": Charmides* 169d.

154. *"a babbler, incapable of finding out anything whatsoever by means of argument": Charmides* 176a.

Chapter 12: Crisis and Cruelty

158. *some took the desperate step of ignoring the oracle of Delphi:* Thucydides 2.17.1–2.

158. *he scrupulously observed his own case to record the progression of the disease:* Thucydides 2.48–51.

159. *according to some estimates, the epidemic had killed a third of the polis's population:* Kagan, p. 78.

160. *"No one was held back in awe, either by fear of the gods or by the laws of men":* Thucydides 2.53.4. (Thucydides, *On Justice, Power, and Human Nature.* Translated by Paul Woodruff. Hackett, 1993.)

163. *"the most violent man at Athens":* Thucydides 3.36.6.

163. *"the horrid cruelty of a decree":* Thucydides 3.36.6.

164. *"had only just had time to read the decree":* Thucydides 3.49.4.

165. *"I'm not one of the politicians": Gorgias* 473e–474a.

167. *"[N]o man will survive who genuinely opposes you or any other crowd": Apology* 31d.

Chapter 13: Definitions of Courage

170. *"He was observing everything quite calmly"; "[I]t was easy to see that he was remarkably more collected than Laches"*: Symposium 221b.

170. *"I can tell you that if the rest had been willing to behave in the same manner, our city would be safe"*: Laches 181b.

171. *"to cast the deciding vote"*: The quotations in this paragraph and the one that follows appear in Laches 184c–185a.

172. *"are considering a form of study for the sake of the souls of young men"*: Laches 185e.

174. *"Good heavens, Socrates, there is no difficulty about that"*: Laches 190e.

174. *"I wanted to learn from you not only what constitutes courage for a hoplite"*: Laches 191d–e.

175. *"a sort of endurance of the soul"*: Laches 192b.

176. *"the knowledge of the fearful and the hopeful in war and every other situation"*: Laches 195a.

177. *"Well, it would be a terrible thing, Lysimachus"*: All of the quotations in this paragraph come from Laches 200e–201a.

178. *Aporia is never an excuse to stop looking for answers*: The difficulty of finding answers might turn a person into what Socrates calls a "misologue" (Phaedo 89d), a hater of discussion. Socrates warns his friends away from this destructive attitude. Misologues fail to recognize that the fault lies in their arguments, not in argumentation itself. "We should not allow into our minds the conviction that argumentation has nothing sound about it; much rather we should believe that it is we who are not yet sound and that we must take courage and be eager to attain soundness . . ." (Phaedo 90e).

Chapter 14: The *Clouds*

179. *the City Dionysia was in full swing*: Tradition ascribed an interesting origin to this festival. In the mists of the past, Eleutherae, a town on the outskirts of Attica, had opted to become part of the polis of Athens. The Eleutheraeans worshiped Dionysus, and to symbolize their new membership in the polis, they brought to Athens a sacred wooden statue of their god. But the Athenians rejected the statue, and Dionysus punished them with a plague that attacked the male genitalia. The plague ended only once the Athenians accepted the cult of Dionysus, and part of how they demonstrated their change of heart was by instituting the City Dionysia.

180. *the audience included women*: This point was long debated, but today most scholars believe that women indeed attended the theater, if only in a separate section in the back. The main reason for this view is that dramatic performances were religious events, and Athenian religion, unlike Athenian politics, welcomed the participation of women. (Henderson, Jeffrey. "Women and the Athenian Dramatic Festivals." *Transactions of the American Philological Association*, vol. 121 [1991]: pp. 133–147.)

180. *one contest for tragedies and another for comedies:* Playwrights entered the first of these contests by submitting three closely related tragedies followed by a satyr play, a short parody that was loosely connected to the plays that preceded it and that provided much-needed comic relief. To enter the comedy competition, playwrights submitted just a single play. Comedies treated their subjects with biting humor, and anyone was fair game.

181. *may have been specially designed to capture the philosopher's distinctive ugliness:* Kenneth Dover raises this possibility, which he grounds in the incident I relate at the end of this chapter—that Socrates stood up to identify himself to foreign visitors during the performance of the *Clouds*. As Dover points out, the story assumes a resemblance between the Socrates who was standing in the audience and the Socrates who was being portrayed onstage—otherwise, how would the foreigners have grasped the connection between them? ("Socrates in the *Clouds*," p. 51.)

181. *the title was apparently the name of Socrates's music teacher:* Menexenus 235e–236a.

181. *"among few men the best, / And among many vainest":* Diogenes Laertius 2.5.27.

183. *"O Lord God Immeasurable Ether, You who envelop the world!":* Clouds 264–265 (Arrowsmith, p. 36).

183. *"These are the only gods there are. The rest are but figments":* Clouds 365 (Arrowsmith, p. 43).

184. *"devised a Method for the Subversion of Established Social Beliefs"; "this little invention of mine":* Clouds 1038–1043 (Arrowsmith, p. 91).

184. *"[D]id you lick me when I was a little boy?":* Clouds 1409–1412 (Arrowsmith, p. 122–123).

185. *"[W]hy did you blaspheme the gods?":* Clouds 1506–1507 (Arrowsmith, p. 132).

185. *"So the gnat has a bugle up its ass!":* Clouds 165 (Arrowsmith, p. 28).

185, 186. *"doing research on Hades"; "a minor in Astronomy":* Clouds 192, 194 (Arrowsmith, p. 36).

186. *"cheated of an immense discovery":* Clouds 169, 177–179 (Arrowsmith, p. 34).

187. *One is told by the Roman author Aelian:* Historical Miscellany 2.13 (Ferguson, pp. 237–238).

188. *a sign, says Aelian, of the philosopher's utter contempt for comedy and his fellow Athenians:* Dover explains what Aelian might have had in mind. By silently standing up, Socrates was in effect announcing, with indignation, "Do I look like the sort of man who's playing the fool on stage?" ("Socrates in the *Clouds*," p. 51).

188. *Aelian's larger account of the history and reception of the play is fraught with glaring inaccuracies:* Aelian claims that Aristophanes wrote the play on the urging of Anytus and the other men whose accusations led to Socrates's trial and death sentence; the goal of the play, says Aelian, was to inflame public opinion against the philosopher and thus ensure a guilty verdict. In fact, almost a quarter of century passed between the production of the *Clouds* and the accusations of Anytus and his confederates. Aelian further claims that the *Clouds* was a resounding success. In fact, the play came in last place in the comedy competition of 423 BCE (Ferguson, pp. 237–238).

188. *A second story, traditionally but probably mistakenly attributed to Plutarch: On Bringing up a Boy* 9c (Plutarch. *Selected Essays of Plutarch.* Translated by T. G. Tucker Clarendon Press: 1913.)

Chapter 15: Family and Divine Mission

191. *Amphipolis, an Athenian colony that Sparta had seized shortly before the truce:* When Sparta marched against Amphipolis in late 424 BCE, the colony impatiently awaited help from Athens. But the Athenian forces were delayed, and by the time they arrived, the beleaguered city had already surrendered to the enemy. The strategos responsible for the delay paid with a twenty-year exile from Athens. Fortunately for us, that strategos was Thucydides. Those twenty years gave him the opportunity to write his monumental history of the Peloponnesian War, by far our most important source on the conflict.

195. *now that the war had depleted the ranks of marriageable men:* Ten years after the war ended, the adult male population was about half the size it had been at the beginning of the war (Kagan, p. 471). According to Diogenes Laertius (2.5.26), the shortage of men may have induced Socrates, like many other Athenian men, to marry more than one woman. Tradition identifies Socrates's second wife as Myrto, the daughter of the statesman Aristides the Just.

195. *Plato depicts her as a sensitive and loving wife: Phaedo* 60a–b. For another sympathetic but quite different presentation of Xanthippe, I recommend Amy Levy's poem "Xantippe," which was originally published in 1889. Levy's Xantippe is an old woman looking back at her life with Socrates. Although she entered the marriage with great hopes for intellectual growth, she quickly realized that Socrates wanted her to be a serving woman, not a thinking companion. In one especially moving memory, she endures the contempt of Socrates and his followers when she tries to contribute to their discussion of women. After that incident, she forced herself into silence: "I spun away / The soul from out my body, the high thoughts / From out my spirit."

Levy's Xantippe is a product of imagination rather than historical research, but several ancient Greek thinkers boldly confronted the ways in which their society restricted women. In Book 5 of the *Republic*, Plato declares that the natural ability to govern is not restricted to men and that all potential leaders, whether male or female, should benefit from the same education and have the same opportunity to lead the polis. And in several of his plays, Aristophanes presents strong-willed, outspoken women who defy their society's expectations—for instance, by taking over the Ekklesia. Aristophanes was a dyed-in-the-wool conservative, and when he showed women in power, he was probably trying to demonstrate just how far out of hand the situation had become. Nonetheless, at least some women in his audience must have identified with the anger of women like Lysistrata, the leader of a women's rebellion in the play that bears her name:

> *When the War began, like the prudent, dutiful wives that we are,*
>
> *we tolerated you men, and endured your actions in silence.*
> *(Small wonder—you wouldn't let us say boo.) . . .*
>
> *Too many times, as we sat in the house, we'd hear that you'd done it*
>
> *again—manhandled another affair of state with your usual*
>
> *staggering incompetence. Then, masking our worry with a nervous laugh,*
>
> *we'd ask you, brightly, "How was the Assembly today, dear? Anything*
>
> *in the minutes about Peace?" And my husband would give*
>
> *his stock reply.*
>
> *"What's that to you? Shut up!" And I did. (Lysistrata, lines 507–524.)*

It is striking that Aristophanes's Lysistrata and Levy's Xantippe have so much in common, despite the 2,300 years that separate them.

195. *"a wife who is of all living women"; "[P]eople who want to become good horsemen":* Xenophon, *Symposium* 2.10.

196. *"Did I not say that Xanthippe was thundering now":* Diogenes Laertius 2.5.36.

196. *replacing the water with more pungent liquids:* Athenaeus brings up the idea of slops, which he mistakenly attributes to Plato (*Deipnosophistae* 219b). The more specific notion of a chamber pot seems to be a later twist on the tale. I have not been able to find a specific source, but the internet is full of references to that colorful idea.

196. *a rare glimpse of Socrates as a father:* Xenophon, *Memorabilia* 2.2.1–14.

200. *the* omphalos, *or navel, of the world:* According to myth, Zeus identified the spot by releasing two eagles from Mount Olympus, one to the east and the other to the west. Eventually the eagles met at Delphi, proving it the center of the world.

200. *The attending priest helpfully restated the oracle's words in more comprehensible language:* Plutarch served as one of these priests in the first century CE, and much of what we know about the oracle of Delphi comes from his writings. Unfortunately, we cannot be sure that the procedures in his own time, which he describes in detail, were identical to the procedures that were in place almost six centuries earlier, when Chaerephon made his visit.

201. *"Whatever does the god mean?":* The quotations in this paragraph and the three that follow come from the *Apology* 21b–23b.

Chapter 16: Melos, Alcibiades, and the Teachability of Virtue

206. *"[Y]ou know as well as we do":* Thucydides 5.89.1.

206. *"[W]e are just men fighting against unjust":* Thucydides 5.104.1.

207. *"Of the gods we believe":* Thucydides 5.105.2.

208. *"ambitious in real truth of conquering the whole":* Thucydides 6.6.1.

208. *he must have been appointed when he was close to thirty, the lowest eligible age:* Thucydides points out Alcibiades's exceptional youth upon becoming a general (5.43.2).

208. *Now, in masterful speeches in the Ekklesia:* One of Alcibiades's many talents was his ability to speak well. According to Xenophon, even before Alcibiades was twenty years old, he managed to outmaneuver Pericles in a discussion about the nature of law and its relation to persuasion and force (*Memorabilia* 1.2.40–47). Since Pericles was the most influential and highly acclaimed speaker in Athens at the time, Alcibiades's achievement was no mean feat.

209. *"by far the most costly and splendid Hellenic force that had ever been sent out by a single city up to that time":* Thucydides 6.31.2.

PERSEPHONE'S RETURN TO DEMETER: In this image, Persephone is being led out of the underworld, where she has been condemned to spend half of every year with Hades. Hermes escorts her, and Hecate, a goddess of fertility and magic, guides the way with torches. On the far right, Demeter awaits her daughter.

Terracotta bell-krater (bowl for mixing wine and water), ca. 440 BCE. Attributed to the Persephone Painter, Greek, Attic. The Metropolitan Museum of Art, New York.

210. *The cult of Eleusis:* This religion, named after the city where it was based, was one of numerous mystery cults that supplemented the public, civic religion of Athens. Most of these cults were based on myths of the gods' death and rebirth. The cult of Eleusis focused on the story of Demeter and her daughter Persephone, who was kidnapped and dragged to the underworld by Hades. At least some of the rites seem to have reenacted Demeter's search for her missing daughter.

212. *"very drunk and very loud"; "I'm plastered": Symposium* 212d–e.

212. *"As for the house slaves and for anyone else who is not an initiate":* *Symposium* 218b.

215. *he fathered a child with the wife of one of Sparta's two ruling kings:* Plutarch, *Lives, Lysander* 22.3, *Agesilaus* 3.1. The rumor is probably related to the Athenian belief that Spartan men shared their wives, an idea that appears in Xenophon (*Constitution of the Lacedaemonians* 1.7–9) and Plutarch (*Lives, Lycurgus* 15.6–9), among other sources.

216. *As Thucydides interprets these maneuverings, Alcibiades's real goal was to return to Athens:* Thucydides 8.47.1.

216. *topple the Athenian democracy and replace it with an oligarchy:* According to Thucydides, self-interest was Alcibiades's only motivation. Alcibiades "cared no more for an oligarchy than for a democracy, and only sought to change the institutions of his country in order to get himself recalled by his associates" (8.48.4).

217. *"general-in-chief with absolute authority":* Xenophon, *Hellenica* 1.4.20.

218. *"It longs for him, it hates him, and it wants him back":* Aristophanes, *Frogs* 1425 (Lattimore, p. 109).

219. *Xenophon claims that Alcibiades was flawed from the very beginning:* *Memorabilia* 1.2.14–16.

219. *"Socrates is the only man in the world who has made me feel shame"; "I know perfectly well that I can't prove he's wrong": Symposium* 216b.

220, 221. *"no matter how handsome and rich and well-born he might be";* *"anyone can stand up and advise them": Protagoras* 319c–d.

221. *"[T]he wisest and best of our citizens": Protagoras* 319e.

222. *"[I]t is madness not to pretend to justice": Protagoras* 323c.

223. *"mindless vindictiveness of a beast": Protagoras* 324b.

223. *"As soon as a child understands what is said to him": Protagoras* 325d.

225. *"Since it has turned out that our salvation in life": Protagoras* 357a–b.

225. *"Now, Protagoras, seeing that we have gotten this topsy-turvy": Protagoras* 361c. Socrates is not embarrassed to learn that his initial position may have been wrong; just before this passage, he quips that if the discussion "had a voice of its own, it would say, mockingly, 'Socrates and Protagoras, how ridiculous you are, both of you'" (361a). Protagoras fails to share the good cheer, but perhaps he can be forgiven. The sophist is in a rather tricky situation. For professional reasons he should be thrilled by Socrates's conclusion that

virtue is teachable; Protagoras purports, after all, to teach young men virtue. But if he embraces that conclusion, he has admitted defeat in a debate, certainly a humiliating outcome for an instructor of rhetoric, especially since the discussion in the *Protagoras* takes place before a large audience.

226. *after her second marriage and the birth of Socrates's half brother:* We know almost nothing about Socrates's mother, but in *Theaetetus* 166a–c, Socrates and his interlocutor consider it an obvious fact that women become midwives only after their childbearing years.

226. *"the labor of their souls":* Theaetetus 150b.

227. *"[T]he most important thing about my art":* Theaetetus 150b–c.

227. *the teacher as sage, several notches above the students whom he or she graces with tidy bits of wisdom:* The *Protagoras* presents just that sort of relationship between Protagoras and his followers. Before Socrates engages Protagoras in conversation, the famous sophist is walking up and down the portico of a private home, and a large crowd follows deferentially in his wake. Socrates describes the scene with mischievous humor:

> He enchants them with his voice like Orpheus [the mythological character who charmed even trees and stones with his music], and they follow the sound of his voice in a trance. There were some locals also in this chorus, whose dance simply delighted me when I saw how beautifully they took care never to get in Protagoras' way. When he turned around with his flanking groups, the audience to the rear would split into two in a very orderly way and then circle around to either side and form up again behind him. It was quite lovely. (315a–b.)

The members of Protagoras's audience hang on his every word, and he revels in their obsequious attention. Socrates found both sides of this relationship absurd.

Chapter 17: The Conscientious Objector

229. *"They were beaten at all points and altogether":* Thucydides 7.87.5–6.

230. *the polis was forced to melt down some golden statues of Nike:* Kagan, p. 452. The original source of this information is a *scholium*, or ancient commentary, on Aristophanes's *Frogs*, line 720. The line mentions "recent coinage," which according to the scholium came from the statues of Nike.

230. *one of the most dramatic events of that period:* Thucydides is no longer our source; it seems that he died before he was able to complete his history, which breaks off in 411 BCE, near the end of the war's twenty-first year. After that point, our chief source is Xenophon's *Hellenica*, which picks up in 411 and continues through the end of the war and its aftermath.

232. *"for not picking up the men who won the victory in the naval battle":* Xenophon, *Hellenica* 1.7.9.

234. *"I was the only member of the presiding committee":* Apology 32b.

234. *"that complaints be brought against any who had deceived the people":* Xenophon, *Hellenica* 1.7.35.

239. *Alone of the men charged with the job, Socrates refused to comply:* Socrates recounts the incident in the *Apology* 32c–e.

240. *"I showed again, not in words but in action":* Apology 32d.

241. *he had enjoyed the company of Critias and Charmides:* Socrates's relationship with Plato was another connection to these two men. Charmides was Plato's maternal uncle, and Critias was the first cousin of Plato's mother.

241. *the same individuals with whom he discusses temperance in the* Charmides: The *Charmides* depicts the two men at a younger and more innocent point in their lives: Charmides is a teenager, his guardian Critias is about thirty, and the atrocities of the Thirty are a quarter century into the future. But Plato, who wrote the *Charmides* long after the rule of the Thirty, ends the dialogue with a hint of what is to come. Critias instructs Charmides to become Socrates's pupil, and Charmides says that he will submit to his guardian's instructions. Socrates, who has overheard the exchange, asks what the two have been "plotting" and wants to know whether he has any say in the matter:

> *"Are you going to use force," I asked, "and don't I get a preliminary hearing?"*
> *"We shall have to use force," said Charmides, "seeing that this fellow here has given me my orders. So you had better take counsel as to your own procedure."*
> *"What use is counsel?" said I. "Because when you undertake to do anything by force, no man living can oppose you"* (176c–d).

The exchange is playful, but Plato's hint of the sinister future is unmistakable.

PART THREE: *The Last Days*

Chapter 18: The Charges and the Question of Piety

245. *"[T]he Athenians appear both in private and public":* "Aristotle," *The Athenian Constitution* 40.2. (Aristotle. *The Athenian Constitution; The Eudemian Ethics; On Virtues and Vices.* Translated by H. Rackham. Harvard University Press, Loeb Classical Library: 2004.)

247. *the polis's mythical founders:* These were Cecrops and Erichthonius. According to various legends, Cecrops oversaw Athena's contest with Poseidon and introduced the worship of Athena to the region. Erichthonius later established the Great Panathenaea, along with its more modest counterpart, the Lesser Panathenaea.

248. *"Socrates is a malefactor":* Xenophon, *Memorabilia* 1.1.1.

250. *The Thirty had banished Anytus from Athens and stripped him of his property:* Anytus appears in Plato's dialogue *Meno*, where Socrates, arguing that virtue cannot be taught, identifies several fathers who have failed to encourage virtue in their sons. Anytus, who believes that he is being slandered over a son who has gone astray, issues a veiled threat that foreshadows his role in Socrates's trial: "I think, Socrates, that you easily speak ill of people. I would advise you, if you will listen to me, to be careful. Perhaps also in another city, and certainly here, it is easier to injure people than to benefit them" (95a).

253. *"[T]heir ideas of the divine attitude to piety and impiety"*: Euthyphro 4e.

253. *"[T]he pious is to do what I am doing now"*: Euthyphro 5d–e.

253. *Zeus punished his father, Cronus, for an act of injustice, just as Cronus had previously punished his own father, Uranus:* Uranus hated his youngest offspring, the one-eyed Cyclopes and hundred-handed Hecatoncheires, and imprisoned them in the deep, dark abyss of Tartarus. His wife, Gaia, appealed to her other children for vengeance, and Cronus, envious of his father's power, responded. Cronus castrated Uranus, cast his testicles into the ocean, and deposed him as ruler of the universe. Cronus got his comeuppance later. After hearing that he, too, would be deposed by his own offspring, he swallowed each of his children as they were born. To save Zeus, her sixth child, Cronus's wife, Rhea, gave her husband a stone to swallow instead of the baby. When Zeus was grown, he freed his siblings from Cronus's belly, and together they overthrew their father and imprisoned him in Tartarus.

253. *"Indeed, Euthyphro, this is the reason"*: Euthyphro 6a.

254. *"the pious is what all the gods love"*: Euthyphro 9e.

257. *"If you had no clear knowledge of piety and impiety"*: Euthyphro 15d.

258. *"And now I must go to the King's Porch"*: Theaetetus 210d.

Chapter 19: The Trial

262. *Socrates had never appeared in court before:* Apology 17d.

262. *"Really, Socrates, ought you not to be considering your defence?"*: The conversation appears in Xenophon, Apology 3.

263. *The end of Xenophon's account does not sit well with Plato's characterization of the philosopher:* Xenophon recognizes the unusual nature of his depiction, but he believes that it reflects the failure of other accounts: "What they didn't make clear . . . is this: he had already decided that for him death was preferable to life" (Xenophon, Apology 1).

266. *"practice the teachings of Socrates and all be thoroughly corrupted"*: Apology 29c.

268. *"I do not know, men of Athens"*: Apology 17a.

268. *"got hold of most of you from childhood"*: Apology 18b.

269. *"fight with shadows"; "cross-examine when no one answers"*: Apology 18b.

269. *"Do not create a disturbance, gentlemen, even if you think I am boasting"*: Apology 20e.

270. *"Tell me, my good sir, who improves our young men?"*: Socrates's grilling of Meletus, which I present here and in the next four paragraphs, appears in the *Apology* 24d–28a.

273. *"Meletus had officially charged Socrates with introducing "new spiritual things"*: *Apology* 24b–c.

275. *"I could claim that a gust of the North Wind blew her over the rocks"*: *Phaedrus* 229c–d.

277. *"I think it will be to your advantage to listen"; "Indeed, men of Athens"*: *Apology* 30c–e.

278. *"Do you think I would have survived all these years"*: *Apology* 32e.

279. *"[T]hey know that Meletus is lying"*: *Apology* 34b.

279. *"pitiful dramatics"*: *Apology* 35b.

280. *"This is far from being the case, gentlemen"; "I leave it to you and the god to judge me"*: *Apology* 35d.

280. *Some sort of contraption kept the votes hidden from prying eyes*: Boegehold, Alan L. "Toward a Study of Athenian Voting Procedure." *Hesperia: The Journal of the American School of Classical Studies at Athens*, vol. 32, no. 4 (1963): pp. 366–374.

Chapter 20: Sentencing and Imprisonment

283, 284. *"So be it"; "What is suitable for a poor benefactor"*: *Apology* 36b–d.

284. *"Nothing is more suitable, gentlemen"*: *Apology* 36d.

285. *"The Olympian victor makes you think yourself happy"*: *Apology* 36d.

285. *"Since I am convinced that I wrong no one"*: *Apology* 37b.

285. *"I should have to be inordinately fond of life"*: *Apology* 37c–d.

286. *"Well, then, that is my assessment"*: *Apology* 38b.

288. *"[I]t is best and easiest not to discredit others"*: *Apology* 39d.

288. *"[S]tay with me awhile"; "a surprising thing"*: *Apology* 39e–40a.

288. *"[T]hose of us who believe death to be an evil are certainly mistaken"*: *Apology* 40b–c.

289. *"true jurymen who are said to sit in judgment there"*: *Apology* 41a.

289. *"I could spend my time testing and examining people there"*: *Apology* 41b.

289. *"In any case, they would certainly not put one to death for doing so"*: *Apology* 41c.

290. *"[W]hen my sons grow up, avenge yourselves"*: *Apology* 41e.

290. *"Now the hour to part has come"*: *Apology* 42a.

290. *the Eleven, the officials responsible for maintaining public order and overseeing the penal system*: To supplement their own efforts, the Eleven seem to have managed a police force of three hundred publicly owned slaves known as the Scythian archers. Ancient Scythia was located to

the north of the Black Sea, and the original slaves may have indeed come from there. It is unclear whether subsequent members of the force were Scythian or even whether they were archers.

294. *was thought to be the one that had originally carried Theseus:* Plutarch says that the original ship was preserved until the time of Demetrius Phalereus, who governed Athens in the late fourth century BCE (*Lives, Theseus* 23.1). The preservation, Plutarch adds, raised an interesting philosophical question. Since all the old timbers had been gradually replaced with new ones, could it really be said that the preserved ship was the same one that Theseus had sailed? This question, often called the Ship of Theseus, is especially intriguing in relation to our own identity. Virtually none of the cells that compose our bodies existed when we were born, and our thoughts, emotions, and behaviors change radically over the years. What makes us the same people as the infants we once were?

294. *the garlanding of the ship took place the day before Socrates's trial: Phaedo* 58a.

SCYTHIAN ARCHERS:
This pottery fragment presents a typical depiction of a Scythian archer. Aristophanes is our major source on the Scythians in Athens. His comedies depict them dragging a drunkard out of the marketplace, ushering a citizen out of the Ekklesia, and beating, whipping, and arresting disorderly individuals. Another duty was crowd control; the Scythians apparently wielded the red-dyed rope that corralled reluctant citizens onto the Pnyx for sessions of the Ekklesia. Aristophanes makes fun of their accents, so whether or not the archers were Scythian, they do seem to have been foreigners.

Terracotta fragment of an amphora (jar), 550–540 BCE, Greek, Attic. The Metropolitan Museum of Art, New York.

294. *the voyage lasted thirty-one days:* Xenophon, *Memorabilia* 4.8.2.

296. *"Often in the past throughout my life":* Crito 43b.

297. *"I used to ask Socrates about the points I couldn't remember":* Theaetetus 143a.

297. *"Socrates, practice and cultivate the arts"; "the highest kind of art":* Phaedo 60e–61a.

298. *"the like of whom I shall never find again"; "Surely there can be no worse reputation":* Crito 44b–c.

299. *"Your present situation makes clear"; "Would that the majority could inflict the greatest evils":* Crito 44d.

300. *"Tell me, Socrates, what are you intending to do?"; "Or do you think it is possible":* Crito 50a–b.

303. *"for anyone who destroys the laws"; "[W]hat will you say":* Crito 53c.

304. *"Crito, my dear friend":* Crito 54d.

304. *"I have nothing to say, Socrates"; "Let it be then, Crito":* Crito 54d–e.

Chapter 21: The Fatal Drink

308. *Socrates, this is the last time your friends will talk to you:* Phaedo 60a. Plato gives us only a tiny glimpse of Xanthippe, but her lament reveals how deeply she understands and respects her husband's love of philosophy.

308. *"two creatures with one head":* Phaedo 60b.

310. *"People get heated when they talk":* This exchange with Crito appears in Phaedo 63d–e.

310. *"I had a strange feeling":* Phaedo 59a.

311. *"as if we had lost a father":* Phaedo 116a.

311. *the other women of his household:* Phaedo 116b. Some have argued that the plural "women" supports the notion that Socrates had more than one wife (see the second note to chapter 15, on page 333). Since women commonly clustered into Athenian households, however, this proof is dubious.

311. *"I shall not reproach you as I do the others, Socrates":* Plato's account of the officer and his words appears in Phaedo 116c–d.

312. *"I do not expect any benefit from drinking the poison a little later":* Phaedo 117a.

312. *"Well, my good man":* The exchange between Socrates and the bearer of the poison appears in Phaedo 117a–c.

313. *"I am told one should die in good omened silence":* Phaedo 117d–e.

313. *"Crito, we owe a cock to Asclepius":* Phaedo 118a.

314. *"Such was the end of our comrade":* Phaedo 118a.

A Note on the Sources

ALTHOUGH SOCRATES WAS A REAL HISTORICAL FIGURE,
he left behind no written body of work. Everything that we
know about his life and ideas comes from other sources, and
these sources are all problematic in one way or another.

The accounts of Socrates's contemporaries, individuals
who knew the philosopher, obviously carry a great deal of
weight. Primary among these contemporaries are Plato,
Xenophon, and Aristophanes. Others who lived in the same
period wrote about Socrates too, but their records have either
vanished over time or come down to us only in bits and pieces
that were quoted by others.

No straightforward portrait emerges from these
contemporaries of Socrates, who sometimes contradict
one another. For instance, although Plato shows Socrates
abandoning natural philosophy as a young man,
Aristophanes depicts a middle-aged Socrates who still busies
himself with the world of nature. These contradictions are
mostly manageable. In the example I have just given, the
problem vanishes when it is understood that Aristophanes's

Socrates is not a portrait of a particular individual but a composite of several intellectuals.

Greater challenges arise with Plato, Xenophon, and Aristophanes individually. Plato was over forty years younger than Socrates, so their meaningful interactions were limited to the last decade or so of the older man's life; additionally, Plato almost certainly composed his dialogues only after Socrates's death. In other words, Plato was not present at most of the exchanges he recorded, and his memories of the ones he did witness would have faded before he ever sat down to write. Furthermore, Plato's principal goal was to wrestle with philosophical ideas, not to write history, and that goal may have admitted a certain flexibility with the facts. For instance, he staged a conversation between Socrates and Parmenides even though those two thinkers may never have met. To complicate things further, the line between what Plato thought and what Socrates thought is never entirely clear; some scholars have gone so far as to accuse Plato, at least in some of his dialogues, of presenting his own ideas through his character "Socrates."

Like Plato, Xenophon knew Socrates only in the older man's final years, but Xenophon had even fewer possibilities for firsthand interactions with the philosopher. Xenophon lived about nine and a half miles from the city, on the other side of a mountain range, and his love of horses kept him happily occupied in the countryside. On top of that, Xenophon left Athens two years before Socrates's trial and never returned. But what is most disturbing is that Xenophon's account lacks sparkle. Xenophon's Socrates offers a good deal of solid, homey advice, but it can be hard to see why this Socrates would inspire people for centuries.

As for Aristophanes, the art of comedy inevitably distorts the truth. To whatever extent his Socrates reflects the individual man who went by that name, the depiction is a caricature, not a realistic portrait. Furthermore, Aristophanes had a clear agenda. He was a staunch traditionalist who bitterly opposed what he perceived as his society's decay, and he was determined to cast Socrates as a chief cause of the problem.

Later sources abound; some of the most important are Aristotle, Diogenes Laertius, and Plutarch. Although Aristotle was born too late to have known Socrates, he had the benefit of studying at Plato's Academy, where Plato and some of his colleagues could share their firsthand memories. Plutarch and Diogenes Laertius lived much later—Plutarch in the first century CE and Diogenes in the third century CE—and both are gossipy and unreliable. It would be foolish, however, to dismiss them entirely. Both had access to oral lore and written sources that we no longer have today.

So what does a biographer do with such a tangle? Like many others who have written about Socrates, I have relied most heavily on Plato's account, and primarily on the dialogues in which Socrates deals with ethical questions, not with speculations about the Forms or other esoteric issues. Whatever its flaws may be, Plato's depiction is the one that has most profoundly shaped the way Socrates has been imagined for the last two and a half thousand years, and Plato's depiction is the one that makes Socrates seem worth our attention.

I have brought in other sources too, sometimes to further my account and sometimes to complicate it; throughout, I have tried to balance academic responsibility with concern for the smoothness of my narrative. A book of this sort can provide only the smallest glimpse of the ancient sources, not to mention the current, vibrant scholarship on Socrates and his age. I hope that some of my readers will undertake their own explorations of this exciting terrain.

TENDING TO THE DEAD: In this scene, the first part of a Greek funeral, the deceased has been washed, anointed with oil, dressed, and laid out on a high bed within the house, and now family members and friends have come to visit, some tearing their hair in a sign of mourning. Next will come a procession, probably before dawn, and finally the body will be buried or cremated.

Terracotta funerary plaque, ca. 520–510 BCE, Greek, Attic. The Metropolitan Museum of Art, New York.

Bibliography

In general, information about sources that I cite only once or twice appears in the relevant notes, not in this bibliography.

Ancient sources

When I cite a dialogue without indicating its author, I am referring to Plato. His writings have traditionally been divided into "Stephanus numbers," or numbered and lettered sections that follow the pagination of an edition published in 1578, and I have followed the standard practice of referring to those divisions rather than to the page numbers in my modern edition. I have done the same with other ancient sources that have traditional numbering systems, but I also provide modern page numbers when they make it significantly easier to find quotations in the translations I am using.

Unless I indicate otherwise, I have used the translations listed below. When I supply a different translation for reasons of clarity or style, I provide the bibliographic information in the notes.

Aristophanes. *The Birds*. Translated by William Arrowsmith. Mentor, 1961.

——————*The Clouds*. Translated by William Arrowsmith. Mentor, 1962.

—————— *Four Comedies: Lysistrata, The Acharnians, The Congresswomen, The Frogs*. Edited by William Arrowsmith. Translated by Douglass Parker and Richard Lattimore. Ann Arbor Paperbacks, 1969.

Athenaeus. *The Deipnosophists or Banquet of the Learned of Athenaeus*. Translated by C. D. Yonge. Henry G. Bohn, 1854.

Diogenes Laertius. *The Lives and Opinions of Eminent Philosophers*. Translated by C. D. Yonge. G. Bell and Sons, 1915.

Herodotus. *The Persian Wars*. Translated by George Rawlinson. Modern Library, 1942.

Pausanias. *Description of Greece*. Translated by James Frazer. Macmillan, 1898.

Plato. *Complete Works*. Edited by John M. Cooper. Hackett, 1997.

Plutarch. *The Rise and Fall of Athens: Nine Greek Lives*. Translated by Ian Scott-Kilvert. Penguin Books, 1960.

—————— *Plutarch's Moralia in Fifteen Volumes*. Harvard University Press, Loeb Classical Library, 1968.

Thucydides. *The Complete Writings of Thucydides: The Peloponnesian War*. Translated by Richard Crawley. Modern Library, 1951.

Xenophon. *Conversations of Socrates: Socrates' Defence, Memoirs of Socrates, The Dinner-Party, The Estate-Manager*. Translated by Hugh Tredennick and Robin Waterfield. Penguin, 1990.

—————— *Hellenica, Books I–V*. Translated by Carleton L. Brownson. Harvard University Press and William Heinemann, Loeb Classical Library, 1961.

Anthologies of ancient sources

Curd, Patricia, ed. *A Presocratics Reader: Selected Fragments and Testimonia*, 2nd edition. Translated by Richard D. McKirahan and Patricia Curd. Hackett, 2011.

Ferguson, John. *Socrates: A Source Book*. Open University Press, 1970.

Modern scholarship

I include here the sources that I cite directly as well as the texts that informed my thinking and writing in more general ways.

Anderson, Mark. "Socrates as Hoplite." *Ancient Philosophy*, vol. 25, no. 2 (2005): pp. 273–289.

Dover, Kenneth J. *The Greeks*. University of Texas Press, 1981.

————"Socrates in the Clouds." *The Philosophy of Socrates: A Collection of Critical Essays*. Edited by Gregory Vlastos. Anchor, 1971: pp. 50–77.

Flacelière, Robert. *Daily Life in Greece at the Time of Pericles*. Translated by Peter Green. Macmillan, 1965.

Goldstein, Rebecca Newberger. *Plato at the Googleplex: Why Philosophy Won't Go Away*. Pantheon, 2014.

Hughes, Bettany. *The Hemlock Cup: Socrates, Athens, and the Search for the Good Life*. Knopf, 2011.

Johnson, Paul. *Socrates: A Man for Our Times*. Viking, 2011.

Kagan, Donald. *The Peloponnesian War*. Penguin, 2003.

Martin, Thomas R. *Ancient Greece: From Prehistoric to Hellenistic Times*, 2nd edition. Yale University Press, 2013.

Nails, Debra. *The People of Plato: A Prosopography of Plato and Other Socratics*. Hackett, 2002.

————"Socrates." *The Stanford Encyclopedia of Philosophy* (Spring 2020 Edition). Edited by Edward N. Zalta. https://plato.stanford.edu/archives/spr2020/entries/socrates/.

Navia, Luis. *Socrates: A Life Examined*. Prometheus, 2007.

Stone, I. F. *The Trial of Socrates*. Anchor, 1989.

Taylor, A. E. *Socrates*. Beacon Press, 1932.

Taylor, C. C. W. *Socrates: A Very Short Introduction*. Oxford University Press, 2000.

Vlastos, Gregory. *Socrates: Ironist and Moral Philosopher.* Cornell University Press, 1991.

JACT (Joint Association of Classical Teachers). *The World of Athens: An Introduction to Classical Athenian Culture,* 2nd edition. Cambridge University Press, 2008.

Bibliography

ATHENA AND HER OWL: In this little statuette, Athena wears her customary helmet and holds out her hand to release her favorite bird.

Bronze statuette of Athena flying her owl, ca. 460 BCE, Greek, Attic. The Metropolitan Museum of Art, New York.

Glossary

A note on pronunciation: For entry words with versions in both English and Greek, I have usually opted for English and provided the American pronunciation. Italicized entries indicate Greek words and an approximation of ancient Greek pronunciation—or at least of one of the widely accepted renderings of ancient Greek pronunciation, which is an issue steeped in controversy.

A few letter combinations in my pronunciation guides may not be intuitive:

a = short "a," as in "cat"

ah = the "o" in "bottle"

g = hard "g," as in "girl"

s = the "s" in "silly"

uu = the vowel sound in "few"

Acropolis: (uh-KRAH-puh-lis) rocky plateau and religious district in the center of Athens, featuring the Parthenon and other temples

Agora: (A-guh-ruh) literally "the place of assembly," the central precinct of Athens; a combination of government district, religious zone, marketplace, and social hangout

Alopeke: (ah-loh-PEH-kee) Socrates's deme, just to the southeast of the city of Athens

andreia: (ahn-DRAY-ah) literally "manliness," steadfastness in both civic leadership and military engagement, the quality of courage that is under discussion in Plato's *Laches*

Apaturia: (ah-pah-TOO-ree-ah) a joyous three-day festival when children officially became members of their family clans; the holiday's timing during the Arginusae affair contributed to the tragic fate of the generals

apologia: (ah-poh-loh-GEE-ah) speech made in one's own defense, the source of the title of Plato's *Apology*

aporia: (uh-POR-ee-uh) the inability to resolve the objections or contradictions that arise in philosophical discussion; this impasse is the usual endpoint of Socrates's dialogues

archon: (AR-kon) one of nine officials who were appointed by lot to oversee the polis's religious and judicial affairs

archon basileus: (AR-kon ba-sih-LEH-oos) literally "king archon," the archon in charge of religious rites and accusations of impiety, the official who conducted Socrates's pretrial hearing and who may be represented on the Parthenon frieze by the man holding the peplos

Areopagus: (a-ree-AH-puh-guhs) a hill to the south of the Agora that served as the meeting place of an aristocratic council whose powers waned with the rise of democracy

arete: (ah-reh-TEH) excellence in body, mind, and soul—the ideal of an Athenian education, often translated as "virtue"

athlon: (AHTH-lohn) Greek for "prize" or "reward," related to the Greek word *athletes*, literally "one who competes for a prize"—a powerful indication of the link that ancient Greeks drew between sports and competition

Attica: (A-tih-kuh) eastern Greek peninsula that constituted the territory of the Athenian city-state, with Athens as its major urban area

bema: (BEH-mah) the speaker's stand at the front of the Pnyx, where any citizen had the right to address the crowd

Boule: (boo-LAY) the five-hundred-member committee responsible for setting the Ekklesia's agenda

Bouleuterion: (boo-loo-TAY-ree-ahn) the building on the west side of the Agora where the Boule met

caryatid: (ka-ree-A-tid) a statue of a draped female figure that is used as a pillar

cella: (SEL-uh) a Greek temple's central hall, usually featuring a statue that represented the god to whom the structure was dedicated

City Dionysia: (die-uh-NIE-see-uh) a springtime holiday dedicated to the god Dionysus, focusing mainly on theatrical competitions; Aristophanes's *Clouds* came in last in the comedy competition of 423 BCE

Corybant: (KOR-uh-bant) a worshiper of a nature goddess named Cybele, whose rites were passionate and wild

cosmology: the study of the physical world and its origins, the focus of much natural philosophy

daimonion: (die-MOH-nee-ohn) literally a "divine something," the internal voice that accompanied Socrates all his life, warning him against taking specific actions

Delian League: (DEE-lee-uhn) the alliance that Athens organized after the Persian Wars to liberate Greeks still under Persian control; the name, which is modern, refers to the island of Delos, the original location of the League's treasury

deme: (deem) one of the 139 subdivisions of the polis of Athens, each with its own government, holidays, and lists of citizens

dialogue: a philosophical genre that presents lengthy conversations among people; the dialogues of Plato, who helped to popularize the genre at the beginning of the fourth century BCE, almost always include Socrates as a character

drachma: (DRAK-muh) a monetary unit that was worth the standard daily wage of an average laborer

Ekklesia: (ek-lay-SEE-ah) the assembly of Athenian citizens that met on the Pnyx and made all major decisions for the polis

Eleusinian Mysteries: (eh-loo-SIH-nee-uhn) a cult that was open only to formally initiated members and that focused on Demeter's loss and recovery of her daughter Persephone; just before the Sicilian expedition, Alcibiades was accused of profaning the cult's secret rites

the Eleven: officials responsible for maintaining public order and overseeing the penal system; after his trial, Socrates left the courtroom in their custody

Erechtheion: (uh-REK-thee-uhn) a temple on the Acropolis, completed in 406 BCE, with a peculiar combination of architectural styles, religious shrines, and furnishings, including the famous Porch of the Caryatids

Forms: perfect abstractions like Beauty or Justice, compared to which all instances in the sensory world fall short; the idea is most closely associated with Plato

Great Panathenaea: (pan-ath-uh-NEE-uh) the most important Athenian holiday, celebrated once every four years, featuring a grand procession that carried a new *peplos* to a sacred statue of Athena as well as sports competitions that attracted athletes from all over Greece

gymnos: (guum-NOHS) the Greek for "naked," related to the Greek *gymnasion*, roughly the equivalent of the English "gymnasium," a reflection of the Greek custom of practicing sports in the nude

Hellenes: (HEH-leens) the Greeks' name for themselves, after the mythical figure Hellen, to whom they traced their ancestry

helot: (HEL-ut) state-owned slaves in Sparta, descendants of Peloponnesian Greeks who were conquered early in Sparta's history and who posed a constant security threat to Sparta

herm: a statue consisting of a head perched on top of a column featuring male genitals; herms often depicted the god Hermes and were used as boundary markers

himation: (hih-MAH-tee-ohn) a large rectangle of wool used as a cloak

hoplite: (HOP-lite) a heavily armed foot soldier who carried a shield and spear, the mainstay of the Athenian army

humanism: a worldview that emphasizes human potential and rationality rather than submission to gods or supernatural forces

idiotes: (ih-dee-OH-tehs) a person who does not engage in public affairs; the English word "idiot" conveys the disdain that Athenians felt for such a person

isonomia: (ee-soh-noh-MEE-ah) equality under the law, the Athenians' early term for their democracy

kalon: (kah-LOHN) something highly valued, usually translated as "the beautiful" or "the fine," the quality discussed in *Greater Hippias*, a dialogue sometimes attributed to Plato

klepsydra: (klep-SUUD-rah) a clock consisting of two pots, the upper one emptying water through a hole near its base into the lower one; the device enabled the timing of speeches during trials

kleroterion: (kleh-roh-TEH-ree-ohn) an allotment machine for the random appointment of citizens to civic duties; the device consisted of a large rectangular stone with slots for pinakia and a tube through which black and white balls emerged

Long Walls: defensive walls that connected Athens to its two ports to the southwest, creating a protected triangular region with some of the military advantages of an island

mina: (MY-na) a silver coin worth one hundred drachmas, roughly equivalent to a laborer's wages for one hundred days of work

natural philosophy: early science, notable mainly for its attempt to explain phenomena such as earthquakes, comets, and lightning without recourse to myth

Nous: (noos) in Anaxagoras's philosophy, the Mind that set the universe into motion and continues to regulate its operations, an idea that briefly interested Socrates as a young man

oligarchy: (OH-lih-gar-kee) rule by a small group of aristocrats

omphalos: (OM-fah-lohs) the earth's navel, or geographical center, which ancient Greeks identified with the spot at Delphi where the oracle sat

oracle: (OR-uh-kuhl) a priest or priestess regarded as a mouthpiece for the gods; the most famous of these in Greece was the oracle of Delphi

orchestra: (or-KEHS-trah) the circular performance area of a Greek theater, largely defined by the curve of the audience's seats

paidagogos: (pie-dah-goh-GOHS) a slave or hired man who escorted young boys to school, ensured their physical safety, and handled disciplinary problems

palaestra: (pah-LIE-strah) a colonnaded courtyard used for athletic training, primarily wrestling and boxing

Parthenon: (PAR-thuh-non) temple to Athena on the Acropolis, built in the 440s and 430s BCE as part of Pericles's ambitious construction program

pederasty: (peh-duh-RAS-tee) a romantic relationship between an adult man and an adolescent boy, widely considered an essential part of the boy's education

Peloponnesian League: (peh-luh-puh-NEE-zhun) Sparta's alliance of city-states, which probably arose to help Sparta keep its helots under control, named after the Peloponnese, Greece's large southern peninsula, where Sparta was located

peplos: (PEP-lohs) a body-length robe made of a rectangular piece of cloth folded down at the top, wrapped around the body, and pinned over the shoulders

phalanx: (FAY-lenks) a tight formation of hoplites moving together as a block

phallus: (FA-lus; plural, in Greek: *phalloi*) a representation of an erect penis

pinakion: (pih-NAH-kee-ohn; plural: *pinakia*) a small bronze plaque bearing a citizen's name and the name of his deme, used in the kleroterion for the random selection of jurymen and civic officials

Pnyx: (pnix) hill to the southwest of the Agora where the Ekklesia held its sessions

polis: (PAH-lis) Greek city-state, including at least one urban center as well as the surrounding countryside

proxenos: (PROK-seh-nohs) an individual appointed by a foreign polis to serve its interests in the polis where he was a citizen; the proxenos provided visitors and delegates from the foreign polis with hospitality, useful introductions, and legal guidance

prytany: (PRIH-tuh-nee) the fifty-member subgroup of the Boule that was responsible for executing the decisions of the Ekklesia

satyr: (SAY-ter) a mythological wild man, lustful and usually drunk, generally represented in Greek art with a horse's ears and tail

satyr play: a short parody that was loosely connected to the cycle of three tragedies that preceded it; all four plays were submitted together as a single entry in the tragedy competition of the City Dionysia

scholium: (SKOH-lee-uhm; plural: scholia) a marginal note made by a commentator on a text written by someone else

Scythian archers: (SIH-thee-uhn) the Athenian police force, consisting of three hundred publicly owned slaves

Silenus: (sie-LEE-nuhs) the mythological individual named Silenus was a satyr who took care of Dionysus when the god was just a baby and remained his teacher and companion; "sileni" (plural of "silenus") may be just a different name for satyrs—wild men who had the tail and ears of a horse and spent most of their time drunk and sexually aroused

sophia: (soh-FEE-ah) originally a term for artistic skill, but eventually a word for wisdom—as in *philosophia*, the love of wisdom

sophist: (SOF-ist) an itinerant, paid teacher of rhetoric and sometimes other subjects; many sophists subscribed to a relative view of truth and morality

sophrosune: (sohf-roh-SUU-neh) self-restraint and discretion, accompanied by an awareness of one's duties toward oneself and others, often translated as "temperance" or "moderation"; the quality under discussion in Plato's *Charmides*

spolia: (SPOH-lee-uh) materials taken from older structures for use in the building of new structures; in the northern retaining wall of the Acropolis, spolia from destroyed temples served as a monument to the Persian Wars

stoa: (STOH-uh) a roofed portico, generally walled in the back and colonnaded in the front, designed to provide a sheltered, open-air space for the public

Stoa Basileios: (STOH-uh bah-sih-LEH-ohs) the Stoa of the King Archon, also known as the King's Porch, the headquarters of the archon basileus in the northwestern part of the Agora; the building, which was the location of Socrates's pretrial hearing, featured a display of the Athenian legal code and a stone platform where government officials took their oaths of office

Stoa Poikile: (STOH-uh poy-KEE-leh) the Painted Stoa, a popular hangout in the northern end of the Agora, named after its display of murals depicting Athens's military victories

strategos: (strah-teh-GOHS; plural: *strategoi*) a military general, an extremely powerful official who was one of the few who were elected by the people rather than selected by lot

substance: that from which everything else is derived, a major concern of the natural philosophers

symposium: (sim-POH-zee-uhm) a formal men's-only dinner held in wealthy homes, including wine, song, poetry, and serious discussion, as well as dance and instrumental music by women who may have also offered their services as prostitutes

Temple of Olympian Zeus: a massive temple to Zeus that stood between Alopeke and the center of Athens and that remained uncompleted for all of Socrates's life

tetradrachm: (teh-truh-DRAM) a silver coin worth four drachmas that bore images of Athena's head, an owl, and sprigs of olive; the coin promoted trade by serving as a common currency throughout the Aegean region

Theater of Dionysus: (die-oh-NIE-suhs) the enormous outdoor theater of Athens, located on the southern slope of the Acropolis, where the comedy and tragedy competitions of the City Dionysia took place

the Thirty: the group of aristocrats who ruled Athens after the polis's defeat in the Peloponnesian War, remembered especially for their brutality toward anyone they perceived as an adversary

Tholos: (THOH-lohs) a round building on the west side of the Agora that served as the headquarters of the prytany; it was nicknamed *skias* (skee-AHS), literally "sunshade," because its round, peaked roof resembled a sunhat

trireme: (TRY-reem) a fast and maneuverable ship with three tiers of rowers on each side, the backbone of the Athenian navy

Index

All page numbers followed by f indicate figures.